Cross-Border Marriages

Cross-Border Marriages

Gender and Mobility in Transnational Asia

Edited by
Nicole Constable

PENN

University of Pennsylvania Press

Philadelphia

Copyright © 2005 University of Pennsylvania Press
All rights reserved
Printed in the United States of America on acid-free paper

10   9   8   7   6   5   4   3   2   1

Published by
University of Pennsylvania Press
Philadelphia, Pennsylvania 19104–4011

Library of Congress Cataloging-in-Publication Data

Cross-border marriages : gender and mobility in transnational Asia / edited by Nicole
Constable.
   p. cm.
   Includes bibliographical references and index.
   ISBN 0-8122-3830-3 (cloth : alk. paper) — ISBN 0-8122-1891-4 (paper : alk. paper)
   1. Intercountry marriage. 2. Intercountry marriage—Asia. 3. Social
mobility. 4. Asian women—Foreign countries. I. Constable, Nicole.

HQ1032.C67 2005
306.84'5'095—dc22
                                        2004052017

Contents

Chapter 1
Introduction: Cross-Border Marriages, Gendered Mobility, and Global Hypergamy

Nicole Constable

The narrator and protagonist in a surrealistic short story by Yoko Tawada (1998) entitled "Missing Heels" is identified as a Japanese "mail-order bride." The story opens with her arrival in an unspecified European country to live with the husband she has yet to meet face-to-face. In an attempt to learn more about the local culture, she recruits the help of a woman teacher. The interaction between the two women encapsulates some of the stark contrasts between perspectives of and about foreign brides. The story, told from the bride's first-person perspective, also hints at some of the paradoxes of the idea that women aspire to and often achieve upward mobility through such marriages. The bride recounts how the woman teacher carefully looked her over and then informed her that

recently women of an inferior sort were being brought into the country from poorer parts of the world, and since far too many of the men were interested in them, marriage opportunities for her more liberated countrywomen were becoming more and more limited. She sat there waiting for my reaction.

"I didn't know that," I replied.

"These are people who marry only for money," she went on, "who come from poor villages, and get divorced and go back to them when they've saved up enough. They're uneducated, which makes it extremely difficult to teach them what living as man and wife really means. . . ."

"But I'm not like those women," I declared. "I gave this decision lots of thought, and came here of my own free will."

"Poor people have no will of their own," she said in a scathing tone of voice. "Whatever they do, they have no choice in the matter—poverty drives them to it." Having spoken her mind she sat, perhaps in anticipation of a counterattack, with her hands in lightly gripped fists and her chin thrust slightly forward, waiting for an answer.

Although I'd never made up my mind about anything before, *this marriage had definitely been my own decision, so being told that poor people have no choice in anything was more than I could stand.* "What do you know about someone you're meeting for the first time?" I fired back (Tawada 1998:104–5, emphasis added).

This fictional interaction between a bitter European teacher and an immigrant bride is noteworthy not only because it neatly elucidates many common stereotypes of foreign brides or so-called mail-order brides, but also because of the bride's refusal to accept such claims. The passage complicates common assumptions about the connection between poverty, opportunism, women's mobility, and the assumed "lack of free will" or lack of agency of foreign women who marry local men. It draws attention to ideas about global patterns of inequality that are thought to pressure poor women to immigrate to richer countries, where their marriages deprive "superior" local women of husbands. Yet it simultaneously suggests the limitations of such views, since the bride is from Japan (a wealthy and "advanced" nation) and has married into a small and seemingly remote European town of her own free will, as she insists. European husbands are depicted as scarce and desirable instruments of mobility, who are eager to marry "inferior" but available foreign women, and who in so doing upset the local status quo. Yet the husband also emerges as a complex figure, despite the fact that he remains invisible throughout most of the story. He provides his wife with shelter in a large house and leaves her a daily allowance. She hears him move about, imagines him in various forms in her dreams, and occasionally glimpses him watching her. Only in the last scene does he finally appear, in the bizarre form of a dead squid.

This story is remarkable for the way in which it challenges prevailing assumptions about "mail-order brides" as simply victims or trafficked women. It allows the bride to speak for herself, assert her self-determination, and tell her own story. Her voice as narrator simultaneously denies her the lack of agency and the victimhood that the local teacher and others attribute to foreign brides. Ultimately, we know little about her background or that of her husband, but what we do know is enough to disrupt the popular logic of the passive and desperate Asian bride who escapes from poverty and backwardness to a wealthy and advanced West.

The chapters in this book draw on stories, conversations, interviews, vignettes, and ethnographic descriptions, as well as materials from the popular media, introduction agencies and marriage brokers. The authors examine the varied perspectives, motivations, and experiences of brides and grooms—and, in some cases, their family members—as they imagine, enter into, resist, or promote particular sorts of cross-border marriages. While our modes of writing differ from Tawada's, our purpose is in some ways similar: collectively, we question many of the bald assumptions about the passivity or desperation of foreign brides; disrupt simplistic notions about upward marital mobility; and offer close ethnographic scrutiny and deep analysis of the local and global processes that make such marriages imaginable and realizable. We seek to convey the variety of experiences among a diversity of Asian women. Like Tawada, several contributors question the popular stereotypes of foreign brides as mail-order brides, commodities, or trafficked women. Yet while we stress the existence of women's and men's agency, we also recognize the limits and different degrees of agency they exhibit, and in some cases the presence and pressure that may be exerted by parents, siblings, and children. We also consider the varied and uneven ways in which economic factors, familial obligations, cultural fantasies and imaginings, and personal motives may come into play. Collectively, we call to mind the multiple ways in which international cross-border marriages are linked to wider regional, national, global, and transnational processes, while at the same time we acknowledge many of the ways in which such international marriages are not entirely new. Drawing on ethnographic studies of marriages that span geographically from China's hinterlands, the Philippines, Vietnam, South Korea, and Japan, to India, and to Canada and the United States, we consider what types of borders are crossed, how, and by whom. How are such border crossings gendered? How are such marriages initiated, arranged, or negotiated? In what sense can these marriages be considered "hypergamous" (upwardly mobile for women), and what are the paradoxes of marital mobility that might simultaneously be considered upward, downward, or lateral, depending on whether we consider class, lifestyle, education, social status, or geographical mobility? As we suggest, greater distances may be associated with new forms of empowerment and also disempowerment for women. Moreover, we pay special attention to how such marriages build on brides' and grooms' contradictory transnational fantasies, desires, and imaginings of marriage, tradition, and modernity.

Gender and Global Marriage-Scapes

In recent decades, amid new and expanding forms of globalization and capital flows, increased time/space compression facilitated by rapid electronic forms of communication, and the emergence of what Arjun Appadurai calls a "global imagination" (1996), marriages that cross the borders of nation-states have become increasingly common, although they have—until recently—captured relatively little scholarly attention. Such marriages are especially interesting because they do not represent a global free-for-all in which all combinations—regardless of class, nationality, ethnicity, or gender, for example—are possible. Rather, they form marriage-scapes that are shaped and limited by existing and emerging cultural, social, historical, and political-economic factors. They are also shaped by what Patricia Pessar and Sarah Mahler call— building on the work of Doreen Massey—the "gendered geographies of power" that underlie all transnational migrations (2001:5).

Recently emerging transnational marriage-scapes undoubtedly reflect certain broadly gendered patterns. A majority of international marriage migrants are women, and most of these women move from poorer countries to wealthier ones, from the less developed global "south" to the more industrialized "north"—from parts of Asia, Latin America, Eastern Europe, and the former Soviet Union, to Western Europe, North America, Australia, and wealthier regions of East Asia—echoing some of the common patterns of women's labor migration (see Ehrenreich and Hochschild 2002, Piper and Roces 2003).

The Philippines is a popular place of origin of marriage migrants, as it is for labor migrants. Immigration figures from the Philippines clearly illustrate one facet of the gendered pattern of marriage migration. Of the over 175,000 Filipinos engaged or married to foreigners between 1989 and 1999, over 91 percent involved Filipino women. The geographic distribution of the foreign partners is not surprising when we consider the historical, colonial, and postcolonial ties between the Philippines and the United States and Japan. Approximately 40 percent (over 70,000) of the foreign partners are from the United States; 30 percent (over 53,000) from Japan; 8.8 percent from Australia; 4.2 percent from Germany; 3.8 percent from Canada; and 1.9 percent from the United Kingdom (Commission on Filipinos Overseas 2000). The remaining 11 percent represent marriage partners or fiancés from other parts of the world, mainly Europe or Asia. Several chapters in this volume reflect the diversity of destinations and experiences of Filipina brides. Nobue Suzuki writes about marriages between Filipinas and Japanese men; Nancy Abelmann and Hyunhee Kim look at a failed marriage—arranged through the Unification Church—between a Filipina and a South Korean man; and Nicole Constable describes the range of Internet introduction services that facilitate introductions of Filipinas and Chinese women to U.S. men.

Women are disproportionally represented among immigrants to the United States, especially among marriage migrants. Marriage migration to the United States almost tripled between 1960 and 1997, increasing from 9 percent to 25 percent of all immigration. Out of almost 202,000 legal marriage migrants to the United States in 1997, 61 percent of those who married U.S. citizens and 85 percent of those who married permanent residents—presumably many of whom were their co-ethnics—were women (USDOJ-INS 1999a). Hung Cam Thai's chapter describes a pattern of intra-ethnic, familially arranged marriages between women from Vietnam and Viet Kieu men living in the United States.

Gendered patterns of marriage migration are also striking in Japan. Between 1965 and 1970, the small number of Japanese international marriages were between Japanese women and foreign men, but after that, especially after the late 1980s, the number of marriages between Japanese men and foreign women increased dramatically (Piper 1997). According to the Japanese Welfare Ministry, there were 5,000 marriages to foreigners in Japan in 1970, 10,000 in 1983, and 20,000 in 1989, and almost 27,000 in 1993 (Sadamatsu 1996, cited in Piper 1997). Out of over 50,000 Filipino-Japanese couples overall in the late 1990s, all but 1 percent are said to involve Filipinas and Japanese men (Ministry of Health, Labour and Welfare 2000, Suzuki in this volume). In 1993, 75 percent of Japanese international marriages were between foreign women and Japanese men. Filipina women accounted for 32 percent, North or South Korean women 25 percent; Chinese women 23 percent; and Thai women 10 percent (Piper 1997, see also Nakamatsu 2002, Suzuki 2003a).

In the People's Republic of China, we see other gendered patterns of marital migration, which are clearly linked to recent political and economic changes in the post-Mao period. Rural de-collectivization, labor surplus in the countryside, booming cities, and declining enforcement of the household registration (*hukou*) system have led to dramatic increases in the rate of rural-urban migration since the early 1980s. Domestic marriage migrations have also followed suit, with vast increases in the number of women who marry across greater geographic distances (Fan and Huang 1998, Gilmartin and Tan 2002). With China's "opening up" to the outside, the number of women marrying foreign residents also began to increase. The first post-Mao marriages between Chinese and foreigners in the 1980s involved mainland Chinese women and overseas Chinese men in Hong Kong, Taiwan, and elsewhere (Kang 1998, see also Clark 2001). The number of Chinese international marriages increased dramatically after the mid-1980s, with approximately 20,000 Chinese marrying abroad each year until 1990; over 30,000 per year in the early 1990s; 50,000 a year by 1998; and almost 80,000 in 2001 (China Statistical Yearbook 2002). The increased popularity and visibility of marriages between mainland Chinese women and men in Taiwan is attested to by a limit imposed in 1996 on the number of brides who can legally enter Taiwan (A. Huang 1996, cited in Scholes 1997:3). The quota for Chinese migrant partners in Taiwan is 3,600 per year, a fourth of the total applicants, thus propelling the market for brides from Vietnam and elsewhere (Wang and Chang 2002:111). Growing public and social concerns about the rapid increase in such international cross-border marriages are expressed in the Taiwan, Hong Kong, and U.S. overseas Chinese popular media (see Shih 1998 and 1999, Li 2001).

Several chapters in this volume reflect the diversity of marriage patterns involving women in or from the People's Republic of China, and collectively they suggest some of the wider national and global implications of increased marriage mobility, as women marry into more desirable locations within and beyond China's borders, creating a shortage of brides in more remote rural regions (see also Fan and Huang 1998, Gilmartin and Tan 2002). Emily Chao analyzes the highly publicized cases of "kidnapped" rural brides within China and of Naxi minority women from the minority region of Lijiang in southwestern China, who have recently begun to marry across more distant borders. Chao examines the changing meanings of elopement (*paohun*) and kidnapping (*guaihun*) within the Naxi context and suggests that marriage strategies have been influenced by China's family and population policies and by the uneven pattern of development that characterizes the post-Mao period of reform. Louisa Schein looks at two recent forms of out-marriage undertaken by Miao minority women. The Miao, a large minority group from southern mountainous agricultural regions of China, have historically tended to be endogamous (to marry within their group). In recent years, however, Miao women have been courted and wed by two different kinds of suitors: Han Chinese men from more populous coastal regions of China; and occasionally, Hmong co-ethnics who emigrated from Laos to the United States in the post–Vietnam War era. Ellen Oxfeld traces a pattern that involves Hakka Chinese women from the Hakka community in Calcutta, India, who marry Hakka men in Toronto, Canada, thus creating a marriage shortage for Hakka men in Calcutta, who increasingly turn to the Hakka "homeland" in rural Mei Xian in Guangdong Province, in South China, as a possible location in which to find Hakka women as brides. The contemporary pattern, Oxfeld argues, is not entirely new, but represents in some ways a marked continuity with older, prerevolution patterns of marriage. Collectively, these three chapters and the following one, by Caren Freeman, illustrate how different patterns of marriage mobility within and beyond China are interconnected and how the bride generally has a much more active say in choosing her own marriage partner than was once the case. But that is not to say that these marriages do not at times recall certain continuities with the past, especially with regard to the importance of marriage for creating familial networks and alliances, as Oxfeld's case reminds us. Nor is it to say that the brides do not experience new forms of disempowerment in the new settings.

Caren Freeman describes a pattern in which tens of thousands of Chosŏnjok women (ethnic Koreans from the People's Republic of China) have emigrated to South Korea since the early 1990s as part of an officially sanctioned government effort to relieve the rural bride shortage (see also Abelmann and Kim in this volume). Marriages between women in China and men in South Korea began in the 1990s. The annual rate increased each year until 1997, with 1,463 such marriages in 1993; 7,683 in 1995; and over 10,000 in 1996. In 1997, the number dropped to just over 7,000, and in 1998 decreased again to just over 6,000, the drop most likely attributable to the Asian financial crisis (Kang 1998; Caren Freeman, personal communication). The marriage of Chosŏnjok women into South Korea in turn created a shortage of Korean brides for Chosŏnjok men in China, who have looked to North Korea as a possible source of marriage partners. An estimated ten Chosŏnjok-Korean marriages per year are between Chosŏnjok men and Korean women, again illustrating the severely skewed gender imbalance of marriage migration.

Tradition, Modernity, and Gendered Imaginings

Whereas many contemporary marriage-scapes fit the pattern of brides from poorer countries and grooms in richer ones, it is important to stress that such migrations are shaped not only or simply by economic geographies but also by "cartographies of desire" (Pflugfelder 1999) or what Margaret Jolly and Lenore Manderson (1997) describe as "sites of desire" that are formed by confluences of culture, border crossings, exchanges, and fluid terrain, rather than simple unidirectional flows of power or desire. Recent marriage-scapes both reflect and are propelled by fantasies and imaginings about gender, sexuality, tradition, and modernity.

Men's openly stated assumptions about the "traditional" moral values and character of Asian women as well as their less openly expressed ideas about their erotic sexuality, and women's assumptions about "modern" outlooks, power, or attractiveness of Western and other foreign men are factors in their motivations to meet and marry. Chinese women, Vietnamese women, and Filipinas are among those who express the desire to marry men from foreign countries so as to escape local patriarchal gender expectations. Many women expect foreign husbands to have embraced more modern and open-minded ideas about gender roles than local men at home. While much has been written about "America" as a site of desire (Cannell 1999, Constable 2003a, Kelsky 2001, Manalansan 2003), these essays indicate some of the ways such desires expand to Japan, South Korea, India, Canada, and other "modern" sites that are also associated with fantasies of modern husbands and modern marriages.

While women may look for modern husbands, many men turn to Asia for traditional wives. White, middle-class U.S. men look for Asian wives whom they imagine to be more "old-fashioned" and committed to family values than U.S. women (see Wilson 1988, Constable 2003a and in this volume). Similarly, the Viet Kieu men described by Thai turn to Vietnam for prospective marriage partners whom they imagine will be more traditional, less demanding, and less liberated than their U.S. counterparts. Men from Hong Kong, Taiwan, and Singapore are motivated to look for wives in mainland China for similar reasons (Li 2001). Hong Kong women—like their U.S. counterparts—are described as spoiled and demanding, too materialistic, too feminist or career-oriented, and less committed to their families than mainland women. The paradox of such marriages is that while the men seek what they imagine to be traditional wives, the women often seek and hope for more modern husbands and marriages than are possible in their homeland (see Freeman, Thai in this volume). As Schein observes, young Miao women are clearly part of Hmong men's fantasy of "homeland women," but to the dismay of the women and their kin, few of the intimate and sexual relationships between Hmong men and Miao women actually result in marriage.

Men may thus be drawn to cross-border marriages because of the presumed values and qualities of foreign women versus local ones, who are believed to be too liberated, demanding, or independent in their outlook. Men—or their families on their behalf—may also look for foreign partners because their local opportunities for marriage are limited or because they are low on the local marriage market. Min, the South Korean rural farmer in the chapter by Nancy Abelmann and Hyunhee Kim, is doubly disadvantaged on the local marriage market because he is a poor farmer and because he is disabled. Min's mother thus seeks to find him a Filipina bride whom she imagines will be less liberated and less independent than South Korean women; furthermore, Min's mother imagines that the Filipina will be more attracted to the marriage because South Korea—even by way of marriage to a poor and disabled man—promises upward mobility from the "less developed" Philippines. The decision to move and marry, however, is not so simple as this imagined geographic hierarchy might suggest. Although she claims to be committed to Min, his fiancée does not show up for the group wedding ceremony, thus casting doubt on her own and her natal family's possible marriage motives.

Just as Min's mother expects Filipinas to share more traditional familial values, so do many men assume that Filipinas take marriage more seriously than do Westernized or urban U.S., Japanese, or Hong Kong women. This may be true of some Filipinas, since they have been raised in a Roman Catholic country that officially and legally prohibits divorce, but it is clearly not true of all Asian women, or of Filipinas who leave the Philippines (see Constable 2003b). Men are sometimes surprised to find that gender stereotypes of Asian women are more imagined than real. And women, among them Chosŏnjok and Vietnamese brides, may be surprised to find that husbands and in-laws from "modern" countries often embrace conservative and "old-fashioned" gender outlooks and familial expectations. Several of the Chosŏnjok brides in Freeman's chapter use the threat of divorce to negotiate with South Korean in-laws and husbands who will not allow them economic independence or to work outside the home. Ping, the Chinese woman whose story is told in Constable's chapter, considers returning to China or divorcing her husband, who, to her dismay, despite his education and cultured background, has very unenlightened ideas about marriage and women's roles.

In addition to common desires for traditional wives and modern husbands, we collectively consider many other discourses and stereotypes about foreign women against and in relation to actual marital experiences. Stereotypes of subservient Asian women and discourses about prostitutes, sex workers, and trafficked women do not accurately reflect the experiences of most of the women described in this book. Yet in many cases, such discourses and images are not far from the surface and inform many common ideas about foreign brides. Such images, inaccurate though they may be in the particular cases we describe, nonetheless contribute to the sense of loneliness and alienation experienced by immigrant women (on sexual images, see Tajima 1989, Wilson 1988, Constable 2003a, Suzuki 1999 and 2003b, Tyner 1996). Freeman illustrates the complex realities and actual experiences of Chosŏnjok brides in relation to the overly simplistic South Korean discourses on Chosŏnjok brides in the 1990s as the government-endorsed "saviors of the Korean countryside," and the later more critical discourse on foreign "runaway brides" who, motivated by the promise of migration and citizenship, actively deceive and abandon vulnerable Korean men. Abelmann and Kim locate the notion of international marriages of Korean men to foreign Asian women alongside the increasingly negative images of marriages between Korean women and non-Korean (mainly U.S.) men, and more recent images of Southeast Asian sex workers. In the cases of Miao or Chinese women who are mistresses or secondary wives, but not first wives, of overseas men, the presumed distinctions between "prostitutes" and "wives" is more difficult to maintain (Schein, Oxfeld in this volume). Chao's chapter also suggests that we need not look far into local Naxi discourses on marriage to discover the blurs and tensions between coercion and agency, kidnapping and elopement. Such examples doggedly remind us of the delicately constructed cultural categories and the hazy area that blurs what are often assumed to be rigid distinctions between marriage and prostitution, agency and coercion, romantic desire and exploitation.

Paradoxes of Global Hypergamy

As noted above, marriage mobility commonly involves the movement of brides from more remote and less developed locations to increasingly developed and less isolated ones, and globally from the poor and less developed global south to the wealthy and developed north. This pattern might aptly be labeled "global hypergamy." It is global in the sense that it involves men and women from different regions of the world. It can be considered hypergamous—building on the conventional anthropological definition of "hypergamy" as women marrying up into a higher socioeconomic group—if we conceive of "up" as referring to a hierarchy or a chain of geographical locations, or what William Lavely has called "spatial hypergamy" (1991, see also Fan and Huang 1998). The concept of global hypergamy is useful, however, only insofar as it can be used to raise questions rather than to foreclose on them. Thus we must ask what the existing global patterns are and why certain regions of the globe are excluded. Not all regions of Asia are represented, nor are all equally represented as the place of origin or the destination of brides. Hypergamy begs the question of how, for whom, and in what sense such marriages represent upward mobility. As Freeman keenly observes, patterns of marital mobility entail a number of paradoxes, including those of nationality/ethnicity, gender, geography, and economic class. To assume that such marriages are simply upward is to overlook the contradictory and paradoxical social and economic patterns that are not necessarily linked to geographic mobility and to overlook interesting underlying questions about gender.

Most contemporary marriage-scapes involve women who move to marry; rarely is it the men. Contrary to popular assumptions, the brides are not necessarily poor, nor do they categorically marry men who are above them on the socioeconomic ladder. Even though the women may appear to be moving up from a less developed country to a richer or more developed one, they do not necessarily move "higher on the chain of economic resources," as Oxfeld argues is the case for the Hakka women she describes. Many brides—including some of the Chinese, Filipina, and Vietnamese women described in this volume—are professional and well-educated women who would be considered middle class in their countries of origin. They may be from countries with low aggregate economic indicators, but where a middle-class income can afford them meals out, maids, entertainment, and other luxuries that are far more expensive and difficult to come by in the United States, Western Europe, or Japan.

Suzuki describes Filipinas who have learned to adjust their fantasies and earlier expectations to the realities of life in urban Japan, but whose relatives back home find it hard to believe that Japan's streets are not "lined with gold." Her description of "Millie" illustrates striking contrasts and contradictions between Millie's intermittent visits to the Philippines (where she lives as a privileged "señorita" in luxury with household help and has earned familial respect for her remittances) and her life in urban Japan as a hardworking and isolated housewife. In a striking example of downward class mobility, Thai describes the marriage between Tranh, a highly educated woman from an elite family in Vietnam, and Minh, a Viet Kieu low-wage earner in the United States. Tranh and Minh constitute part of a wider pattern of Vietnamese-Viet Kieu marriages in which the bride's standard of living can be expected to decrease significantly after marriage and migration.

Most of the chapters in this book thus call into question scholarly and popular assumptions that women who migrate to marry, marry up socially and economically, to men who are wealthier and better educated. The grooms' social and economic statuses vary, as do those of the brides. Japan, South Korea, Western Europe, and North America, for example, are generally considered higher on the ladder of economic development than the Philippines and China, but many Japanese, South Korean, European, and North American men who seek foreign brides are poor by local standards. As rural bachelors, South Korean or Japanese men may find it difficult to find local wives, so they seek brides from other poorer regions of the world. Suzuki's chapter tells the less well-known stories of Filipina marriages to urban Japanese men, and of Japanese-Filipina couples' shared "fantasy of reversal" in which they may one day retire in the Philippines and live elevated lives. U.S. husbands of Asian women also span a spectrum. Some are well above average in terms of education and income, whereas others work at low-wage jobs and their lifestyles represent a step down for their foreign wives (Jedlicka 1988, Constable 2003a). Such examples suggest that whether, and in what sense, such marriages can be considered hypergamous remains a key question.

Women do not simply marry up because of material logics. As mentioned earlier, other sorts of desires also come into play. Some women count love among the factors that motivate them to marry. Several Hakka women mentioned in Oxfeld's chapter opted to marry local Mei Xian Hakka men of their own choosing rather than marry wealthier Hakka men in Calcutta. Other women actively seek to marry farther afield not to find a husband in more desirable locations or because they prefer to live abroad but because of local constraints on their marriage opportunities. Some women are less marriageable locally because they are considered too old, too educated, divorced, or too experienced by local standards to be considered good wives. As Constable observes, Chinese women who are over thirty or divorced consider their opportunities to marry better with foreign (non-Chinese) men. Thai finds that Vietnamese women who are "too successful" or over thirty may choose—as did Tranh—to marry up globally to a U.S. low-wage worker, rather than remain unmarried or marry down locally. Filipina entertainers or single mothers may be considered marriageable by foreign men but not by local Filipinos (Suzuki 2003a and 2003b, Constable 2003a). As several of the women described in the following chapters illustrate, pragmatic or practical considerations in cross-border marriages do not necessarily preclude love and nonmaterial forms of desire (Abelmann and Kim, Freeman in this volume, see also Constable 2003a, Suzuki 2003a and 2003b, Jolly and Manderson 1997).

Crossing Geographic Borders and Gendered Agency

All marriages cross borders of some sort, and marriages in many parts of Asia have often involved a patrilocal postmarital residence pattern in which a bride is, under normal circumstances, expected to relocate to her husband's home or community. Yet Oxfeld reminds us that there have long been exceptions and variations to this rule in the context of older Chinese international marriages. In nineteenth- and early twentieth-century marriages between Chinese women and their overseas Chinese husbands, the wives often remained in China with their in-laws while their husbands lived abroad. In other cases the women emigrated as well, thus more closely resembling the transnational marriages of today.

Despite some similarities, many of the international marriages we describe are—both quantitatively and qualitatively—new and different from their older manifestations. By the late twentieth century, the distances crossed were often greater, and women were geographically farther away from their natal kin. The technology and transportation were faster and more widely available. Even in very rural and poor communities, as Schein observes, distances were sometimes bridged by telephones or even computers and the Internet, which allowed even women in rural and otherwise isolated villages to communicate with their natal kin in even more remote areas of China and with prospective overseas suitors. Greater distances from their natal kin can provide women with greater freedom, but as Schein and Chao so vividly illustrate, it can also render them more isolated and vulnerable within their new communities.

The older anthropological literature took such movement of a bride from her natal community into her husband's community as an indication of her lack of agency, her necessary obedience to marriage arrangements, and her assumed subordinate status and vulnerability among her in-laws. Claude Lévi-Strauss's classic work on the exchange of women insightfully reflected the ways in which the exchange of women among bride givers and bride takers create and reinforce social ties (1969, see also Rubin 1975). Yet Lévi-Strauss's approach regards brides as objects of exchange, overlooking the bride's perspective and agency. Within the Chinese context, Rubie Watson has stated that "patrilocal residence has been singled out as one of the major reasons for women's continuing oppression in postrevolution China" (1991:351). Schein and Oxfeld both suggest, however, that we carefully rethink the significance and possible varied meanings of women's postmarital mobility within particular contexts. Schein argues that in the contemporary context, patrilocal marriages can offer women certain advantages and disadvantages. As Oxfeld observes, the older Hakka women she interviewed may have followed the dictates of their kin, expressed little choice or say in the matter of whom they married, but the younger Hakka brides she knew expressed far greater agency, initiating their own marriage plans or declining to marry against their will.

Overall, the chapters in this volume contribute to a critique of the notion of wives as simply objects of exchange, and highlight instead women's agency in relation to wider structural constraints. Many of the women described herein made their own marriage choices. Even in the more coercive examples of Naxi women in southwestern China who are kidnapped or who elope, Chao clearly illustrates how women try to use marriage to maneuver for themselves, to achieve residence in more desirable locations, to escape the confines of local patriarchal marriages, or to lead what they envision as more modern lives. Such mobility is not simply or necessarily a familial strategy, as most Chinese marriages once were, but may serve in some cases to reduce or escape familial control. That is not to say, as chapters by Thai, Freeman, and Suzuki clearly illustrate, that women's imaginings and hopes about modern marriages or more leisurely lifestyles will be achieved or that they necessarily marry to escape familial commitments and obligations. Nonetheless, Naxi women sometimes use marriage to escape familial controls and to marry by what they see as more modern means, and, like Miao women who marry Han Chinese men, they can use marriage as a means to move to more desirable locations, instead of waiting, as Chao describes, for the Chinese state's promise of rural development and prosperity to reach the isolated regions of the country.

Abelmann and Kim's chapter on a failed Filipina–South Korean marriage is less concerned with the perspective and agency of the bride or groom than with that of the prospective groom's mother. The authors document this would-be marriage in its familial, national-historical, and transnational context and draw on interviews with the rural mother and the unmarried son's sisters in order to examine the diverse (even within a single family) ways in which a poor man's rural plight and the possibility of transnational marriage are variously signified. Abelmann and Kim argue that this case is important for what it tells us of the Korean mother's agency as expressed in her attempts to achieve "maternal citizenship"—by arranging the most favorable marriage imaginable for her only son. Her ability to travel to the Philippines with her son and to contemplate a transnational marriage (regardless of its failure) calls for theorizing beyond market logics, raising the issue of this mother's social location within a modernizing and globalizing South Korea that made her efforts possible in the first place.

That women express agency and choice is not to idealize the resulting marriages. As several contributors suggest, a woman may actively pursue marriage to an outsider or a foreigner and she may actively choose one man over another, or she may decide to marry a local man and remain at home. But none of these choices guarantees that her marriage will be happy or successful. Nor do greater border crossings guarantee that the marriages will be "upward" in the ways that women may imagine. Moreover, as the chapters by Abelmann and Kim, Suzuki, Oxfeld, and Thai so vividly remind us, women's agency and choice should not blind us to the varied influence and pressure that may be exerted in certain cases by parents, siblings, and even children.

Gendered Geographies of Power

Doreen Massey's notion of "power geometry" suggests that we consider not only who moves but also how people are differently located in relation to access and power over the flows and interconnections between places. As Massey writes, some people "initiate flows and movement, others don't; some are more on the receiving-end of it than others; some are effectively imprisoned by it. . . . [There are] groups who are really in a sense in charge of time-space compression, who can really use it and turn it to advantage, whose power and influence it very definitely increases. . . . But there are also groups who are also doing a lot of physical moving, but who are not 'in charge' of the process in the same way at all" (1994:149).

This volume builds on and questions some of Massey's ideas. Massey's work begs the question of why it is usually women who move by virtue of marriage and not men, and whether this means that women are simply, and across the board, on the "receiving end" of mobility that is controlled by men and their kin. As the story of Min's mother suggests, some women are empowered to arrange marriages for sons who have little say in the matter. The following chapters also illustrate that women, by virtue of their social positioning, can take advantage of opportunities for mobility that are sometimes unavailable to men. As noted above and demonstrated in the chapters that follow, marriage can be used to achieve upward geographic mobility and independence (Freeman, Schein); to provide economic support for families back home (Suzuki, Oxfeld, Constable); or to escape less than ideal marital opportunities or gender constraints at home (Constable, Thai). It can also serve as a critique of the state or a means to resist the state's family-planning policies and unequal development schemes (Chao). As Freeman observes, brides may not be "in charge" of their mobility, in the sense that they may depend on marriage brokers, government policies, and prospective grooms and in-laws for their mobility. Correspondingly, men are not necessarily in charge of this process, nor are they necessarily the only ones on the receiving end of such mobility. Whereas Massey's work implies a certain linear pattern to mobility, or one in which some are beneficiaries and others are not, such a clear-cut pattern is not borne out by the localized paradoxes of mobility on the ground.

In their work on "gendered geographies of power," Pessar and Mahler have built on Massey's work and pay close attention to people's "social location" or their "positions within power hierarchies created through historical, political, economic, geographic, kinship-based and other socially stratifying factors" (2001:6). Herein we illustrate some of the varied ways Asian women's social locations are linked to their ability or inability to meet foreign partners and their decisions to marry or not marry across particular borders. The number of Chinese women marrying outside of China decreased during most of the Maoist period and increased during China's period of economic liberalization, and Chinese-Korean marriages decreased in the late 1990s because of the downturn in the Asian market; these facts point to the relevance of politics, economics, and history to people's social locations. Such large-scale patterns are important, but they do not tell the whole story.

Pessar and Mahler also consider the "degrees of agency" that people are able to exert in their particular social locations (2001:7). As they observe, agency is "affected not only by extra-personal factors but also quintessentially individual characteristics such as initiative" and "cognitive processes such as the imagination as well as substantive agency"

(2001:8). Such considerations help to explain why someone occupying a particular social and geographical location might initiate change or imagine the possibility of cross-border marriage and migration whereas another person in the same position might not. Women may choose not to leave home even when the opportunities present themselves (see Abelmann and Kim, Oxfeld), whereas others might eagerly embrace such possibilities (see Freeman, Suzuki). Men might wish for their own opportunities for marriage migration but find that such opportunities are mostly available only for women (Constable, Freeman).

In the chapters that follow, we deal with different but sometimes overlapping gendered patterns of marriage mobility. Each story of cross-border marriage illustrates the importance of social positioning, imagination, and initiative, as well as political, historical, social, and cultural logics. While most of the cases are of men and women who marry across geographic and social borders of various sorts, we also ask about those who do not. To what extent does social location (including gender) influence one's ability or inability to initiate correspondence or courtship across borders? To what extent does a global imagination—and the global fantasies and desires of brides and grooms and their family members—influence, as Appadurai suggests, one's ability to dream and imagine oneself in a different social and geographic location? In the cases we examine, women are expected to cross borders when they marry. Although men cross borders to meet prospective spouses, women usually cross them more permanently. Relatively few men have the option of becoming marriage migrants themselves, and men at the lower end of the global and spatial hierarchy are unlikely to have the power and ability to facilitate the mobility of wives. Marriage mobility can be used by women—sometimes in accordance with their family's wishes, sometimes in opposition to them—to their own advantage. Greater distances can mean greater vulnerability as women are separated from their natal communities, but they can also mean greater freedom and opportunity. Insofar as transnational global marriage-scapes are concerned, sometimes it is difficult to tell which way is up.

Chapter 2
Cross-Border Hypergamy? Marriage Exchanges in a Transnational Hakka Community

Ellen Oxfeld

In the summer of 1993, while visiting Mei Xian, a county in Guangdong Province, China, I witnessed an attempt at international matchmaking. My travel companions were two sisters who had grown up in a Hakka Chinese community in Calcutta, India, where I had engaged in field research during the 1980s. The Hakka are a distinct ethnic and linguistic group who are dispersed throughout a number of provinces in southeastern China as well as throughout the diaspora.[1] They are nonetheless considered to be members of the majority Han Chinese rather than members of an ethnic minority.

I wanted to travel to Mei Xian because it was the ancestral homeland of the Calcutta Hakka. So I accompanied Ruolan, who now lived in Hong Kong, and Lilan, her sister, who still resided in the Hakka community of Calcutta. They were returning to see relations in Mei Xian, particularly those in Moonshadow Pond, their father's native village. During lunch at the overseas Chinese hotel where we were staying, the two sisters tried to interest one of the waitresses in a young Hakka Chinese man from Calcutta. They spoke to her about how diligent he was. He had his own business, a tannery, and her standard of living would rise if she married into his business family.

Later, they explained to me that there were many fine young men in the Calcutta Chinese community who were having a hard time getting married.

"Everyone there is leaving the country," they said. "So now men are looking for brides from Mei Xian."

This chapter looks at marriages that cross the borders of three interconnected communities: 1) the village in Mei Xian that I call Moonshadow Pond; 2) Calcutta, India, where there has been a community of Hakka from Mei Xian for many generations; and 3) Toronto, Canada, where many Calcutta Hakka have migrated, especially since the early 1980s. Over the course of two decades, I have engaged in fieldwork in all of these communities. My research in the Calcutta Chinese community took place in 1980–82 and again in the summers of 1985 and 1989. In 1986, I conducted fieldwork among emigrants from that community who were living in Toronto (see Oxfeld 1993 for a more extensive study of both communities). Subsequently, I visited and conducted field research in Moonshadow Pond in 1993, 1995–96, and 1997.

The concept of marriage exchange in classic anthropological theory entails the assumption that marriage is part of a system of alliance in which the exchange of women by men forges ongoing relationships between bride givers and bride takers. In these theories, hypergamy refers to a specific kind of marriage exchange in which women marry into families of slightly higher social status than their own (see Barfield 1997:254, Dumont 1966:116). After examining marriages among the three communities referred to above, I will ask to what extent they can be understood as transnational, cross-border variants of hypergamy. And I will ask if the assumption that marriage exchange is the exchange of women by men—an assumption that has been frequently criticized—makes any sense in this particular case.

In my conclusion, I will suggest that concepts such as "hypergamy" and "cross-border" need to be modified to understand the nature of the marriages among these three communities. I will also agree with earlier critics of marriage-exchange theories who point out that women may also have agency in constructing these relationships and that the notion of "men exchanging women," while accurate in some instances, is hardly all-encompassing when trying to understand the forging of relationships among groups and individuals through marriage.

Hypergamy and Marriage Exchange in Anthropology and China

Disagreement over the content and even validity of the concept of marriage exchange has a long history in anthropology. For Claude Lévi-Strauss, marriage exchange was the foundation of culture itself, forcing people to mate beyond the borders of their biological families and to establish links and communicate with outsiders (Lévi-Strauss 1969). Without this, he contended, one could not even have society, but rather would only have families who reproduced among themselves and who lived out their lives in isolation from everyone else.

Yet Lévi-Strauss and other exponents of these approaches were subsequently criticized for portraying women as lacking agency in these exchanges—in other words, for describing women as mere tokens in a game of culture played by men (Weiner 1975). In addition, the implication that marriage is only about relations between groups—and not also about individuals who have their own agendas and desires, worked out within the limits of their social and cultural milieus—has also been roundly critiqued (Bourdieu 1977). Finally, as Gayle Rubin reminds us in her now-famous essay on the traffic in women, to the degree that the exchange of women by men is an element of societies and cultures, we must keep in mind that these exchanges could not proceed at all unless cultures first constructed the gendered categories and emotional orientations of "masculinity," "femininity," and "heterosexuality"—that is, the social structures and emotional orientations needed to reproduce male exchangers and female exchanged (Rubin 1975).

Despite these criticisms, there is no doubt that the early theorists of marriage exchange were right when they pointed out that marriage is always in some ways about borders and boundaries. At its very minimum, the incest prohibition ensures that most humans go beyond the border of their biological family to mate, and subsequent rules and practices of exogamy and endogamy only add specificity to this project.

In China, the boundaries and borders created by marriage are given further definition by the normative practices and principles of patrilocality and patrilineality. As numerous scholars have pointed out (see M. Wolf 1972, Baker 1979), it was daughters who married "out" and who had to be integrated into a new family. Much has been said in the literature about the problems of that integration—the new daughter-in-law is needed if the patriline is to reproduce itself, yet there are "dangers" in integrating this new and "foreign" presence into the family (see, for instance, Ahern 1978). How will the new bride adjust? Will she get along with her mother-in-law? Or, as in the boundary crossing discussed by Mary Douglas (1966), will the border crossing of the new daughter-in-law into her husband's family create chaos, disorder, and danger (Ahern 1978)?

Hypergamy fits well with the assumptions in this normative model. Since it was the bride rather than the groom who had to accommodate to a new family, it was logical to assume that "a bride from a high-status family might not adapt well to humble surroundings" (Lavely 1991:288–89). In *The House of Lim* (1968), for instance, Margery Wolf tells the story of one disastrous marriage in rural Taiwan in which the wife came from a wealthier family than that of her husband. Interestingly, this marriage was contracted against the advice of the matchmaker. The groom's family had been financially successful, but not successful enough, it turned out, to make up for the discrepancy between the families, and the wife was never reconciled to her new position (1968:123).

Although hypergamy in the case above is based on class, it has also long held a spatial component in Chinese society. An urban versus a rural locale, or even life in the valleys versus the mountains, could have tremendous influence over a family's economic welfare (see Schein in this volume). William Lavely calls this "spatial hypergamy" (1991:291) and points out that it was quite pronounced during the Maoist era, when it was very hard for rural residents to move up through "higher education, the army, advancement through the party, or temporary work in state units" (Lavely 1991:290). Migration within rural areas or from rural to urban areas was also tightly controlled and almost impossible during this time. Under these conditions, marrying one's daughter to a more prosperous area was one of the only ways a family member could move up.

Before moving on to our specific examples, we need to think through what is new and old in our charge. We need to keep in mind that marriage is "cross-border" by definition. And in the patrilineal, patrilocal Chinese context, it is women who are the border crossers. Given the demands on Chinese brides to adjust to their new families, it is logical that hypergamy would be a favored pattern, and this has long held a spatial component. In fact, one could argue that marriage has always been a form of migration in the Chinese context. What is different in the cases to be considered in this chapter is that the marriages under investigation create links across global space, and over national as well as merely village, county, or provincial borders.

Indeed, in the Chinese case, marriage has always helped create links between the mainland and the diaspora.[2] In early stages of Chinese migration to many countries (see, for instance, Loewen 1971, Patterson 1975), men left without their brides, and often mated with local women. But as Chinese communities overseas grew and consolidated, women joined them. Their arrival usually made it easier for the community to close ranks and maintain a sense of ethnic and cultural distinctiveness from the host culture (see for instance, Patterson 1975, Bonacich 1973). As such, the phenomenon of Chinese brides crossing national borders as well as familial ones and creating alliances across global as well as national space is not new.[3]

At the same time, as the cases below illustrate, the nature of these transnational marriages may not always be summed up simply as "cross-border hypergamy." As we shall see, some "transnational" marriages created links across borders but did not result in the actual migration of a bride to her husband's home in a foreign land. Other marriages crossed national borders but remained within the confines of a de-territorialized ethnic community, and hence in certain respects did not involve the crossing of community borders at all. Finally, the hypergamous nature of these alliances is not always as clear-cut as one might think at first glance.

Entrepreneurs, Workers, and Peasants

With these preliminary observations in mind, we now turn to the three interconnected Hakka Chinese communities that I have observed at different points in time over the last twenty years. Although Mei Xian is the ancestral homeland of both the Calcutta and Toronto Hakka, people's daily lives are lived within these individual communities and in the interactions with the wider societies of India, Canada, or China. The Calcutta Hakka are successful entrepreneurs, primarily leather manufacturers, but also shoe-shop owners and restaurateurs (especially since the late 1980s, when the popularity of Chinese food among Calcutta's middle-class citizens soared). On the other hand, Calcutta Hakka who have migrated to Toronto have rarely gone into business. Instead, they have sought blue- or white-collar salaried employment to support themselves. Many live in the Toronto suburbs, but they are spread out over a fairly wide area and do not live clustered together in one place, as do their Calcutta relatives (Oxfeld 1993).

By contrast, most of the Mei Xian relatives of the Calcutta and Toronto Hakka still live in rural villages like Moonshadow Pond. There they mix agriculture with other economic activities that can bring more cash into their families. For instance, among families in Moonshadow Pond, some individuals will work their shares of land in order to grow rice and pay taxes, as well as to provision their families with vegetables (these are usually activities engaged in by middle-aged women). Other family members usually add to the family income through small business (running small shops or cultivating fruit or fishponds) or by migrating to larger cities to work in factories or as cooks or drivers.

While many marriages connect families within rather than between these three communities, there have also been a number of marriages over the last century that have linked Mei Xian to Calcutta, Calcutta to Toronto, and finally Mei Xian to Calcutta once again. At first glance, these marriages appear to be cross-border because they link individuals and families across international borders. They also appear to be hypergamous, because they link the bride to a family that is slightly higher on the chain of economic resources than her natal family. However, for the purposes of this paper, I will not take either of these assumptions for granted. Rather, I will seek to understand the nature of marriage exchanges between Mei Xian, Calcutta, and Toronto Hakka. I will ask whether and to what degree they can be understood as both hypergamous and cross-border.

Prerevolutionary Transnational Marriage Exchanges

"Widows" and "Little Daughters-in-Law"

As an area of China from which many emigrated in the first half of the twentieth century, Mei Xian is not a newcomer to cross-border marriages. These marriages could take several forms. Sometimes, young men who immigrated to India or Southeast Asia married before leaving Mei Xian. If they established themselves economically in their new homes, they would send for their wives.

Still, in some cases a husband might emigrate and send money home, but never return or send for his wife to join him. Some of these men were never heard from again and, in fact, remarried while abroad.

The experience of Xuelan, a woman in her seventies in Moonshadow Pond, was not atypical of this kind of marriage. Like many in her generation, she was a "little daughter-in-law," that is, she was sent to live in her future husband's home while still an infant, and the relationship was consummated without fanfare when the bride and groom both came of age. (Most elderly residents of Moonshadow Pond now explain these arrangements as stemming from their former poverty. They usually point to the fact that the few prosperous families in the village prior to liberation did not give their daughters away in this manner, and waited until they were young adults to arrange their marriages).[4]

Like many "little daughters-in-law," Xuelan told me she had no feelings for her natal family, but she did develop feelings of attachment for her mother-in-law, who played the role of an adoptive mother. Unfortunately, her mother-in-law died when she was only eight, and her father-in-law's second wife treated her harshly. She could still recount with anger specific incidents, such as the time her new mother-in-law beat her because she had accidentally burned the rice she was cooking.

Meanwhile, her future husband migrated to India with his younger brother. He later returned to China to consummate the relationship, and she bore a son. Her husband went back to India. He returned to China one more time, and she conceived her daughter. After that, she never heard from her husband again. Although Xuelan had children of her own, many of the women left behind in this way never bore children. To ensure their own security, these women often adopted a child or children who were raised as members of their husband's descent group and who were responsible for their mothers in their old age.

Were these cross-border marriages? Were they hypergamous? In theory, marriage to an overseas emigrant would be a step up. But in those cases where the wives remained in rural Mei Xian, they had the worst of all possible worlds: they did not receive the economic benefit of emigration; and they were often called "widows" at home because of the long-term absence of their husbands. Left to live with their in-laws, but without a spouse to provide material and moral support, their situations were often bleak.

This phenomenon is clearly not limited to my Mei Xian sample. One finds references to it in other works that focus on areas of China from which there were high rates of emigration. For instance, Graham Johnson found evidence of a disproportionately high number of widowed household heads among families in the Pearl River Delta. He explains this phenomenon as resulting from the out-migration of husbands, many of whom "never returned" or "broke contact with their homeland villages. Some may have remarried abroad and established separate families" (Johnson 1993:128). Two moving portrayals of women who were left behind by émigré husbands are found in Maxine Hong Kingston's novel *The Woman Warrior* (1975). In the chapter "To the Western Palace," the narrator describes a futile visit by her elderly aunt to Los Angeles to find her émigré husband, who had long ago remarried in the United States. In the famous opening scene of the book, the narrator introduces us to the story of her aunt, the "No Name Woman," who became pregnant while her husband was away in America, and who ultimately took her own life in order to spare her family shame.

Such lonely and bleak endings were not always the fate of these preliberation transnational marriages. In some cases, reunification occurred after long years of separation. One woman in Moonshadow Pond told me the story of her mother-in-law, who stayed in China with her son when her husband left Mei Xian for India. Liberation and the tumultuous events of the Maoist period (see below) made it difficult for her to follow her husband to India until the early 1980s, when she was already over sixty years old. Although she had been separated from her husband for thirty-five years, they were ultimately reunited. And, unlike many others, he had not remarried during this long interval.

Such a long wait was not always the case, even for an adopted daughter-in-law. During my research in Calcutta, I gathered stories about a number of first-generation Hakka immigrants. Some of them had marriages that could be classified as "minor marriage"—marriage arranged before adulthood, contracted without the exchange of dowry and brideprice, and without elaborate ceremony or feasting. In some of these cases, while the bride-to-be had already entered the groom's family in Mei Xian as an "adopted daughter," the marriage was not consummated until after both husband and wife had arrived in India. For instance, Mao Yisheng, who later became a successful tannery owner, arrived in India in 1936, when he was twenty-two years old. A few years after his arrival in India, his fiancé, who had lived with his family in Mei Xian as an adopted daughter-in-law, traveled to India with his younger brother. Another emigrant, Qiao Tanming, arrived in India in 1939 at age eighteen. Nine years later, his "sister" came to Calcutta, and they began to live together as husband and wife.

Major Marriage

Success abroad might change a man's marital prospects. If an emigrant had not already been matched in childhood to an adopted bride, and if he had established himself economically while abroad, he could return home to marry an adult bride, and to enjoy the elevation in status that came with this type of marriage.

I encountered a number of older men in the Calcutta Chinese community whose cases conformed to this pattern. Typically, the emigrant would arrive in India as a young, unmarried man. After many years of hard labor in a tannery, he might succeed in starting his own business. At that point, he would return home to Mei Xian to marry and come back to India with his bride. For instance, Wei Guangrong arrived in India in 1906 at age sixteen (I didn't meet him, since he was deceased by the time of my field research, but his descendants told me his story). In his twenties, he returned to China to marry and then came back to India, where he built his own tannery in 1941. Similarly, Xi Feiyuan arrived in India at age sixteen in 1928. After ten years of hard work, he built his own tannery in 1938. He then returned to Mei Xian for his wedding, and came back to India with his new wife.

The story of Yuan Qide's family nicely illustrates the change from transnational minor marriage to transnational major marriage. Yuan Qide emigrated in 1897 with his father, mother, and his bride-to-be, who had been an adopted daughter-in-law in their family. He established one of the first Chinese tanneries in Calcutta, in 1913, and became financially successful during World War I, when the demand for leather increased rapidly. Indeed, he was so successful that he sent his own son back to Mei Xian for a grand wedding in 1931. This son then returned to India with his adult bride.

There were also cases where an adult bride traveled to India and the wedding was held there. Since it was considered dangerous for a young woman to travel alone, however, another family member would have to accompany her. This family member, often a brother, would then be the next migrant. In this way, marriage pulled in a successive chain of Chinese immigrants to India. As women married, they traveled with members of their natal families, who could then begin the process of establishing themselves in India (see Oxfeld 1993: chap. 5).

Traditional theories of affinal alliance and marriage exchange come close to describing the reality in these cases, even if they never envisioned such alliances taking place over global spaces. The brides in these situations certainly married up in terms of economic status. In addition, the marriages provided an important link for their natal kin to climb up the economic ladder.

However, even here the notion of "hypergamy" may not completely capture the nature of these marriage links. First, by marrying adult women, these emigrant men enhanced their own status (by comparison with those who married their adopted "sisters"). If they returned to China for the wedding, there was the status enhancement of an elaborate ceremony and banquet in one's ancestral village. While one might say that such status enhancement devolves to the groom in all major marriages in China, the return home added additional status, since the wedding was not only status-enhancing in itself, but underscored the returning groom's material success while abroad. As such, bride givers and bride receivers each had something to gain through these arrangements.

Transnational Marriages After Liberation

Several factors influenced transnational marriage links among Hakka in Moonshadow Pond, Calcutta, and Toronto after liberation. First, after the revolution in China in 1949, it became much more difficult for marriages between overseas Hakka and those in Mei Xian to occur. The policies of the Communist government did not favor families with overseas relatives. Not only were there practical difficulties in traveling in and out of China, but a woman's natal family could actually suffer as a result of having an overseas Chinese relation. During the 1950s and early 1960s, the kinfolk of overseas Chinese were able to receive some remittances, but return visits from emigrants were not encouraged and rarely took place. Then, during the Cultural Revolution era (officially 1966–68, but continuing in influence through the early 1970s), almost all contacts between overseas Chinese and mainland kin were cut off. Overseas Chinese who returned, such as refugees from Indonesian political violence, were "attacked for their bourgeois values and wasteful practices" (Godley 1989:333).

"If you had an overseas Chinese relative," one villager told me, "they might even accuse you of being a spy. So most people, if they had any connections, just kept it a secret." In such circumstances, no one benefited from transnational marriage negotiations. It was only after 1978 that the policy toward overseas Chinese was reversed and contacts actively encouraged (see Godley 1989). Confiscated property and bank accounts were reimbursed to overseas Chinese who had returned to China (Godley 1989; Woon 1989). On the national and provincial levels, investment by overseas Chinese capitalists played an important role in the expansion of China's economy, especially in the southeastern area, from which the bulk of the émigré population originated. Even at the township and village level, overseas Chinese have played an increasingly important economic role in villages that were once their home or the home of their ancestors. A result of this opening was that many Hakka families in India began to reconnect with their kin in Mei Xian.

Simultaneously, developments in the Calcutta Chinese community began to lead to emigration from their community to North America and Europe, particularly to Toronto. During the Sino-Indian conflict of 1962, many Chinese in India were deported from the country or interned in a camp in Rajasthan. Although the vast majority of Chinese born in India are now citizens, the conflict left community members feeling insecure as a tiny minority in their adopted home of India. Further, life in Calcutta in terms of everyday public amenities is still much more difficult than life in Toronto, even if it means discarding life in a family business for an ordinary working-class job.

By the early 1980s, emigration of some family members had become an important strategy for the Calcutta Chinese, economically and politically, and there are now few Calcutta Chinese families who do not have at least some family members who live abroad. Marriages between Calcutta Hakka and former community members living abroad, particularly in Toronto, are one means of sending new family members abroad, and these marriages, in turn, have an impact on the marriage market for those who remain in Calcutta.

Since the beginning of the reform regime in China, several new forms of transnational marriage between Calcutta Hakka, Toronto Hakka, Mei Xian Hakka, and Hakka from other parts of the diaspora have emerged. These marriage exchanges are mutually implicated. Below, I examine these new cross-border relationships in more detail and ask what kinds of dilemmas they attempt to resolve. I also try to understand the ways they differ from their predecessors in the first half of the twentieth century.

From Calcutta to Toronto

I begin my examination with the third link on this transnational marriage chain, that between Toronto and Calcutta Hakka. As I found during my research in Calcutta in the 1980s, young men from the Calcutta community often immigrate to Canada before they marry. Once they are established, they often look to the Calcutta Chinese community to provide a mate. During the 1980s, almost every Chinese family in Calcutta had at least one family member who lived abroad, and daughters were no less likely to emigrate than sons (Oxfeld 1993:187). But the motivations behind emigration for men and women sometimes differed. Daughters were much more likely to emigrate in order to marry, rather than prior to marriage (Oxfeld 1993).

While many families wanted at least one son to stay behind in Calcutta to continue running the family business, there was no reason to pressure daughters to stay behind in India. Family businesses were still passed down patrilineally, and children in Canada were viewed as critical in providing connections for other family members who might ultimately seek to emigrate. Even if parents had put pressure on daughters to marry in Calcutta, it is doubtful they would have been as successful as their predecessors in determining their daughters' marital fates. While many marriages in Calcutta continued to be arranged by parents, there were also many couples who chose their own mates. Even those who did not choose their own mate had veto power by the 1980s. Elders could suggest a match, but everyone had to agree.

For instance, Henry Wang immigrated with his family to Toronto in the late 1960s as a teenager, so he was one of the early emigrants. About ten years later, he returned to Calcutta for his grandfather's funeral. While he was there, his relatives started to drop hints about a particular girl. They asked him, he said, "whether you have any interesting ideas about her, and then it sort of sunk in my mind that that is what they were trying to match."

In Henry's case, the potential bride was interested, and she eventually emigrated to Toronto, where they were married in 1980. All other things being equal, a husband in Toronto often looked much more attractive than one in Calcutta. There were and are a number of reasons for this. Although Calcutta Hakka who lived in Toronto often spoke nostalgically about the human touch, slow pace, and interpersonal interactions in Calcutta, there is no doubt that Toronto was considered a more peaceful and economically secure place to settle over the long haul. Moving to Toronto was usually seen as a step up.

For instance, Susan Qin, who had immigrated to Toronto in 1974 so that she could marry her fiancé, spoke about how sad her family felt when she decided to leave. However, she then added, "I guess it's mixed feelings, because you know how I told you that going abroad is a big thing there. . . . [W]hen you have somebody going abroad your status goes up."

Another factor may also influence Calcutta Hakka women and make a marriage in Toronto look desirable: the balance of power in the Toronto families is quite different from that in Calcutta. When a Calcutta Chinese couple starts a family in Toronto, they may also sponsor the groom's parents for immigration. A major motive in this decision is child care, because in most of these cases, both husband and wife are employed in Toronto. Unemployable, and sometimes unable to speak English, the elders in these situations can be at the mercy of their adult children, and the authority of the elders over their adult children is vastly weakened as compared with the situation in Calcutta. It was very clear that in Toronto, the elders lived in their son and daughter-in-law's house, rather than their son bringing a bride to live with him in his parents' home (Oxfeld 1993:261).

Such a situation might actually look appealing to a potential bride, who could consider a future in Canada with either no mother-in-law resident in the home at all, or with a mother-in-law who would function more as an unpaid child care worker than as a figure of authority (Oxfeld 1993:259).

The case of Susan Qin, whom I interviewed in 1986, helps illustrate this. As I have written elsewhere,

> when Susan emigrated from India in 1974, she had not been that keen on leaving India. There, as the only daughter among five siblings, she received lots of attention. But she felt that her fiancé, Thomas, who had already emigrated in 1972, had no other option. As Susan told me, Thomas came from "a big family, and the tannery is not big enough to house all of them [his nine other brothers]. So, he was smart to branch out." Within a few years of their marriage, however, both Susan and Thomas found themselves busily occupied with jobs and with the task of raising three small daughters. Thus, when Thomas's mother visited in 1977, they encouraged her to stay and applied for a change in her immigrant status. Thomas's mother now takes care of the children after they come home from school each day, and she also does laundry and cooking on weekdays. (Oxfeld 1993:259)

Of course, this situation may not look so appealing to the senior generation. In Calcutta, I heard many horror stories about elders who had emigrated abroad in order to join their adult children. Some even returned to Calcutta and to their tanneries rather than remain abroad with their married children (Oxfeld 1993:259). Ironically, though these elders went to live with their own children, their isolation from the host society, and their inability to control their destiny in their new surroundings in some ways parallel the situation of brides who marry abroad, discussed in this volume.

In contrast to the larger and more amorphous group of Hmong/Miao from Laos, Vietnam, and China described by Louisa Schein, or the even less well-defined group of Korean small farmers described by Caren

Freeman (this volume), the Hakka brides from Calcutta were not so isolated in their new surroundings in Toronto. They married into a group
of transplanted co-ethnics who were well known—if not to themselves,
at least to their relatives—in the small and well-defined Calcutta Hakka
community. For the most part, they spoke English and worked upon
arrival in Toronto.

Looking Once Again for a Bride in Mei Xian

For all the reasons stated above, Calcutta Hakka men were finding it
more difficult to find a bride by the late 1980s. Some men began to look
to Mei Xian as a possible remedy for this bride shortage. For reasons I
will explain below, this strategy was not always successful.

While in Moonshadow Pond, I did witness one wedding between a
returning overseas Chinese from Taiwan and a Mei Xian woman. Young
women from Mei Xian may experience a rise in their living standard if
they marry abroad, including marriage into the Calcutta Hakka community; but unlike the rural women who were married to emigrant men in
prerevolutionary China, contemporary Mei Xian women now have a
much greater say in their marital fates.

The reasons for these changes are numerous and well known. With
the establishment of the People's Republic, China instituted significant
changes in marriage law. Economic roles of women have also changed
significantly. Young women from Moonshadow Pond now work for several years prior to marriage, often by migrating to one of the large cities
in Guangdong Province and seeking factory employment. Although
some of their earnings are remitted to their natal families, these women
are no longer completely dependent upon these families. Further, China's marriage law prohibits parents from forcing their children to marry
against their will, and even if ideology is far from a reflection from practice, rural Chinese women have grown up in a society that at least pays
lip service to gender equality on the ideological level.

While "love marriages," or marriages where the partners choose each
other based on an emotional and romantic bond, are still in the minority, almost all marriages in Mei Xian are at least undertaken by mutual
consent. A matchmaker may introduce a couple, or try to set up a chan-
nel of communication between them, but ultimately the decision is
theirs.

In Ruolan's attempted marriage negotiation, referred to at the beginning of this chapter, nothing further transpired. It turns out that the
young Mei Xian woman whom Ruolan was trying to interest in a Calcutta
Hakka groom already had a boyfriend of her own, and was uninter-

ested—an outcome that could not be imagined for Mei Xian women in the first half of the century.

Here we find one of the most significant differences between the cross-border marriages of the past (Mei Xian to Calcutta) and those of the present (Calcutta to Toronto, plus Mei Xian to Calcutta once again). Women now have an agency that was unthinkable earlier. Indeed, during my time in Mei Xian, I heard about many more attempts at international matchmaking than actual matches. My landlord's family, for instance, told me that several years earlier a visiting overseas relative approached them about a match for their daughter that would have taken her to the United States. Despite the connections this might give her family, as well as the opportunity to immigrate to a presumably wealthier locale, she was not interested. As in the case above, she already had a boyfriend in Mei Xian, a fellow villager whom she later married.

Of course, some matches between Mei Xian and Calcutta were successfully negotiated. For instance, Tan Qiyun had a successful tanning business in Calcutta. One son remained in Calcutta and two immigrated to Canada. The elder son, however, was divorced in Canada in the late 1980s, something that was still unusual in this community. Unable to find a bride in Canada, he returned to Calcutta to help with the family business. There, he had more than one strike against him: he was somewhat older (in his thirties), and had already been divorced. He ultimately was remarried to a woman from Mei Xian. In this case, his somewhat older age and divorced status were compensated for by his economic status.

Second Wives and Concubines in the New China

Interestingly, the reform era in China has also led to one more example of cross-border liaison. In this case, an old practice has been reinvigorated by economic globalization. This is the taking of a secondary wife, or concubine. A contemporary phenomenon in China is that of overseas Chinese businessmen who take mistresses on the Chinese mainland. Mei Xian villagers view these relationships as secondary marriages (the women involved are often referred to as *xiao laopo*, or the "small wife"). Of course, such "marriages" have no legal validity. Nonetheless, this does not stop villagers from talking about them.

During the course of my fieldwork, I witnessed discussion about one local case of this type. A wealthy overseas cousin of one of the older men in the village returned from Taiwan frequently to visit Mei Xian, where he said he had a "wife." Since he already had a wife in Taiwan, villagers referred to the Mei Xian "wife" as his secondary wife, or *xiao laopo*. Moonshadow Pond residents did not view either party to these "marriages" in a favorable light. In the eyes of Moonshadow Pond residents, both the "wife" and her reputed husband were out for gain. In this case, they said that the "wife" had "thick skin." Presumably, the financial windfall from being involved with a wealthy but elderly overseas Chinese had made her impervious to the concerns of status and face that villagers thought would ordinarily deter people from this kind of relationship. The older man's motivation was explained not in terms of money, but sexual image. Villagers poked fun at him, saying he was obviously concerned with projecting a virile image that should no longer have been important at his age. When his mistress became pregnant, they noted with sardonic glee that he was very quick to take paternal credit for himself.

The low status of these relationships for the residents of Moonshadow Pond is partially based on the less than savory motivations that villagers attribute to the partners. But unlike traditional marriage exchanges, these cross-border relationships are not embedded in a larger context of alliance and exchange. In the relationships between returning overseas men and mainland women, there are no gains or new relationships for natal kin. In other words, there are no in-laws created.

The absence of alliance and the creation of new affinal connections make these relationships different from many of the other marriage exchanges between Mei Xian, Calcutta, and Toronto Hakka described earlier in this chapter. Indeed, as I have shown, the ability for natal families to forge overseas connections is one of the attractive elements in some of these other alliances.

There is a final irony regarding these secondary marriages between mainland women and overseas men, at least from the point of view of Moonshadow Pond villagers. While they will tell you that both parties in this relationship think they have gained something—either money or a virile image—the villagers see each party as the fool. From the villagers' point of view, these matches are far from hypergamous. While both the man and the woman think they have gained, the villagers "know" they have not.

Conclusion

Categories have a way of escaping your grasp just when you would like to use them. In this chapter, I have examined marriages that cross the borders of three interconnected Hakka communities. But although one might categorize these as cross-border, hypergamous marriage exchanges, each of these categories is rendered somewhat less certain through my own analysis.

Let's begin with "cross-border." I noted at the beginning of the chapter that, all marriages are, by definition, cross-border. But beyond this definitional sense of "border," how do the marriages in this case hold up? Of course, these marriages created links across national borders. Yet, they occurred among Hakka Chinese from Mei Xian. As Arjun Appadurai has reminded us, "as groups migrate [and] regroup in new locations . . . the ethno in ethnography takes on a slippery, nonlocalized quality" (1996:48). And, he continues, though there are "stable communities and networks of kinship, friendship, work, and leisure, as well as birth, residence and other filiative forms . . . the warp of these stabilities is everywhere shot through with the woof of human motion" (1996:48).

It may be that we are not dealing with cross-border marriages at all in this case, but with marriage in a de-territorialized community (a situation quite different from the much more amorphous grouping of co-ethnics described by Schein, Thai, and Freeman in this volume). The de-territorialized community in this case is created at least in part by the very marriage alliances across national borders that this chapter describes. These marriages are therefore central in the reproduction of the de-territorialized community. In Toronto, the weddings themselves are central to maintaining "Calcutta Hakka" life in Toronto. One Calcutta Chinese immigrant to Toronto stated, "In social life Calcutta is better, here there's no social life at all, it's only work, work, work." Weddings, he said, "are the only time we meet" (Oxfeld 1993:264). Many others told me that the larger the Calcutta Chinese community became in Toronto, the bigger and more elaborate these weddings became, until there was a considerable element of competition and status as people compared and assessed each wedding.

The notion of "hypergamy" becomes similarly slippery when one tries to understand the cases in this chapter. While it might be easy to view the marriage exchange from Mei Xian to Calcutta to Toronto as a one-way flow of brides to higher-status locales, it doesn't work quite as neatly here, either. First, in the case of the marriages between women in rural China and overseas husbands who never returned, one might argue that women did not step "up" and that these marriages amounted to the promise of hypergamy left undelivered. Second, where grooms from abroad returned home to marry, their brides may have moved up economically by marrying into a family and locale with greater economic resources. But their husbands also raised their own status by contracting a "major marriage" and putting on an ornate wedding in their home village. As mentioned above, this gain in status is more than the gain from all major marriages; it is also the gain that accrues because the wedding is a way for the returnee to demonstrate his success while abroad.

In such cases, it may be better to describe the process as some kind of reciprocal or equivalent gain in status. This reciprocal gain in status may also be the case for the liaisons between overseas Chinese men and their mainland mistresses, at least in their own eyes. However, in these cases community bystanders view the gains as illusory and think that these liaisons are laughable.

The idea of marriage "exchange" is also tricky in some of these cases. As I have shown, women had virtually no agency in the preliberation marriages between "little daughters-in-law" and their overseas Chinese husbands. But, of course, as little daughters-in-law they had no agency in any event, even if it was not a transnational marriage. Later on, however, women began to determine their own marital fates, in the Calcutta community as well as in Mei Xian. Describing marriage as solely the exchange of women by men is difficult to defend in these circumstances.

Finally, there is the category of marriage itself. Anthropologists have argued frequently about the validity of using this one term to describe the great variety of practices across the globe that link partners, usually men and women, in a socially recognized bond. Certainly, some cases discussed above also stretch our definitions—in particular, the preliberation bond of virtual widows and their overseas husbands who never returned, or the postliberation relationships between overseas Chinese men and their mistresses or "secondary wives."

Despite these caveats, one thing should be clear: the creation of marriage alliances across broad transnational spaces is not a new phenomenon in the Chinese world. While we may question the categories we use to describe these practices, we cannot deny that such exchanges have long been a template for a large array of goals and desires.

Chapter 3
Cautionary Tales: Marriage Strategies, State Discourse, and Women's Agency in a Naxi Village in Southwestern China

Emily Chao

Although the Chinese state represents rural marriage practice as regionally determined and the legacy of local culture and history, I argue that elopement strategies in rural Lijiang (the Naxi Autonomous Prefecture in Yunnan Province, China) and related constraints on women's agency are recent phenomena shaped by the state's economic policies and population discourse. Specifically, I address how state discourse about the nationwide problem of kidnapping in the 1980s and 1990s influenced local marriage practice and women's agency in Lijiang. Although kidnapping and elopement initially appear to be significantly different practices, a closer examination of kidnapping discourse and local elopement practice reveals certain similar characteristics. By subsuming a wide range of local practices (abduction, arranged marriage, marriage, elopement) under only two categories—"marriage" and "elopement" —Lijiang residents differentiated local practices from those practices recently condemned in the national media and targeted in local campaigns to educate residents in the context of widespread violations of the marriage law. But beyond this narrow Lijiang typology of marriage and elopement, a much broader range of local practices—on one side of the continuum, the coercion of women and, on the other, female agency—may be identified. Unregistered clandestine marriages and women's elopement are both informed by and contrapuntal to marriage law, parental authority, population policy, and national models for economic development. Depending on which end of the continuum such practices fall, they suggest that women exercise both more and less agency than they did prior to the post–Mao era economic reforms.

This chapter is based on fieldwork among the Naxi conducted in rural Lijiang between 1990 and 1997. The Naxi are an ethnic group living primarily in northern Yunnan Province, southwestern China. The practices of elopement, abduction, and kidnapping addressed in this chapter took place in rural villages in the Lijiang Naxi Autonomous Prefecture (referred to hereafter as Lijiang) as opposed to the semi-urban town of Lijiang (referred to as Lijiang town). The following account, which is one of many similar stories I heard in rural Lijiang, illustrates the complex role of female agency in marriage practices:

A young girl walking home from the market meets a handsome young man. He flirts with her; she is flattered and attracted to him. They agree to meet secretly several times, and one day he suggests that she become his wife. He tells her his home is in a beautiful place where sparkling water flows and crops grow abundantly. She listens, impressed by his account, and agrees to go with him, but just to have a look. He tells her his home is not far away. They walk. A day passes, they climb over a hill, but they still haven't arrived. She asks how much farther, and he says they are almost there. They walk over another hill and another day passes. They walk over more hills and into the mountains. They stop at a run-down shack, and the man says, "We've arrived. This is my home." The young girl, understanding that she now faces a completely impoverished existence, is horrified. Far away from her parents and home, she is helpless and unable to make her way back. The young man has tricked her.

Such narratives warn Lijiang women of the perils of crossing borders into unknown regions, a form of female agency that is equated with danger. To some extent, marriage always entails border crossing, but this practice becomes more perilous when it is undertaken without parental guidance and at a moment when both regional localities and the broader national landscape are fraught with danger. This particular narrative also offers a more subtle commentary about mobility and agency. The movement across borders is a metaphor for economic mobility. The young woman thinks she is moving to a better place and improving her standard of living but, unbeknownst to her, she is actually heading toward permanent poverty. The narrative outcome suggests that marriage requires a choice between desire and economic improvement. The hapless young woman thinks both are possible, but the attractive young man skilled in flattery represents downward mobility. The gravity of finding herself in a remote locality is based on the assumption that "localities" occupy fixed positions in an economic hierarchy. Actors patrilocally tied to such localities are locked into economies that are immutable, providing a life sentence of poverty for the young man who owns the run-down shack, as well as for the woman he has lured there.

The narrative also addresses tensions over conflicting generational views of marriage and mobility informed by the experiences of two vastly different economic periods. In the eyes of parents with daughters of marriageable age, marriage fixes one's position in both a hierarchy of place and an economic hierarchy. The *hukou* system of residential permits instituted in 1955 (which restricted the movement of populations by issuing residence permits according to where one was born or assigned to work) prohibited rural migration to urban centers. Because of the significant economic differences between localities (a factor of the state's economic policies), spatial mobility meant economic mobility. For women, marriage entailed border crossing that could result in upward mobility (Lavely 1991:286). Hence parents viewed it as a crucial moment necessitating parental guidance and mediation. But since the post-Mao era (roughly, from the 1980s), the potential for economic mobility and spatial mobility has changed. De-collectivization (1980 in Lijiang), which increased flexibility in work schedules, and the rise of private-sector employment in urban centers enabled rural residents to supplement livelihoods formerly based solely on farming. Farmers could engage in moneymaking sidelines, and many rural men from poorer localities sought migratory work as a means of improving their economic status. For many young people, in particular, the economic reforms were embraced and associated with the promise of a new, more prosperous life. Locality was still associated with where one stood in an economic hierarchy, but the new mixed economy offered other means of economic mobility.

At the same time, in the Lijiang countryside courtship and elopement began to eclipse parentally arranged marriage. Young people with more flexible work schedules and leisure time participated in social activities with agemates. Groups of young men and women from rural villages descended on Lijiang town on weekends to window-shop, see movies, or simply cruise the streets to check out the opposite sex. The rise of consumer culture fostered new constructions of maleness, femaleness, modernity, and romantic desire. For young people, the older ideas defining a suitable marriage partner in terms of family, economic standing, and reputation as a worker were in tension with newer models of desirability in which appearance, ability to socialize, and "modern" outlook were valued. While economic standing was still considered relevant, the ability of young men to effect an aura of modernity conferred a kind of cultural capital associated with progress and economic potential. For parents and rural residents who held stock in older ideas of marriage, the characters in the narrative represent new actors on the social landscape. The young man with honeyed words is a cunning trickster, and the young woman, wooed into running off with him, is the victim of her own vanity and naïveté. In sum, this cautionary tale is informed by a gen-

erational construction of marriage that criticizes elopement; it argues
that contracting a marriage requires choosing between trickery and honesty, romantic desire and economic security, individual right and familial authority, female agency and parental respect.

The young woman's agency is limited to deciding whom she will follow, her parents (implicitly) or the young man who has courted her. Her
movement across borders and back is not independent, but is necessarily facilitated by others. The finality of her journey is based on the
assumption that she could not independently leave and find her way
back to her parents' home. But this representation of female agency
appears contradictory. According to the Lijiang storytellers, who are
mostly middle-aged village residents, young women are vulnerable, if
not gullible and easy prey, to the deceptive manipulations of others. At
the same time, young women, the intended audience of these tales, are
clearly being cautioned about the dangers of female agency. The story's
depiction of the young woman is paradoxical—she is both helpless and
simultaneously responsible for her actions. This tale is about elopement,
but it also echoes state discourse on the problem of kidnapping since
the late 1980s. Both practices are characterized by a contradictory depiction of female agency and the problematization of the spatial mobility
of women.

This problematic depiction of female agency was most conspicuous to
young female informants who explained that these tales caution against
two potential dangers facing young local women: *paohun* (a popular type
of elopement) and *guaihun* (a form of kidnapping in which local women
were courted with promises of marriage or lucrative employment, only
to be sold to wifeless Chinese farmers in distant coastal provinces).
These tales intrigued me because they were the only contexts in which
elopement and kidnapping were alluded to as being in any way comparable. I found it extremely puzzling that kidnapping, a crime that
deprives a woman of her freedom, could in any way be likened to elopement, a form of marriage based on a woman selecting her future husband. Among local residents, government officials, the Public Security
Bureau, and Chinese and Naxi anthropologists, elopement and kidnapping were classified as completely distinct. This is evidenced by the use
of different terminology to refer to each practice, as well as by the
emphatic remarks of informants who described elopement as an "ethnic
custom" distinctive to the Lijiang basin, in contrast to kidnapping,
which they defined as a crime perpetrated by outsiders. In order for the
meaning of these local representations to become clear, they must be
contextualized within the political campaigns and national discourse of
the late 1980s and 1990s.

Lijiang Under Scrutiny

In the late 1980s, marriage practices in Lijiang came under political scrutiny for two reasons: cohabitation and kidnapping. Government surveys of marriage registration in Yunnan Province found that an alarming number of early marriages and cohabitations were taking place in Lijiang. Responding to these violations of the marriage law, the provincial Civil Affairs Department launched a reeducation effort to teach and enforce marriage law. At the same time, the Public Security Bureau attempted to eradicate the kidnapping of local women—who were being sold as brides as far away as Zhejiang and Jiangsu Provinces—a problem that grew in the 1980s and mid-1990s.

The movement of Lijiang women to Zhejiang and Jiangsu, whether by kidnapping or voluntary migration, is part of a broader phenomenon occurring throughout rural southwestern China. In the 1990s, Yunnan Province had the highest out-migration of women for the purpose of marriage in all of China (72.7 percent) (Fan and Huang 1998:241). The growing phenomenon of migration for work or marriage is the result of the substantial economic differences that exist between regions. The coastal provinces of Zhejiang and Jiangsu are among the most prosperous provinces in China; Yunnan is among the poorest (Gilmartin and Tan 2002:206). When Lijiang women leave the area, it is usually unclear whether they have engaged in migration for labor or for marriage, or if they have been kidnapped and sold. There is little doubt, however, that all forms of migration were economically motivated and that long-distance marriages were conceived of as hypergamy. Increased long-distance migration linked to marriage caused particular alarm because, prior to the 1980s, it was rare for minority women to marry outside of their communities, and such marriages did not involve parental agreement. By creating local shortages of women, long-distance migration and kidnapping contributed to the rise of elopement in Lijiang.

Kidnapping and Long-Distance Marriage in Lijiang

The long-distance "kidnapping" of rural Naxi women began between 1982 and 1984, when, according to my informants, Chinese men from Zhejiang began traveling to Lijiang to look for women. The Lijiang countryside is inhabited by a number of ethnic groups, including the Han Chinese, but the Naxi are the most populous. Most rural Naxi women speak some Yunnanese, a Chinese dialect, but Naxi is their first language. It is not clear if the earliest Zhejiang arrivals were marriage brokers and kidnappers, or just unmarried men in search of wives. According to Qing, a woman whose sister had *taohun*ed[1] (ran off to be married) to a man in Zhejiang, Zhejiang men needed wives because of the shortage of women due to the substantial migration of local women to "better places like Shanghai or Jiangsu." Qing's sister had willingly gone to Zhejiang to be introduced to a prospective groom after being persuaded by a female friend, who had herself married a Zhejiang man. Qing's sister made her decision after hearing that men did all the farm-work in Zhejiang, leaving women responsible only for housework. According to informants in East Wind, the basin village where I carried out my fieldwork in 1990–1992, 1995, and 1997, other village daughters who went to Zhejiang sent back small amounts of money for their mothers and letters reporting that they were well. However, at least one young woman from Qing's village died mysteriously in Zhejiang. Villagers as well as the Lijiang Public Security Bureau suspected that Lijiang women were being "tricked" (seduced, or raped and sold) into going to Zhe-jiang, coerced into remaining there, and even pressured into luring other Lijiang women to similar fates. One young woman from Lijiang town, Li, was traveling with another young woman to find work. When they ran out of money, Li's friend sold her into a marriage with a Sichuan farmer and told her family that she had died in an accident. Li's journey had begun solely for the purpose of finding lucrative work; she had a boyfriend in Lijiang and planned to marry him when she returned. After Li was sold into marriage, she gave birth to a daughter—much to the disappointment of her "husband's" family. When she became pregnant with her second child, her husband's family allowed her to return to Lijiang to "hide" until the second child was born. After returning to Lijiang, she had an abortion and found a job working in a hair salon. She reunited with her former boyfriend and had no plans to return to Sichuan.

From the late 1980s until the late 1990s, *youguai* (kidnap involving deception or enticement) and *guaihun* (kidnap marriage) have increased throughout China (see Schein in this volume). According to authorities and Lijiang residents, the kidnapping of Lijiang women is perpetrated by "outsiders" who effect a unidirectional flow of Lijiang women out of the region. While at the national level most kidnapping is intra-ethnic, Naxi women leaving the area were crossing ethnic as well as regional boundaries, a phenomenon with dire consequences for rural Naxi men at the bottom of the local marriage hierarchy.

National Kidnapping Discourse

National and provincial efforts to eliminate kidnapping in in Yunnan culminated in 1989 when the kidnapping and sale of women and chil-dren was included as a targeted evil in the national "Six Evils Campaign." Directly following this campaign there was a decline in kidnapping, but a resurgence in 1990 prompted another national campaign in 1991. Throughout the Lijiang countryside, there was widespread awareness of the "kidnapping problem" in rural villages such as East Wind.

State discourse on kidnapping is articulated in the criminal law itself and in the media (because the press is government-controlled). While the criminal law clearly condemns kidnapping by repeat offenders and gang leaders, it is more ambivalent toward the men who purchase kidnapped women. Government and media treatments of kidnapping typically explain the practice in terms of economic rationality. Men are portrayed as understandably willing to purchase brides because of the shortages of women and the exorbitant expenses associated with marriage to local women. The "difficulties" of local men are blamed on the persistence of "feudal customs"—specifically, bride-prices and the expectation that women's families will demand elaborate marriage celebrations (W. Huang 1991:25). State and media accounts are generally sympathetic to men seeking wives and often claim that women's families who arrange for marriages to more prosperous areas are creating the underlying shortages in women.

Conflicting portrayals of women depict them as passive victims and, simultaneously, as responsible for the crimes committed against them. In the national media accounts of kidnap victims, women are portrayed as vulnerable, naive, and oppressed by backward customs and discrimination; their helplessness appears to rationalize their victimhood. This view implies that kidnapping may be attributed to the behavioral inadequacies or spiritual shortcomings of the victims themselves. These shortcomings require the legal system's leadership to educate potential victims and urge women to take responsibility for changing the economic conditions in their localities. The "great masses of women" are encouraged to "consciously resist the ugly habit of buying and selling marriage, to build up their own pride, confidence, independence, and self-strengthening spirit, to rely on their own efforts to change the situation in their localities, and to eliminate poverty and achieve affluence" (Feng 1990:3).

At the same time, these reports imply that kidnapping occurs as a result of misguided female agency. Women who independently seek employment or marriage in more prosperous areas make themselves vulnerable to kidnappers. It should be emphasized, however, that this is only considered problematic when such activities entail trans-regional border crossing. It is regional border crossing as opposed to all women's agency that is associated with danger. Hence, women who leave the familiar to cross distant borders may be perceived as seeking out danger, thus calling into question their morality. Women who leave their home region are associated with dishonesty, misguided behavior, and the fostering of social disorder (Biddulph and Cook 1999). Most rural women marry within a radius of ten kilometers, usually finding husbands within the same county (Gu cited in Gilmartin and Tan 2002:205). Given the implication from state and media directives that women are responsible for changing the economic situation in their localities, the minority of local women leaving the area may be perceived as disloyal to their community, or even as defecting to other areas. Conversely, morality is associated with remaining within the borders that define one's home region. Indeed, the notion of space is implicated in the very definition of kidnapping. The distinction between "selling marriage," a violation of the marriage law, and the more serious criminal violation of "kidnapping" is based on where and by whom the woman is sold. Selling marriage occurs when a woman still in her home region is forcibly sold by her family head or guardian, while kidnapping occurs when a woman who has left home is sold by a stranger, not her guardian or kin (Biddulph and Cook 1999:1459–60). Hence, the definition of kidnapping intentionally excludes families or guardians from criminal prosecution for coercing daughters or female charges into marriage. Whereas both selling marriage and kidnapping violate the free will of the woman, leniency toward selling marriage is based on the practice being a form of arranged marriage, and incomparable to the profit-making intention of a kidnapper.

An examination of the definitions of kidnapping also reveals cultural values about the legitimate function and authority of families and guardians. The criminal law classifies two very different practices as kidnapping: *bangjia,* often translated as abduction by force or drugging; and *youguai,* kidnapping by enticement or trickery. Both crimes entail the intent to sell the victim. The distinction between these practices is that kidnapping by trickery aims at luring a woman "away from her home or guardian" (Biddluph and Cook 1999:1455). It implies that the stewardship of family or guardian is required to determine a woman's departure from her home, and that bringing about any departure without consent of family members or guardians is illegitimate and criminal. The definition of *youguai* provides insight into why practices of kidnapping and elopement are locally understood as similar. Kidnapping (the *youguai* form) is similar to elopement in that the woman is being "deceived" or "enticed" away from her family, home, or guardian. Elopement, like kidnapping, takes place against the wishes of a woman's family or guardian. Kidnapping law permits certain persons—family heads or guardians—to "sell" women without criminal repercussions. Hence, kidnapping law, insofar as who is excluded from prosecution, fails to protect women from their parents and weakens the right of a woman to independently decide whom she will marry.[2] A young man who entices a young woman to elope is in a position structurally homologous to a (*youguai*) kidnapper. The illegitimacy of his act hinges on the absence of parental consent. Particularly for parents who had their own marriages arranged and who came of age when prevailing views were that daughters do not have the right to contract their own marriages, elopement is analogous to the usurpation of parental rights or the theft of property.

Population Containment and the Problematization of Female Migration

State discourse on kidnapping and marriage law cannot be fully understood apart from the state's policies for economic development and population control. The overarching logic that informs economic development is that certain areas (special economic zones and coastal regions) will prosper first, after which other areas will follow their model. Corresponding to this pattern, the reform era has been characterized by the growth of economic inequalities that are understood in poorer areas as inequalities between geographic regions, but are explained by the state and understood in prospering urban areas as a factor of difference between the quality of populations (Anagnost 1997; Cohen 1993). The growing economies of developing areas and the resulting need for low-cost labor created a mass movement of migratory workers known as the *liudong renkou*, or floating population. Like this floating population, kidnapped women and women migrating long distances are associated with social disorder and stigmatized as having questionable quality because they are bodies out of place, a specter of the state's inability to control its population—a control that is essential to its goal of orderly economic development.

Hence, kidnapping discourse stigmatizes women not simply because they cross boundaries, since most marriages require this, but because they fall within the (long-distance) "boundary-crossing" populations that are read as signs of disorder. Dating from economic reforms instituted in 1978, the distances women have traveled for the purpose of contracting hypergamous marriages have increased dramatically (Gilmartin and Tan 2002:205). Women traveling out of their home counties and beyond provincial borders for marriage have become so noticeable that they have given rise to the creation of a separate category in the census. *Qianyi*, permanent migration, has been the only category of "migration" in which women predominate. Twenty-eight percent of all female migration falls into the *qianyi* category (Gilmartin and Tan 2002:204). According to the 1990 census, 21.64 percent of the marriage migrants were women migrating intraprovincially, and 29.9 percent were women migrating interprovincially (Gilmartin and Tan 2002:216). What is interesting about these statistics is both the phenomenon they report and the distinctions they make. Census statistics record interprovincial marriages and intraprovincial marriages contracted outside of the woman's county of residence. Given that most marriages are intraprovincial, why should the subset of intraprovincial marriages contracted outside one's home county be tracked as *qianyi*? In a sense, marriage usually entails border crossing of some sort, whether it be family or village borders. In Lijiang, since most villages consist of one to three patrilines, preferences for exogamy usually require that marriage entail crossing village borders. Why, then, should county borders mark local marriage versus marriage migration? It may simply be that the county, as an administrative unit, is a convenient starting point from which to record population stability and movement. Alternatively, I suggest that marriage migration statistics, like media discourse on kidnapping and marriage, are less concerned with categorizing marriage than with the overarching objective of tracking and containing populations in their native localities. Certainly the moralistic tone of media accounts supports this.

Elopement as Agency and Coercion

Although kidnapping and elopement appear to be inherently contradictory practices, the national discourse suggests that kidnapped women actually do have some agency, just as local elopement accounts stress the absence of it. Why would these practices be represented to the authorities and to me as distinct, and yet be locally understood as comparable? If the tale of the young woman who finds herself stranded at the poor man's door can be categorized as elopement, then elopement is more appropriately categorized as a number of practices situated on a continuum that ranges from male coercion to female agency. On the coercive end of the continuum:

Li, a woman described as having *paohun*ed, detailed the events leading up to her marriage. One evening a young man she was acquainted with, but who had never courted her, invited her to his house. He told her that several of his relatives were visiting and the food would be plentiful and the evening lively. She initially declined, but after much discussion it was getting dark and he refused to walk her home. She reluctantly went with him, as "she had no other choice." When they arrived she was treated very well, given a chicken leg and lots of other food. There were many people celebrating what she would later learn was "her arrival" as the new daughter-in-law of the household. The young man's family members refused to escort her home, as he had assured her they would, forcing her to share a room that night with several of his female relatives. The next morning, his family sent go-betweens to announce that Li had eloped with him.

It wasn't until she returned home a day later to her angry parents that Li herself learned that she had "eloped." Because her future in-laws had not allowed her to return home before her parents agreed to the match, the union was already agreed to by the time she did return.

According to Li's account, because her parents had consented to a match, albeit reluctantly, she feared that rescinding the agreement would cause her parents difficulties and so she was resigned to the "fate of being with her husband's family." Li's father-in-law was a politically powerful official, and her parents had been apprehensive about refusing his proposals of an arranged marriage between the couple. Although Li's marriage is widely viewed as an elopement, she insists that she did not intend to elope and that she had no choice in the matter of her marriage.

On the other end of the continuum:

Quan and Hua, who lived in villages in the Lijiang basin, met and fell in love while working in Lijiang town. They had known each other for more than a year before deciding to marry. Quan went to Hua's father to ask his permission to marry, but her father politely refused. No reason was given, but the couple and others suspected the objection was that Quan's family was from a poorer village. After a second attempt, Hua's father was less polite to Quan and forbade Hua to see him. Hua's parents then attempted to arrange marriages with two other young men from prosperous families, but she refused each time. After setting a date, Hua and Quan rendezvoused in town and she *paohun*ed. The couple sent her parents a telegram from Xiaguan, where they had gone for a traveling wedding. They wrote: "You were not willing to allow us to be together, so this is the way we're taking care of it."

In contrast to Li's case, Quan and Hua's elopement was clearly a strategy to circumvent the objections of Hua's parents. After the couple returned from their traveling wedding, Hua's family, unwilling to drop the matter, sent family members to inform Hua that her mother had suffered a heart attack and needed her. When Hua reached her house, she learned that her mother was fine, though angry, and her parents proceeded to lock her in her room for months, refusing to release her unless she promised to "give up" Quan. Eventually, Hua was allowed to go out to work in the fields with her sisters, and she again escaped to Quan's house and remained there. In this case, Hua's family clearly experienced her elopement as an infringement on parental rights, which they sought to reassert through deception and physical force.

Marriage and Courtship in the 1990s

According to local and official accounts, the only forms of marriage practice in Lijiang were marriage and elopement. Marriage was defined as a practice initiated by the couple or approved by them after their parents enlisted a go-between to make introductions. Elopement, or *pao-hun*, was defined as a situation in which, without her parents' knowledge, a young woman "ran" to her lover's house to be married, after which a go-between went to the woman's parents to apologize and negotiate the marriage. Within each category was a continuum of female agency and varying degrees of anger on the part of the woman's parents. Some parents made no distinction between "trickery" and a daughter's volitional elopement; in both cases, they held the man and his family responsible for taking a daughter without first negotiating with her parents. For these parents, trickery involved a range of practices that potentially included the use of physical coercion, rape, deception (as in Li's case), courtship, and the use of "honeyed words" to persuade a young woman to elope. For this group of parents, the notion of marriage is fused with parental permission and resembles "arranged marriage" because there is no room for any legitimate female agency. Other parents, particularly mothers, were willing to accept elopement if they knew that their daughters were voluntary participants. For this second group of parents, elopement in the abstract is described as volitional, although further probing reveals their understanding of elopement as a category that includes a range of practices from the coercion of women to women's willing participation. The opposition between marriage and elopement did not correspond to categories of legitimate and illegitimate, as it did for the first group of parents, because volitional elopement was considered an acceptable alternative to marriage. Hence, both groups of parents construed at least some forms of elopement as coercive, even though coercion is not mentioned in their generic descriptions of elopement. Suspicions of coercion are further evident in the customary practice of the woman's family sending a group of her relatives to investigate after an elopement has taken place.

Because elopement circumvents early parental investigation and approval, it is assumed that something is problematic or being hidden—that there was something negative about the young man, his family members, or their economic circumstances that made him an undesirable marriage prospect. Naxi parents, referring to the Chinese saying *men dang hu dui* (matching windows and doors), stress that the bride and groom should be from comparable households. Most commonly, men were from poorer families and the women they sought to marry were from more prosperous ones. However, I knew of other cases where couples had eloped in the following situations: the man and woman were patrilineal kin (an increasingly common situation); the young man was disabled; two fathers-in-law had bad reputations (one for being lecherous, the other for being selfish and lazy); a mother-in-law had epilepsy in her family line. Many young people said that the "matching doors and windows" concept was more important to their parents' generation than representative of their own views. While several young women deferred to or even embraced the notion of "matching doors and windows," substantial generational differences characterized the views of most young people. Daughters share their parents' desires for them to marry up, but this was not conceived of as purely economic. For many Lijiang women who eloped, a good match may be defined in ways other than their suitor's financial assets. A young man's abilities and potential are assessed in ways that echo Bourdieu's notion of cultural capital. Thus, young male suitors who take pains in how they dress and in how they perform their masculine and modern identities may appear upwardly mobile to the women they court, despite the shortcomings of their pocketbooks.

Constructions of gender and courtship since the reform era are significantly different from those in the Maoist era, when young people's parents came of age. New generationally based identities have been fostered by the rise of consumer culture. Images in films and advertisements portray new ways of life and modern identities. For the young people from the countryside who congregated in Lijiang town on Friday and Saturday nights near the department stores, movie theaters, and outdoor ballrooms, courtship and romance were imbued with an aura of the modern. Pleasurable rendezvous in town broke the tedium of rural life, but also provided opportunities for the refashioning and display of modern rural identities. The attention to clothing and appearance, politically problematic activities a decade earlier, became a popular preoccupation for the young. For rural men, alcohol and cigarette consumption increased and was popularly equated with masculinity. Marlboro, Wan Bao Lu (the road of ten thousand treasures), was the most prestigious brand—with its masculine image of the rugged cowboy headed down the path to modernity and prosperity. Young women and men from the countryside bicycled to town in single-sex groups to cruise the streets. Young women with arms locked wore matching shirts and combed their hair identically. A group of young men wore black sunglasses (with the gold brand-name stickers prominently displayed in the left corner of the lenses) and identical jackets emblazoned with such English logos as "Nice Guy League."

Most elopements took place on festival days, though many young women simply went into town to the movies and never came back. In the early 1990s, the most popular song was the Taiwan pop tune "Genzi Ganjue Zou" (Go with your feelings), and elopement was virtually replacing arranged marriage in the Lijiang basin. In East Wind village, approximately 80 percent of the "marriages" between 1990 and 1992 were elopements. Young people, particularly the young men who prac-tice it, claim that elopement is new and modern, that it was an innova-tion of rural men faced with women's parents who "only look at money, and not the person." They draw a distinction, suggesting that "charac-ter" and "morality," but not prosperity, should be the only criteria for spousal selection. Much of what has inspired courtship and marriage in the 1990s is the result of a substantial shift in the local economy since the reform era. Fixed assets such as a job in a good work unit, Commu-nist Party connections, education, or good farmland were no longer the only markers of a good husband in the new economy. According to the perceptions of many young people, a man's success is often explained in terms of his character traits (Chao 1995 and 2002). Men who are innovative and daring risk takers epitomize the sort of masculine prow-ess equated with success in the new market economy.[3]

New Practices, Old Resonances

But if elopement is portrayed as contemporary, there are certainly aspects of its practice that resonate with the past. Perhaps most sugges-tive is the way in which elopement draws on protocol virtually identical to bride abduction as practiced in the pre-1949 era. Bride abduction, like elopement, was a practice particularly common among poorer households that had difficulties finding brides for their sons (Chao 1995). A young man, with the aid of male agemates, would abduct a young woman and bring her back to his house. According to the conven-tion, the woman was considered the future daughter-in-law of the house once she entered his courtyard. Following the abduction, the man's fam-ily sent a party of go-betweens and gifts meant to be a bride-price to apol-ogize for the man's actions and to secure the agreement of the woman's parents. During this time, the couple have an ambiguous status; they occupy a liminal state as neither married nor single, associated with sex but not yet married. Hence, the couple is prohibited from socializing or leaving the house beyond working in the fields. Regardless of whether the woman's family agrees, the man's family usually celebrates the union with a special meal or banquet, after which the couple is recognized as married. Prior to 1949, men's families who could afford to do so sought to portray abduction as comparable to arranged marriage. These fami-lies not only celebrated the union with large banquets, but they also sent the young woman back to her parents' house so that they could go through the ritual of fetching the bride.

Although Lijiang's rural residents describe bride abduction as a thing of the past, elopement by deception more closely resembles bride abduction than elopement. This is particularly the case with respect to the coercion of women. The use of protocol after elopement that is identical to bride abduction strongly suggests that elopement is locally perceived as resembling bride abduction. While parents typically have little to do with their son's courtship or "leading a girl home," parents are consulted and indeed orchestrate the negotiations after an elopement. The use of the same conciliatory protocol or ritual language indicates that, regardless of the views of their children, parents feel a need to legitimize the implicitly illegitimate actions that have taken place. In interviews with young men about the course of events following their elopements, most would call in their parents to recount the precise order and meaning of the negotiations after elopement. It was clear that, while the sons may have been the primary actors on the elopement night, their parents were the central actors in the events that followed.

The common description of elopement as volitional appears to be informed by the need to differentiate abduction-like local practices from the kidnapping frequently addressed in the media. As a cynical, but not particularly politically savvy, informant told me: "When outsiders trick your daughter, it's kidnapping; when Lijiang people do it, it's *paohun.*" As this account suggests, despite the disclaimers of local officials and villagers, there is a local perception that elopement resembles kidnapping and bride abduction. This is further suggested by the cautionary tale that treats elopement and kidnapping interchangeably.

Arranged marriage is similarly subsumed within the category of marriage. The open acknowledgment of arranged marriage would place many parents in violation of the marriage law by "selling marriage" or denying their daughters freedom of marriage. Yet if arranged marriage and the parental authority to prevent marriage did not exist, the practice of elopement would not be as prevalent as it has been since the late 1980s. There are clearly more elopements that are planned by couples than there are cases of women being coerced (Chao 1995). In virtually all cases of elopement in my 1990–92 study, the groom either assumed that the woman's parents would not approve of the match or the parents had already indicated their disapproval.

Local officials and residents who claim that only marriage and elopement are practiced in the Lijiang basin have edited their portrayal of local practices to conform with the marriage law and to differentiate them from nationally condemned kidnapping practices. In rural Lijiang, the correlation between, on the one hand, elopement and, on the other, underage marriage and cohabitation is common knowledge. During *zuo tan hui* (village meetings) and *laonianxiehui* (meetings of the village elderly), parents with daughters were advised to be vigilant, and women who had eloped without registering marriages were criticized. This depiction of elopement suggests that women are perceived to have agency and are blamed for elopement; at the same time, however, an eloping man did not come under comparable scrutiny. Strictly speaking, *paohun* is not equivalent to an American definition of elopement because it is not possible for a man to *paohun*. Men do not *paohun*; rather they "lead a girl home."[4] By limiting the representation of their activities to bringing a bride to their parents' household, sons are perceived as engaging in filial conduct and the reproduction of descent. In contrast, the wild sexuality of a daughter who has "run off" with a man can only be perceived as illegitimate. *Paohun* is female agency that stands in opposition to marriage, an institution historically requiring parental consent or control. At the same time, *paohun* is equated with romantic liaisons, desire, and sex detached from marriage. In terms of the symbolism of local gender and ritual discourse, the opposition female:male corresponds to the parallel oppositions sexuality:fertility (social reproduction) and illegitimate:legitimate. The understanding of elopement reflects these ritual oppositions in which sexuality associated with female agency stands in opposition to the social fertility of marriage and male agency. The alignment of women's agency with illegitimate sexuality (sex outside of marriage) is furthered by the pattern of women being the ones who delay marriage registration—the state's certification of marriage.

But there was yet another explanation of elopement that drew on historical antecedents as well as contemporary context. In 1995, the former Party secretary of the prefecture, who had been raised in East Wind village, told me that *paohun* is an "ethnic practice." To some extent, he was attempting to immunize the practice from the realm of the political, from being considered "chaotic," "unlawful," and in violation of population policy or the marriage law. But in doing so, this well-meaning official also characterized elopement as the persistence of a timeless cultural essence as opposed to a strategy situated in the present. Like the state's discourse on kidnapping, which attributes it to feudal sources, the identification of elopement as "ethnic" problematically suggests that such practices are localized phenomena that have miraculously survived decades of socialist rule. Absent from this depiction is the recognition of local marriage practices as part of a broader national arena. The kidnapping of women in less prosperous, inland areas like Lijiang is connected to the shortages of women throughout China resulting from the one-child family policy. And the kidnapping of Lijiang women created a greater shortage of local women, which in turn gave rise to the innovative elopement strategies of Lijiang men from poorer households.[5] While these elopement strategies drew on past forms of marriage practice, they were inspired by a contemporary shortage of women and are better understood as class strategies as opposed to distinctively ethnic institutions. Beyond this, the misrepresentation of national problems as local ultimately shifts blame away from state policies and onto those actors most acutely affected by them.

Women and Muted Agency

The problematization of elopement at the village level has a direct impact on the representation of women's agency. There is no doubt that women did not exercise agency in cases of coercive elopement, but the preponderance of elopements do not fall into this category. Although the same women who insist that they were "not coerced" stop short of claiming an active role in elopement, their agency is more visible in the actions they take. Women's actions have to be contextualized in the broader regional and national landscape characterized by shortages of women. It is well known that, in contrast to a man who "leads a girl home," a woman who has *paohun*ed may easily find another man to marry should she decide not to marry the man she eloped with. Given the shortages of women in rural Lijiang, a man who unsuccessfully led a girl home would have a problem finding another woman to marry. And while men prefer to register their marriages if the women they have led home are of legal marriage age, it is women who often refuse. In many cases, the woman has gone back and forth, living for periods of time at the man's house and then returning to her parents' home before agreeing to register the marriage. Thus, marriage registration typically takes place from several months to a year or more after the elopement and cohabitation have occurred. The following case illustrates this point:

Mei had eloped with a young man from a nearby village. The young man was one of two sons and had promised that he and Mei would have their own set of rooms despite being part of his parents' household. When Mei arrived she was treated well, but there were no separate rooms, as her fiancé had promised. When she went home for a visit, her parents "locked her up" for running off. Some time later, Mei escaped and ran back to his house, but only stayed for a few days. According to her friends, she was disappointed that there was still no separate building. Mei told her prospective in-laws that she had returned home because she was homesick but that her parents had "locked her up again." I later learned that her fiancé did construct a separate building and that she moved in with him. However, when I left Lijiang a year and a half after she first eloped, Mei was living at home with her parents again, uncertain about her plans. It was clear that her parents were not forcibly detaining her.

In Mei's case, while her parents had initially locked her up, they did not forcibly detain her during her subsequent visits home. Nevertheless, she claimed that her parents had prevented her return in order to negotiate better living conditions at her fiancé's home. Since the marriage was not registered, prolonged visits to her parents could continue until an agreement was reached. As Mei's case demonstrates, cohabitation in effect affords women a form of trial marriage, and avoidance of marriage registration enables them to negotiate the terms of their marriages with their future in-laws and husbands. While Mei's efforts required some collusion on the part of her parents, eloping women also resort to prolonged visits to their sisters and other kin. The refusal to acknowledge intention or agency was not distinctive to Mei's case, but was prevalent among eloping women. According to Mei, her visits home were for the purpose of "seeing her parents" and she would not divulge what conditions she required before she would agree to marry.

There was a row of houses on the outskirts of East Wind village called the "village of unfilial sons" (*niezi cun*). I was told that these houses were inhabited by women who had eloped and then persuaded their husbands to set up households separate from their in-laws. While eloping women claim to have no agency, the village's architecture suggests that they do. If illegal cohabitation and the refusal to register marriage are markers of female agency, it is not surprising that women would be reluctant to claim that their actions are intentional. Ironically, it is by failing to conform to the marriage law that eloping women are able to exercise the most agency. It is clear that eloping women do not see the marriage law, which was intended to safeguard the right to freedom of marriage, as protecting a woman's rights so much as those of her husband. An elderly friend recounted that his "son-in-law" had complained to him when his daughter ran off. My friend was sympathetic, but blamed the "son-in-law" for failing to register the marriage. If the marriage is registered, he proclaimed, the government will protect a man's rights.

The negativity associated with female agency in kidnapping and marriage discourse appears to have ultimately silenced Lijiang women, making them reluctant to claim agency in their marriage strategies. Nonetheless, this female agency does exist. Rural women who brave threats of kidnapping to seek employment or marriage in more prosperous regions may be understood as challenging the state model for economic prosperity in which some regions will prosper first, allowing others to learn and follow. Their departure from poor areas suggests an inability to wait for, or a lack of faith in, the state's unfulfilled promise of prosperity. Their actions articulate a critique of the state's orderly development by seeking to prosper before their time and outside their space. And for Lijiang women who have stayed within borders of the familiar, female agency is perhaps most visible in what women do not do (for example, not registering their marriages or staying put at their in-laws), as opposed to the romantic portrayal of their elopements. Perhaps there is less female agency taking place during elopement and more in the silent negotiations before an elopement becomes a marriage.

Conclusion

Rather than exploring practices of cross-border marriage, this chapter addresses its symbolization. Cautionary tales about women leaving Lijiang are freighted with moral meanings that may be interrogated to reveal unexpected similarities between elopement, kidnapping, abduction, and marriage migration. The operations of power and agency in rural Lijiang cannot be understood apart from the legal definitions of these practices, growing economic inequalities, and state population discourse anchored in reform-era economic policies. When women deny they are agents, they articulate an understanding of the moral censure associated with bringing about one's own marriage. By practicing the opposite (that is, by resisting marriage registration) until they have negotiated the terms of their new lives, these women teach us to rethink the forms that agency may take and to broaden our understanding of what counts as having crossed the border.

Chapter 4
Marrying out of Place: Hmong/Miao Women Across and Beyond China

Louisa Schein

"I'm so sorry you couldn't reach me earlier!" apologizes a high official upon our meeting in a small city in Yunnan Province, southwestern China. It was my last day of research in this city, a center of concentration of the Miao minority in China, and I had been trying for at least a couple hours to reach this Miao official at home to set up a meeting. The phone had been constantly busy. Finally, the line freed up and I was able to schedule an appointment. The official arrived, contrite about our communications problems, but ultimately abdicating responsibility for his phone line: "You see, we have a young Miao *baomu* [housekeeper], and during the midday hours she gets phone calls from Hmong American men who want to chat with her." "Hmong American men who are visiting here?" I queried. "Oh no," he explained. "They are calling from the States. Can you believe they spend hours on the phone, international long-distance, just to talk to each other?"

These costly telephone calls, along with letters, Internet and transpacific travel, are not, of course, about "just" talking to each other. They are components of a highly gendered and still-developing set of interchanges between Hmong migrants to Western countries and Hmong/Miao inhabitants of China and Southeast Asia. The term "Hmong" refers to an ethnic group with a distribution that has become increasingly globalized, especially since the 1970s. Originally from China, several hundred thousand Hmong migrated across the southern border into Vietnam, Laos, Thailand, and Burma within the last two centuries. During the Vietnam War, a significant proportion of the Hmong in Laos were recruited to assist the United States in its covert war there, and hence, upon U.S. withdrawal in 1975, became political refugees. Many crossed the Mekong River into Thailand; of these, most were eventually resettled to the United States, France, Canada, Australia, and French Guyana. Some have remained in Thailand, and a few have repatriated to Laos. Almost all of those who had originally settled as agriculturalists in Vietnam, Thailand, and Burma remain there as farmers.

Meanwhile, within China the Hmong have come to be classed as a subgroup of the umbrella category of the "Miao," an ethnonym of dubious derogatory connotation until the Communist state dignified it as an official designation for the implementation of minority policy in the 1950s. There are now over 8.9 million Miao recognized in China, and they are scattered over Guizhou, Hunan, Yunnan, Sichuan, Guangxi, and other provinces. The sprawling group is characterized by sharp internal divergences of culture, language, and livelihood. The Hmong, constituting one of the three linguistic subgroups of the Miao, inhabit the southwesternmost regions of Miao distribution, contiguous with the Vietnam border. In this chapter, although we are dealing with one ethnic group, I shall use "Hmong" to denote those outside China, "Miao" to denote those remaining within Chinese borders, and "Hmong/ Miao" to refer to those Miao within China who identify as Hmong ethnolinguistically.

By the 1990s, Hmong immigrants in the West had developed the means and desires to travel back to Asia in great numbers. Having initially arrived as poor refugees, with no rights to passports and international travel, many had saved money and earned citizenship, all the while nurturing a longing to return to their roots. Such roots-seeking has particular valences for Hmong refugees. First, as involuntary migrants out of Asia, their sense of loss and desire for recovery of their homelands has been especially acute and abiding. Second, as minorities wherever they reside, they harbor a dream of a motherland that could be identified as an origin, even if it was also remembered as a site of oppression by a dominant ethnic group. For many Hmong Americans, this dreamed-of land has bifurcated into two origin countries: that of ancient China, from which their people as a collective derived; and that of Laos, where they as individuals were born.

With all the privileges of the First World travelers that they have become, increasing numbers of Hmong, primarily men, have undertaken to travel in person to find these sought-after lands and peoples. What many have actually found is homeland women. In an intricately patterned set of relationships between East and West, Hmong male travelers have pursued multiform gendered relations with their Asian-counterpart women, seeking them out for flirtation, entertainment, accompaniment, sexual trysts, mistresshood, and marriage.

In order not to exclusively privilege Hmong American men as mobile agents of initiation of cross-border sexual relationships, the bulk of this chapter is narrated through the lens of the Chinese Miao experience of these and related phenomena. My basic premise is that a careful treatment of those translocal relations that eventuate in marriage and other forms of long-distance mobility for rural Miao women requires a multifocal approach and a multisited research design. We need to consider both the women in Asia and the men who come from abroad, and each in terms of their mobilities across distance, nation, and class. In addition, we need to consider the families of such translocal agents, even when the families do not move, and the men in Asia who are implicated in these processes. The larger structural configurations of each society, as well as a more global political economy, also need to be taken as integral to any analysis.

I structure my inquiry here by contrasting two forms of long-distance marriage that have been entered into by Miao women in southwestern China. Before I take up the phenomenon of transnational unions described above, I look at the more common instance of marriages within China, also described for Naxi by Chao (in this volume), that are taking place at unprecedented distances and are denoted in common parlance as *waisheng* or extra-provincial. Unlike those co-ethnic transnational marriages precipitated by the return of Hmong migrants now resident in the West, these unions are notably cross-ethnic, almost always to men of the majority Han ethnicity. Extra-provincial marriages within China have become so common as to be transforming Miao villagers' senses of spatiality and structures of affinal obligation. Transnational marriages, on the other hand, akin to those described for Hakka by Oxfeld (in this volume), are exceedingly infrequent, but are regarded by Miao village and town dwellers within China as so spectacularly significant, so productive of desires and hopes, that they capture much of the imagination and inspire a great deal of strategizing. Whether the two contrasting marriage forms should ultimately be considered in terms of continuum or counterpoint remains for further analysis.

Mobility and Distance

From the standpoint of Miao women (and many less well-off rural women) in China, opportunities for social and economic mobility are increasingly conceived of in terms of some type of long-distance strategy. From the perspective of Chinese society under economic reform policies initiated in the late 1970s, growing industrialization and uneven development that favors coastal and urban regions have precipitated a massive movement of laborers out of farm villages and into many kinds of work and service. This rise in the mobility of the population follows upon several decades of strict enforcement of a *hukou*, or household registration policy, in which Chinese were not permitted to move from their designated place of work and residence. Whereas under Maoism, *nongye renkou*, or agricultural personnel had been expected to remain tied to the land, under the rapid and differential development policies of the last decade especially, surplus farm labor is expected by the state to be on the move, providing cheap toil to the burgeoning production and service industries in the most developed areas.

From the perspective of able-bodied peasants all over the poorer parts of the Chinese interior, and even in the more wealthy Chinese country-side, going out to *dagong* (seek temporary wage labor) has become a routine strategy of more and more rural households. The practice has been transformative of gender structures since, despite the majority of workers being men, vast numbers of women, some as young as their mid-teenage years, have also hit the road looking for earnings. Under the general rubric of migrant labor, there are several particularities that pertain to women: 1) they may find opportunities to work in various gendered labor niches, such as domestic work, service and entertainment work, and even garment work; 2) they may willingly or unwillingly turn to or be tricked into sex work; or 3) their initial labor migration may be transformed into marriage migration. The last happens because they are tricked and sold into marriages upon signing on with brokers for what they believe to be a work or study opportunity (*guaimai*),[1] or because during their laboring sojourn they meet someone whom they agree to marry.[2] This interlocking of labor and marriage migration is consistent with what Roland Tolentino described as a continuity for Filipinas at a transnational scale: women's bodies become the "requisite" for becoming "integrated into the circuits of multinationalism and transnationalism, generating a political economy marked by a sexualized division of labor" (1996:53).

Beyond the labor migration context, there are also increasing numbers of marriages contracted directly with grooms from other provinces or countries. This practice has become so widespread that it has transformed the social landscape of China's interior, as there are growing numbers of families in many villages who are linked by marriage to other provinces. In order to apprehend just how unusual a circumstance it is that young women, characteristically sheltered and secluded, should have opportunities to travel through marriage to much more distant places than their parents or even their brothers might ever go, it is necessary to take account of the abiding structure of patrilocal residence.

Patrilocality

The marriages with which this chapter is concerned take place in a setting in which a kinship system that prescribes patrilocality holds sway virtually uncontested for Miao and for Han China.[3] During my field-work, among peasants and highly educated interviewees alike, canons of patrilocality were consistently iterated in common parlance through the choice of a gender-bifurcated language to describe the act of getting married. Although one occasionally heard the gender-neutral *jiehun* used for both men and women's marrying, it was far more common to hear women described as having been *jia gei* X, or given away in marriage to X, or *chu jia*, married out.

While women otherwise continue to be associated with domicile and interiority, then, the abiding patrilocal kinship structure dictates that at this unique moment in women's lives, theirs will be a major and unparalleled move outward to another locality signaled by the *chu* before *jia*, which literally means "to go out" or "to go beyond." This move, which can be social as well as spatial, as Carolyn Steedman (1986) has so eloquently pointed out, stands to be a unique and transformative moment available only to women. Steedman's project was to contest male-biased critics of English society who genericize the experience of class position as imprisoning, suggesting instead that, for women, the possibility of mobility through marriage produces an entirely different structure of feeling, one of longing and of gendered calculation: "Women are . . . without class, because the cut and fall of a skirt and good leather shoes can take you across the river and to the other side: the fairy tales tell you that goose-girls may marry kings" (1986:15–16). Likewise in China, it will not be possible for men to make such a transformative move in their lifetimes; instead they will *qu*, or "get," a wife or a daughter-in-law, but remain firmly tethered to their class and locational positioning. Even in villages and towns in which women marry within a community, their leaving home and going out is linguistically marked in the same fashion, since they will move, however symbolically, to become members of their husbands' families. In contemporary China, economic factors such as a woman's employment or legitimate household registration in a desirable location *may* mean that a groom moves to live with his bride upon marriage. But across China, these are seen as unusual instances, exceptions that only transgress but do not weaken the rule of patrilocal residence.

The question that arises is what might be different in the case of long-distance marriages. If women have always married out, is this simply a quantitative shift, a marrying to a place that is simply that much farther away, or does it constitute a qualitative shift in the nature of out-marriage? What kind of questions would need to be asked to assess whether such moves have shifted the import of patrilocal residence? Rubie Watson stated: "In recent years patrilocal residence has been singled out as one of the major reasons for women's continuing oppression in postrevolution China" (1991:351). With patrilocal marriage moves transposed to a larger scale—that of the entire nation and sometimes that of the globe—is women's isolation-induced disempowerment merely exacerbated as they lose their bearings and family-support networks to an even greater extent? Conversely, is it conceivable that greater distances and the relocation to a distinctly different sector of society also mean certain advantages for such women, greater possibilities of transcending class, status, or economic stagnation? Might longer moves also imply greater degrees of hypergamy, whether spatial (Lavely 1991) or material? How might these considerations be inflected by the variable of moving within China versus beyond its borders, or by the variable of marrying within one's ethnic group versus marrying out (mostly to Han)?

Trafficking Versus Strategizing

Sheltered from the brilliant sun of a Yunnan sky in a county bordering Vietnam, a Hmong/Miao family clusters in the doorway of their mud-brick home, telling me of the fates of their four grown young women scattered across China. One daughter is in Guangxi Province, explains the mother; one is in Jiangsu, one is in Zhejiang, and one is in Yunnan's capital city, Kunming. The last went out looking for work and is still unmarried. The third daughter willingly married a man from Zhejiang when he came looking for a wife. The mother recounts her own visit to Zhejiang, where she stayed for six months. The land is flat, she offers, indicating that her daughter would be able to farm with greater ease. The life is better.

Things are not so upbeat in her portrayal of the fate of the two eldest daughters. By her account, in the mid-1980s, a man came to the village and convinced the young women that they were going to the nearby city of Wenshan to study. They disappeared, and didn't write back for over a year to let their parents know where they were. Only then did the parents know that the daughters had been married off to such faraway places. It was a *guaimai* situation, the mother affirms at the query of a Hmong/Miao scholar from Kunming; they were tricked and had no idea they were going to be sold into marriages in different provinces. In the intervening years, they have been back to visit only twice. Implying that the children are held hostage by the husband's family so that the wives will not flee, she explains that her grandchildren have never visited, nor has she ever gone to meet them.

It is a sinister story as she tells it, one that plagued the more impoverished parts of China especially in the 1980s, before the government had started to clamp down on the practice of marriage brokering by deception. Such accounts of far-flung families, of brides isolated, sometimes permanently, from their natal homes, are found all over the less developed regions of China. They beg classification as a kind of trafficking in women on the part of middlemen (and sometimes women) out to turn a profit in the liberalized economy. "It's not necessarily *guaimai*, however," protests a local Hmong/Miao official who has accompanied me to this village. He is a native of this county and feels passionately about his people, the economic imprisonment that is their entrapment on the arid, sharply sloped, infertile land that is so forbidding to cultivate. "Sometimes it's just that daughters *tell* their parents they were tricked, when actually they wanted to run off with the men."

The disjunction between the mother's account and that of the official speaks to the ambiguities that complicate any discussions of the marriage mobility of young women in China. It shows such women to be what Watson, following Gates (1989) and Hershatter (1991), referred to as "polyvalent"—as both person and commodity (1991:349). Hence the official's words can be doubly read: he may have been trying to put a positive spin on the daughters' departures because the actual occurrence of *guaimai* is an embarrassment to reform China. But he may have been reflecting an instance of women's active strategizing for marriage mobility—spatial if not social.[4] Importantly, one option does not exclude the other. There may have been a traffic in women in which money changed hands in the transfer of brides and at the same time the women may have gone willingly to their new homes.

In discussing transnational NGO discourses on "trafficking" in relation to sex workers, Sea-Ling Cheng sketches the way in which agency and force become dichotomized and mutually exclusive in the representation of the women in question as passive and powerless: "Instead of asking what the women *want*, this line of anti-trafficking argument focuses on what the women are. . . . The desires of these women are obscured by their victim identity" (2002:279). To be sure, there have been variants of such versions within China as well. In the early 1990s, for instance, shrill reports stated that "rural women in Guangxi Province, lured to cities with promises of jobs, have been raped and then sold for prostitution. . . . [M]ore than 50,000 abductions of women and children were reported in 1991–92" (*China News Digest*, May 24, 1994) and that "police processed more than 15,000 cases of gangs that kidnapped and sold women into marriage" (*China News Digest*, February 24, 1994). But as Emily Chao (in this volume) points out, Chinese discourses about mobile women seeking labor or marriage also often attribute blame to forms of "misguided female agency," to women's desires that prompt them to act imprudently, thus precipitating their victimization at the hands of kidnappers. Importantly for Chao, though, such discourses only bemoan those women's initiatives that take them far from home: "It is regional border crossing as opposed to all women's agency that is associated with danger," for it produces "bodies out of place, a specter of the state's inability to control its population." From the state's perspective of ordering the population into regions, ethnic groups, and labor segments, long-distance, cross-ethnic marriages might present particularly acute and threatening instances of what Veena Das has called a "vision of more flexible boundaries between . . . men and women than the state could tolerate" (1995:232).

Why would the women agree or even seek to marry so far from home? The willingness of Miao women to traverse great distances for marriages into strange settings with unfamiliar men is one of the chief problematics of this article. In the instance above, the official went on to explain that the county government had investigated some of the conditions of married-out women from their county in other provinces. The women insisted, he said, that they went voluntarily—*ziyuande qu*. As Gilmartin and Tan (2002) point out, often the birth of children transforms the initial resistance of women to distant marriages into a kind of resigned acceptance. It may be that in retrospect, when asked, they do not want to disavow marriages of several years simply because they had originally objected. But my research among brides from Guizhou married out to Jiangsu Province revealed other reasons for their going on their own volition.

A Chain Migrant Community of Brides in Jiangsu

In a cluster of neighboring villages in the Han countryside between Shanghai and Nanjing dwell a handful of daughters-in-law who hail from halfway across China. They are Miao women, mostly from the rugged mountains of Guizhou Province, and they were sought out by Han men whose family hardships meant that their quest for brides took them beyond their immediate locality. Exploiting the disparities generated by China's uneven development, most of the grooms had traveled themselves to China's interior, networking through contacts to seek out marriageable women at lower bride-prices who would demand less in terms of living conditions. Such suitors choose minority areas in particular, for these are regions where the implementation of the birth-planning policy has not been so stringent as to already produce a population imbalance with a paucity of young women.

Local officials tell me that in this *zhen* (administrative township), made up of eighty villages and a population of 36,000, there are two hundred women married in from the southwestern provinces of Guizhou, Yunnan, and Sichuan. Marriage migration here follows the chain pattern, with introductions by new brides eventuating in subsequent marriages. Forming a community of co-ethnics to cushion them from the shock of life in a new region with Han in-laws, they actively facilitate the unions of their kin and friends at home with other men of their new community who are still seeking partners. Sometimes the brides even travel home themselves with the express purpose of making other matches for their relatives.

Family members, and the daughters-in-law themselves, assert with vehemence that these unions cannot be described by the much sensationalized interprovincial traffic in women (*guaimai*) that has tricked many would-be wage earners into unwanted marriages with unchosen husbands. "I came here on my own!" one says to me. "They courted by themselves," affirms a father-in-law. The reason, almost without exception, that women give for having agreed to come is a highly embodied one, about the physical difference of spaces. What drew them to accept such distant marriages, they say, was simply the lure of flat land. Never until the recent era was it possible for Miao women to consider using marriage to escape the bitter labor on the steep terraced slopes of their home mountains. While spatial hypergamy was much practiced during the collective era, as Lavely (1991) has shown, it was almost exclusively within regions. But as Fan and Huang (1998:234) suggest, "economic reforms and the ensuing uneven regional development have further underscored the importance of location, motivating women to move up in the spatial hierarchy." Migrants explained this in terms of the variant exigencies of labor: "At home, the moment you step out the door you are carrying something on shoulder poles. Here everything can be pulled by tractors." The Han grooms whom they marry may be of lower status than they are, with less education, and with parents who are peasants rather than salaried workers and officials. Nonetheless, from the perspective of Guizhou natives, these were considered hypergamous marriages for the sole reason of the level land.

Settled into villages surrounded by the sprawl of flat fields outside their doors, now toting the one child they are permitted to bear in this populous Han region, many of these women have become bitter about the move across China. In some cases, they assert that they were duped, using the same language that is used to describe *guaimai* to rewrite a story of marital arrangement in retrospect. They'd been *pian* (cheated, tricked). They'd been promised a life of leisure, of watching TV free of farmwork. Instead it usually turned out that their new families were especially short of labor and that their toil was ceaseless. In many cases, other sons had split off into separate households; the Miao bride and her husband were the ones designated to stay home and take care of aging parents. One woman discovered that, in addition to single-handedly tilling the fields, she was expected to be the primary caretaker for a disabled adult sister-in-law who needed to be bathed and fed daily. Several women asserted vehemently that they wanted to go home at the same time that they somehow let on that they were resigned to their futures in Jiangsu. Others complained that they wanted desperately to go out and *dagong* to make money, but that the domestic responsibilities assigned to them had saddled them to the household and the fields.

Some women described intense loneliness: they knew that their fellow Miao sisters were so nearby, yet their families would not release them from domestic duties so that they could visit with one another. Moreover, almost every husband sojourned most of the year away from home, traveling China to seek wage labor, as has become the strategy of so many peasants everywhere. Alone with strange villagers, whose dialect of Chinese was well nigh incomprehensible to them at first, these Miao brides passed their days as the perennial daughter-in-law, in meaningless toil, taking delight in their only children. What they had not comprehended, or bargained for, was the sheer physicality of space that made home so far away. They narrated their desire for home and relatives with acute deprivation. For most, although they longed to more than anything, they could not go home, whether to visit or even to run away. In the Miao mountains, a bride had usually married within walking distance, even if it was a matter of a couple of days' excursion. Thus her sense of space took shape as a larger regional community, in which she knew both language and specific people. There she had always lived a small-scale translocality, traveling between villages to market days and festivals. There was security in the awareness that should life with in-laws become insufferable, she might simply walk on her two feet out the door onto the well-worn footpaths and go "home." But in this faraway province, the material distance of home constituted an unanticipated sense of immobility. Most brides did not have access to enough cash, or lacked permission from their in-laws, to travel home. In-laws protested that the women were not competent to undertake travel, that they would be vulnerable and helpless. Indeed, in some cases, the women did not have the literacy or other travel skills that would have been required for them to make the trip, but in some cases it was likely that the in-laws feared a home visit would tempt the bride to run away permanently. Similar to the circumstance that has been described for brides who were duped and sold off to faraway villages whose geographical location was actually kept secret from them, these willing brides had likewise become disoriented in space; in a certain sense, they did not know how to find their way home.

In lieu of traveling home, the most fortunate had put their meager resources into the telephone, that instrument of time-space compression that could instantly connect them to the voices of their loved ones.

Some paid for phone calls at local shops; others managed to afford phone hookups in their homes and in those of their parents back in Guizhou.

One night, for instance, I sat in the bare central room of a Miao peasant household in the Guizhou mountains, talking to an old woman about her daughter, who had married out to Jiangsu seven years ago. The old woman had just returned from the fields, where she had been digging up potatoes. She told me of her disorienting boredom when she visited her daughter's new home, as well as the awkwardness of the groom when he came to visit the Miao village. When she showed me a photo of her grandson, I had to squint to make out the picture since the room was dark, with minimal electricity. The old woman was skinny and ate hard, cold rice with some boiled greens directly from a wok. Flies buzzed around and a rat scampered across the adjoining room. One grown son who still lived at home disappeared into the inner rooms to look for an address for his sister. Several discrepant addresses were on various envelopes and the family got agitated, afraid that I would not be able to locate their daughter with an inaccurate address. Suddenly from the back room I heard elevated voices. Gradually, I realized that in order to confirm the daughter's address, the girl's brother had removed the characteristic kerchief that was draped over the family's private telephone, and had simply dialed her up several provinces away! The surroundings could not have begun to reveal to me that this family would have put resources into acquiring a phone or spending on long-distance charges.

The proliferation of telephone communications in the rural hinterland represents one concrete outcome of long-distance marriages. In addition to new forms of isolation for brides, such marriages also create instant linkages between remote areas and any part of China in the form of a weblike, lateral network. For the brides, the comforting physicality of home has been supplanted by that instantaneous but one-dimensional substitute—the plastic headpiece that has made talking to their kin a possibility across their agonizing separation. In shifting economies of value, so cherished is this new form of connection that even the poorest of families may decide that it is worth it to invest in a phone. Yet there was something about these disembodied voices that seemed to exacerbate the experience of distance, and I saw tears fall amply during phone calls home.

The brides still hungered for a more embodied sense of community. In the absence of blood kin, what they eagerly awaited were those brief, sometimes stolen, moments in the company of their co-ethnics. By their accounts, it was this tiny and fragile subcommunity of women that they valued, not the attentions of the Han men with whom they cohabited.

Some openly expressed repugnance for their husbands and indicated that the only way they achieved a sense of belonging was among those who also came from "home." If their in-laws would free them, they would willingly walk for even a few hours to visit their friends' villages. A few were envied as extremely fortunate, for they lived in a large village where at least five Guizhou women had married in, making it possible for them to associate on a daily basis. When together, these women could use Miao dialects, or a more widely intelligible Guizhou dialect, to have private conversations free of the prying ears of their in-laws.

Other than issues of language comprehension, these women narrated most of their experience in terms of bodily disjunctions and fusions. It was through their bodies that they produced not only the mixed child, but also the hybridized lives they continued to live. Most had voluntarily cut their hair to sensible Jiangsu peasant lengths. To explain this style decision, they cited not any canons of coastal cultural discipline, but rather the suitability of short hair to the physical features of their peasant lives—the intensity of their labor and the ovenlike heat of the Jiangsu summer. In this narrative, home was portrayed as a site of greater cultural constraint from which they gained a degree of self-determination upon their exit. Nonetheless, they continued to embroider Miao-style hats to protect their babies' heads, and one woman who'd been there several years said she had begun to grow her hair long again so that she could wear it in proud Miao style for the rare occasion when she might visit home.

Significantly, the accounts of these women also contained fragments of testimony as to how their presence had affected their new communities, altering them ever so slightly. Interestingly, one of these fragments emerged when I asked about the hair decisions of a visiting Miao mother. Miao married women from her part of Guizhou typically wrapped a towel over their tied-up hair to protect it from dirt, creating a ubiquitous and distinctive look. I asked if the mother-in-law had removed her towel out of embarrassment when she visited the Han countryside. At first she had, I was told, but since her head felt cold, she put the towel back on, and discovered that it didn't matter: nobody stared. Local Han, I was told, had already become *xiguan* (accustomed) to the look because so many Guizhou Miao women had married in. Such a tiny anecdote indicates a remarkable shift in place identity. That the presence of Miao and their characteristic looks could become a matter of *xiguan* in the Han countryside suggests that, at least in this instance, what migrants' mobilities were doing was refashioning certain places—even rural villages—in terms of increasingly polyglot identities that included more heterogeneous ethnicities, body practices, and cultural norms.

Food practices, too, revealed this narrative of impact. Brides spoke of how they'd taught their husbands and in-laws to eat spicy food. From home, they'd imported their cherished chillies—a hallmark of southwestern China's cuisine—and introduced them into the local Jiangsu dishes, actually persuading not only their children but also their husbands and in-laws to adjust their taste buds. And if spiciness was not enough, they also introduced the beloved flavor of sour. They lovingly transported huge ceramic pickling jars, so that they could get the right tangy taste for the vegetables they painstakingly cured in Miao style. When they met one another, they would exchange their delicacies, comparing notes on whose product best preserved the hometown flavor. With a mischievous glimmer in their eyes, these custodians of a rarified culinary knowledge seemed to take delight in the opportunity to purvey their flavors among a tiny few of those northern and coastal elite who have protested over history that fiery spice and other southwestern tastes were inedible. Here the politics of bodies could clearly be seen to intersect with those of sociocultural prestige. The Miao brides' bodily micropractices, in other words, may have had the effect of destabilizing any notion of ethnic hypergamy that might have otherwise inflected their marriage to majority Han.

One-Way Traffic?

I want to highlight briefly here a conundrum in analyzing the movement of brides out of China's hinterlands as conceivably a newfangled "traffic in women." I want to draw attention to the possibility of slippage between a more classical sense of the traffic in women derived from Gayle Rubin in her canonical rereading of Lévi-Strauss, and the more contemporary use of "traffic" to mean a commodification of women in translocal marriage markets and sex-trade contexts. The former "traffic" could be characterized as eminently legitimate within its context, constitutive of the social fabric, a substrate of the kinship system that is the basis of social organization. It derives from the formulations of Bronislaw Malinowski, Marcel Mauss, and Claude Lévi-Strauss, who saw the practice of reciprocal exchange as essential to social order. The production of alliance through affines was the chief outcome of the exchange of women by male partners or social groups. In Rubin's words, "If it is women who are being transacted, then it is the men who give and take them who are linked, the woman being a conduit of a relationship rather than a partner to it" (1975:174). In the ideal-typical model, women "are in no position to give themselves away" (Rubin 1975:175).

The situation in translocal marriage markets in contemporary China and in many other parts of the world confounds this simple structure of reciprocity between male groups. First, the women do not "flow" between social units that are practicing forms of solidarity (even if agonistic). Theirs is a unidirectional flow out of impoverished or disadvantaged regions toward wealthier ones, often at the objection rather than the initiation of their menfolk. Their moves are frequently atomized and do not contribute to the constitution of any particular social fabric, at least not one that incorporates their natal families. Even when a larger pattern of marriages becomes established between a sending zone and a destination, it does not result in the elaboration of reciprocal linkages but is rather characterized by sharp asymmetry. Second, in many instances the women do, in a certain sense, "give themselves away," in the instances in which they run off or enter into marriages without the knowledge or consent of their families. Parents recounted to me again and again the sense that, their daughters having chosen their own grooms, there was nothing they could do to intervene. The ensuing weddings did not involve the usual cementing of affinal ties through ceremonies in both bride's and groom's homes together with the exchange of gifts and money. In many of the cases I have researched, the benefits to brides' families were minimal, and the relations between affines nonexistent, stifled by distance.

There is, of course, the other sense of "trafficking," in which a woman is transmuted into a commodity by virtue of the material exchanges that take place in conjunction with her transfer. This type of exchange could apply to the more traditional institution of bride-price, to the remuneration to families or marriage brokers for wives, and also to the contractual payment for short-term sexual services. Yet there is a critical disjunction between the bride-price form, which is socially legitimate, and the other forms that are commonly critiqued as socially dysfunctional. The latter—sex trade and wife purchase—somehow become recast in normative terms, designating a social aberration in which women's volition has been denied to them through "trafficking" activities most commonly regarded as criminal. What accounts for this disjunction? In all cases, the model is premised on the erasure of women's volition. Is it because of the translocal dimension, the vastness of space, and the unidirectional flow of women that the latter forms are criminalized? Is it because the modalities by which alliance and reciprocity are produced have been shattered by distance and by the uneven economy that is a nation-space like reform-era China? To push consideration of this conundrum further, we turn to the scale of the global, to the interchanges between Hmong émigrés to the West and their co-ethnics in China.

The Gender of Hmong Homecoming

The small city of Wenshan is the capital of the Wenshan Miao and Zhuang Autonomous Prefecture, a region in Yunnan Province that borders on Vietnam and comprises several counties. A few of these counties contain some of the densest aggregations of Hmong/Miao in all of China. More important for the purposes of this article, this is one of the regions of China in which the subgroup of Miao bears most cultural and linguistic similarity to the Hmong who have migrated out of China. Of crucial importance is that Miao here refer to themselves with the ethnonym "Hmong" and that their language is entirely mutually intelligible with the émigrés to Southeast Asia and beyond. Wenshan, known in Hmong language as Paj Tawg Laj and in émigré lore as an ancient place of origins, is also a switching point for voyages into the Hmong/Miao hinterland, to villages where "traditional" life may be found intact. For many of the Hmong Americans who come to visit, the physical place Paj Tawg Laj is preceded by rich imaginings: souls of the deceased must return to Paj Tawg Laj, and centuries-old migration routes canonized in oral history invariably name this site. Moreover, Hmong travelers have shot widely circulated seductive videos showing this remembered land of nostalgia. Hmong American viewers have been able to watch the spectacle of craggy mountains, the rugged village life, and the colorful costumes worn by Hmong/Miao women on VCRs in living rooms across the United States (see Schein 2002). Eager anticipation attends any pilgrim to Paj Tawg Laj, and in just over a decade such travelers have already beaten a well-worn path of return to this mystic land.

Local Hmong/Miao who host the travelers have also developed patterns and expectations in the years of reigniting contact. For both sides, the encounter is almost always structured by kin-type relationships. For Hmong anywhere in the world, a patri-clan system prevails in which those with the same surname are recognized as brothers, cousins, or uncles. For Hmong returnees to China, one need only seek out Hmong with the same surname, and elaborate canons of hospitality go into effect, regardless of whether any actual kin connection can be directly traced. Hmong in China regularly house, feed, and accompany their newfound American relatives, providing them with every convenience within their comparatively meager means. The occasion of the month-long spring festival has become a transnational event, in which not only relatives from within China, but Hmong from abroad come to share in the festivities, attend outdoor celebrations, and bask in the glow of what Anna Everett, describing the African diaspora, has called "virtual consanguinity" (2002:139).

The reception of Hmong American relatives has come to be, for local Hmong/Miao in China, an occasion of exuberance and affection mingled with bitterness and hope. Most of the returnees are men, and they have some surprising needs. Many are moneyed enough to stay in good hotels, and if they visit villages it is on day trips, where they are almost like tourists, except that they can speak the local Hmong dialect fluently. They buy ornate traditional costumes, some in bulk to resell in the United States. Indeed, so many Miao costumes are being bought in China for sale abroad that tiny factories and cottage industries have proliferated to meet the demand. They also sightsee, visiting the parks and tourist traps of China, as any distant foreigner might do. They constantly shoot videos, which they take back with them to sell to other Hmong at home. An increasing number are seeking out traditional and herbal medical treatments for ailments that Western doctors are at a loss to help them with. But more than anything else, I was told over and over again, by local men and women alike, these male travelers are coming to *wanr guniang*, to play with girls. For the hosts, their bitterness is about the fact that they have been reduced to such forms of feminized pleasure provision; their hope is that the liaisons formed between local Miao women and the men from the West will enable a few young women to travel to a richer country and a better life halfway around the world. The fact that several dozen have done so to date intensifies their aspirations.

Doing ethnography on Hmong/Miao transnational interchanges, one cannot escape the extreme asymmetries that shape the quest for "virtual consanguinity." We see here the effects of a very particular globalization, in which the Hmong community has been transposed to the global scale, yet it has not achieved a kind of horizontal integration in which all are simply relatives wherever they are in the world. Instead, male migrants to the West return to the East for sexual and romantic pleasures they cannot enjoy in the West, while young women and their families in Asia strategize about how to make this new demand for women work to their advantage. From the perspective of the Miao in China, the unidirectional flow of women and the uneven sexual exchanges have tempered any initial euphoria that they may have felt at being reunited with kin, replacing it with a longing to land their young women in transnationally hypergamous marriages that will ideally shift the whole family's fortunes.

Reciprocal Imaginings and Mismatched Longings

If one were to ask a Miao young woman in China whether she would prefer to marry a Han from another part of China or a Hmong from the West, it is almost certain that she would elect the latter. First, she likely would be marrying not to a farm but to an urban or suburban setting where her opportunities, at least in her calculation, would be much greater. Second, she would be marrying to a country revered for being rich and developed; she would think about the comforts of life in a prosperous foreign land. But third, and crucially important, she would be marrying a Hmong co-ethnic, and hence, in a certain sense, remaining within her "community" at the global scale. So great are these motivators for Hmong/Miao women in China and their families that a great deal of mobilization has gone into positioning young women for courtship with Hmong men from abroad. No sooner have they reached the homeland than Hmong male visitors seem to find themselves tenderly hosted by young, attractive women usually speaking their language, catering to their needs, and often willing to sleep with them. In some cases, women are very young, in their mid-teens, but as long as they are attractive to the male travelers, they take their chances with trying to become a courtship object.

That these local women who fawn over them are often very young is one of the distinct pleasures for nostalgic Hmong men returning to lost lands. As I have suggested elsewhere (Schein 2004), the courting of very young girls, even girls of twelve or thirteen years old, is a practice remembered from experiences in Laos and has become part of the fantasy of what home means. The majority of Hmong men who travel to Asia, however, are not young themselves, but middle-aged and more often than not married. Since many are not in a position to court a young woman and bring her to America as a bride, they enter into a variety of other types of liaisons. Some find girls with whom to have ephemeral romantic-sexual adventures that will not necessarily develop into long-term commitments. Some cultivate such relationships for a relatively longer period by setting the women up as mistresses, keeping in touch by letter, phone, and increasingly by e-mail, and through visiting periodically. Others actually marry the women—officially or otherwise—as second wives, leaving them in Asia and taking up a life of shuttling between the continents where their women reside.

Some of these polygynous relationships, which are much more common in Southeast Asia, are entirely out in the open, reflecting a perduring legitimacy of polygynous practices among Hmong men of means. In rare cases, such men will have even more than two wives and will boast of their multiple relationships as a source of prestige. While there is a great deal of social censure around this issue, especially among more feminist-inclined Hmong American women, it is also not uncommon for Hmong in the U.S. to matter-of-factly refer to men's second or third wives. Other marriages are, by contrast, kept circumspect, with respective wives never knowing of the others' existence. Indeed, among Miao in China, frustrated women and their families and general purveyors of gossip routinely respond to a Hmong visitor's failure to marry and import a bride by surmising that he must already have one, unconfessed, on the other side of the Pacific.

Such normative commentaries about Hmong Americans have become quite common among Hmong/Miao in China. In a striking reversal of what one might expect from those who remain in Asia, they sometimes critique Hmong émigrés along the lines of their *chuantong sixiang* (traditional attitudes), pointing out that polygyny has not only been illegal in China for decades, but that Hmong/Miao no longer believe that it is a defensible institution. One educated, urban-dwelling mother of a Hmong/Miao bride also told me that she was shocked that Hmong in the West had not succeeded in revising the custom of early marriage, that this practice negatively influenced the futures of women, whether in work or education, and that China, in its more progressive social programs, had long since put an end to teen weddings and unofficial cohabitations. These discourses of critique invert the bifurcation of the globe into modern West and traditional East that still suffuses the imaginaries of émigré travelers seeking a home suspended in time. Ironically, while their quests might be for "traditional" women, their practices overseas have inspired some of their co-ethnics in Asia to view them with disdain, as guardians of a retrograde system of male privilege that will only disappoint the women they ultimately find.[5]

Such disappointments are very much a part of the story for that handful of women who do actually marry to the West. They, too, harbor a vivid imaginary—of a life of comfort, self-advancement, and opulent wealth. In terms of social mobility, such a move cannot even be compared with the lowly marriages to Han in other parts of China that so many of their sisters have begun to consider. So strong is this image—across China as well as among the Hmong/Miao—that women go to great lengths to position themselves to be chosen in marriage by foreigners. For the courting correspondents of China and the Philippines described by Nicole Constable (2003a) and for urban migrants such as the Shenzhen laborers studied by Constance Clark (2001), such positioning is through marriage agencies, electronic mail, and such high-tech procedures as bridal advertising through video. It begins with a premise of anonymity. For Miao women and their families, by contrast, positioning begins with the skillful activation of kin ties.

How do particular unions get formed across the Pacific but within the Hmong/Miao universe? A first consideration is clan membership. While Hmong American travelers may seek out "relatives" with the same surname as hosts, codes of clan exogamy absolutely forbid, as incest, any sexual or marital relationship between clan members. This stricture remains virtually unchallenged anywhere that Hmong reside. It is so severe that, for instance, one Hmong American man and his bride, who were of the same surname but from different Miao dialect groups in China, were absolutely ostracized as censure by their kin in the United States, to the point that they dissociated themselves entirely from the

Hmong community and carried out bitter lives in loneliness. Affinal ties, then, become crucial to matching overseas men with women in China, and it is often from the kin of hosts' wives that eligible girls are selected. In some cases, the introductions are made first when, say, a male relative of the potential groom locates a prospective bride and suggests to her family and to the man in the U.S. that a match be made. Among the stories I know of, some involved active calculation on the part of the girls or their families to position the bride as available. Other families were unwitting, suddenly finding themselves at the receiving end of aggressive courtship in the form of visits from the groom or his clan representatives along with letters, phone calls, and other forms of persuasion. Still others were taken by surprise and sometimes quite resistant when their daughter entered into a relation on her own and only later announced her betrothal to her kin. Initial introductions were sometimes followed by a lengthy period of letter writing and other forms of long-distance communication—such as the phone calls recounted at the outset of this chapter—before the prospective couple actually met. In the process, the family or the girl had the opportunity to test the loyalty of the groom, and to ensure that the girl would mature to a respectable age for marriage. If the groom did visit in person, however, premarital sex was not necessarily taboo.

Aside from carefully orchestrated family arrangements, other types of encounters also occurred. Men might locate women incidentally, without relatives' knowledge or intervention, as service persons in the establishments they patronized or in villages where they visited as tourists. Photos and videos also assisted in the matchmaking process. Akin to the older institution of "picture brides" from Asia, photos might be carried by individual travelers who took them back to the States to show to prospective grooms. Videos, on the other hand, often portrayed a more generic sampling of women, often identified by clan name, that viewers in the United States might watch while cultivating their fantasies of unions with homeland women.

The role of media in producing homeland desire cannot, in my assessment, be overestimated. As George Yudice has eloquently put it, "in contemporary U.S. society . . . fantasy is no longer limited to the private psyche but projected on the screen of the social" (2001:229). Likewise for transnational Hmong society, the homeland woman is a product of collective fantasy, reiterated in multiple and mutually reinforcing media formats that serve to stabilize this feminine object as a focal point for myriad desires. Video genres that represent the homeland woman include documentaries, love stories, martial-arts and war-action dramas, and an abundance of music videos. In the most blatant form of marketing, literal cruising might be part of the content of such videos. This is indicated, for instance, by scenes depicting interrogations as to young women's clan names, in which we see a man in the frame directly asking a girl for her clan affiliation to assess marriageability. In one video about China, the idiom of courtship is made even more explicit. Three rural young women are arrayed on a hilltop, colorfully dressed before a backdrop of panoramic scenery. The cameraman asks: "Will you sing a song for me to take back to America to find you a man?" And then: "Are you girls still young and unmarried?"

The girl who is apparently the eldest, but still appearing to be in her mid-teens at most, utters: "Yes, we don't have 'it' [marriage] yet."

"Thank you very much," he replies. The camera hesitates, zooms in on the face of the speaker, then pans to the other two girls. They smile awkwardly and smooth their skirts and aprons self-consciously. The cameraman, now self-appointed matchmaker, narrates: "These are three of our Hmong girls. They are going to sing and I'm going to record a couple of songs to take back to our men in America." He chuckles audibly, then asks one of them the key question:

"What clan are you?"

"Zhou clan," the eldest offers.

Then they proceed to sing, not knowing where to cast their eyes. They appear disoriented at the staging of what, in face-to-face courtship, would have been a dialogue, but now has been rendered as a one-way self-marketing opportunity about which their faces convey primarily awkwardness and ambivalence. Like the paradigmatic catalog brides marketed by mail-order companies, they communicate, but only from a position of what Ara Wilson (1988:119) has called "rhetorical vulnerability," in which they are commandeered to present themselves in codes not of their own making to audiences not visible to them.

To Escort Is Not to Marry

The conventions of Hmong homeland video, then, characteristically seek out and cruise a typified rural woman, usually in costume and in song, as the object of fantasy. In practice, however, it was for the most part women with some measure of education and urbanity, who were already living in small towns or cities, who were ultimately identified by Hmong Chinese and Hmong Americans alike, to be most eligible as marriage partners. Peasant women, it was surmised, would have too great an adjustment problem dealing with life abroad. The importance of the woman's status to transnational marriages was interestingly formulated by a young woman I met at a market in a small town near the Vietnam border.

Strolling down the strip of this town on a market day, the street crammed with stalls peddling agricultural products, tools, clothing, snacks, cigarettes, and other essentials, I was surprised to the hear the grainy strains of Hmong/Miao traditional song blasting from a speaker at one of the stalls. Under an awning providing some shelter from the sun were VCDs (video compact disks) and audiotapes of all manner of popular Chinese movies and music. A discerning shopper might discover that, amid these mass wares, some in borrowed cases—adorned on the outside with Han pop stars sporting electric guitars, sunglasses, and highly fashionable hairstyles—were tucked cassettes of locally recorded Hmong/Miao music.

My eyes shifted to the young woman who was minding the stall. Despite the heat, she wore her hair long and out, highlighted with a reddish dye. Her outfit was a black shirt and long skirt of slinky material over stylish sandals with three-inch heels. Her skin had the telltale ruggedness of having already worn too much makeup in her life. How, I asked her, had she gotten into this business? A graduate only of lower school (sixth grade), she had moved to Kunming, the provincial capital, at the age of seventeen. There she had been retained by a local Hmong/Miao man who hosted many Hmong from abroad. When a group arrived, he would call on her to escort them, sometimes touring around Kunming, but especially if they wanted to go to Hmong/Miao villages. She would take them to the small towns in the region to attend festivals. Sometimes she would even hike with them into villages off the road, villages such as her own. Usually, she recounted with a hint of disdain, they didn't stay there but just ate a meal and went back to the hotels, complete with showers and toilets, in the bigger towns.

After two years of earning money as an escort, she had decided to change her work. She now travels all over the region, even to Kunming and Wenshan, to buy media materials. Then, with her sister, she works the circuit of periodic markets in the area immediately surrounding her home village. Based in the county seat where her uncle lives, each market day they pack several crates of VCDs and cassettes along with folding tables and awning onto a bus to travel to various markets, bringing media to the peasants. Why had she chosen to give up her escort work? You reach a time in your life, she explains, when you start thinking about finding someone. Living alone in the city like that, in her opinion, is no way to find a husband. Now a twenty-year-old, she has returned back to her home region to begin to think about marriage.

I asked whether any of the overseas Hmong men she had hosted had ever sought her out as a bride. It seemed strange that the role she had played as female escort had not involved more overt courtship on the part of the visitors of such a young and attractive local Hmong/Miao woman. She replied, matter-of-factly, in a tone that did not seem to indicate false modesty, that none of those men would want a country girl like her. There was not a shred of doubt in her assessment that her status was not commensurate with a marriage abroad. Indeed, I met other young women who likewise represented themselves this way, seeming almost embarrassed by the intimation that they might merit the attentions of such high-status men.

And yet the costumed, singing country woman remains an object of fantasy consumption for the viewers of Hmong homeland videos, even if she doesn't end up to be so marriageable. Somehow it is as if the more educated and more urbane Hmong/Miao women who actually qualify to enter into transnational marriages are in turn scripted into roles as typifications of the rural past. This allows us to return to the question of the actual conditions for those who end up in the United States and to suggest that the fantasy of the traditional woman is connected to their experiences of disappointment.

Life in a Transnational Marriage

Despite the highly routinized gendered relationship that obtains throughout the Hmong/Miao areas in China as they receive co-ethnic visitors from abroad, only a few dozen women at this writing have actually married out to the United States. A larger proportion of wives from abroad come from Laos and Thailand, but such marriages are also not widespread, although they appear to be on the increase. Among those from China married to U.S. Hmong, experiences have been very mixed. Many of the wives had been working in China, some in professional capacities as performers, journalists, or traditional medical doctors. Some had college or high school educations. In some cases, they had lived apart from their Hmong/Miao communities at home for long periods. They spoke local dialects of Chinese, and sometimes standard Mandarin, but did not have the level of Hmong language that would allow them to communicate with ease in their new in-law families. For almost all of them, their English was nonexistent or extremely limited. The Chinese they spoke fluently was of no use in their lives with Hmong from Laos. Ironically, it had been precisely the life strategies of seeking education and work in towns and cities that had, on the one hand, separated them from their Hmong/Miao backgrounds, but on the other, placed them in the path of Hmong American travelers as service people and performers in the tourist industry. Only a few had managed to parlay these backgrounds into opportunities in the U.S.—one continued her education in business, while a former performer established song and dance classes for Hmong American children.

Wives from China were not prepared for the relative isolation of urban/suburban living in sprawling U.S. cities. Husbands were typically not a focal point for their social and emotional lives, so they yearned for other forms of community. Some who lived with in-laws complained of the relationships, strained by linguistic incompatibility and strict notions of rank; but those in neolocal residences often felt horribly alone. Transportation had become a huge challenge in their new lives; some had learned to drive, but those who hadn't felt intensely housebound. Sometimes they averred that their husbands had not given them sufficient opportunities to study English and to take driving lessons. In Minneapolis-Saint Paul, where several of them lived, they were also unprepared for the bitter cold and deep snows of winter. They had formed a tiny network and, in the absence of any independent means to get around, kept in close touch by telephone.

Childbearing was also a factor in keeping the wives housebound. Some had many children or had husbands who wanted to have many children, in the "traditional" Hmong way. This, too, was an adjustment, since at home they had come to take for granted the Chinese birth-planning policy that would limit their births to one, if they resided in the city, and to an ideal of two if they lived in the countryside. Growing up under this policy, these young women had lost the sense—so common among previous Hmong/Miao generations—that large families were an absolute value. Their feelings toward their children were mixed: on the one hand, children constituted for them a tiny "uterine" family (M. Wolf 1972) to counter their isolation; but children also meant more impediments to acquiring skills and savvy for living in American society, or to a future that would involve work and other forms of participation in a broader life.

Even more than the Miao daughters married out to faraway provinces within China, these women lamented their horrible distance from home. Some had had parents come to visit in the United States, to stay and help them take care of newborn children. But others had very little contact with their parents and felt cut off from their home society with a frightening degree of finality. Distance was ameliorated a great deal for those whose parents in China had telephones, but for those who didn't, there was virtually no communication, and they were not about to write letters telling their parents of the bitterness of their lives. Not only were their new existences virtually indescribable, but that such lives would be disappointing was well nigh impossible to transmit, especially since their marriages implied a kind of hypergamous privilege that no daughter-in-law should bemoan.

Returning to the question of hypergamy, we again come up against the issue of how to evaluate such long-distance moves. To be sure, in terms of any global ranking of the respective spaces, such transnational

Hmong/Miao brides have not only married out, but they have married up several scales. Yet many have fallen in status from their starting point within their own society in which they were moderately or highly educated and working. This loss in status is, of course, a ubiquitous condition of many labor as well as marriage migrants who give up higher status in their home countries for better earnings or more comfortable lives in more wealthy economies. The case, documented by Constable (1997), of Filipina domestic workers who leave their college-educated employment at home to undertake menial cleaning and child-care duties in Hong Kong (or Canada or the Middle East) is one particularly pronounced example.

Yet another status issue comes into play in this instance. In many cases of transnational marriage, the husband himself is low status within his own society, or of dubious desirability as a marriage partner, either because he is much older, is disabled, is divorced or a widower, has problems with his own financial situation, or has otherwise been subjected to social or legal censure. In Hmong/Miao society, marriageability is also marked by height, and it is striking how many suitors who go to China are exceptionally short in relative terms. For most of the married-out brides to the U.S., putting up with a range of such stigmas is also a common part of their experience. Should they betray dissatisfaction with their husband's character or social standing, they might become subject to forms of discipline often reported among immigrant brides (Thiesmeyer 1999). Life in the American dreamland, then, is highly mixed and uneven, presenting unanticipated challenges for women who had initially approached it as the highly mediated global destination of desire that it has become for so many.[6]

Conclusions

Several aspects of the two forms of translocal marriage discussed here remain to be thematized in comparison. First, it is striking that the marriages beyond China's borders, at far greater physical distances than those between China's provinces, constitute unions that are not marked by ethnic difference. The divergent national location of brides and grooms is critically important, to be sure, but it is painstakingly elided in the fantasies of ethnic union that inform these transpacific alliances. For Hmong men from the West, the quest for a homeland bride is a quest for self, distilled and preserved, now alluringly embodied in a feminine counterpart, akin to what Edward Said called a "surrogate and underground self" (1978). In a strange way, then, Hmong reunification across borders has not escaped a certain gendered orientalizing despite such liaisons simultaneously being championed as elements of a global diasporic identity. For women who are Hmong-speaking members of the Miao group in China, this intra-ethnic marriage form is desirable not only because it means access to the high-status West, but also because of the sense of ethnic belonging marked so acutely by language compatibility.

By contrast, as we've seen, Miao women who marry out of their provinces within China are almost always marrying to Han or another ethnic group. The isolation born of distance that afflicts all such translocal outmarriages is intensified by the ethno-linguistic difference that makes brides outsiders once over, even though they remain within China. It is crucially important, then, that the notion of border-crossing that conceptually unites these newfangled marriage forms also be qualified in terms of the national, racial, ethnic, and regional specificities of each particular type of union. Greater physical distance by no means maps seamlessly onto greater ethno-racial distance. Diasporic marriage alliances as forms of transnational exchange have become a key component of the transnational marriage institution that is on the rise globally.[7] Such long-distance joinings, signified in terms of ethnic selfhood, complicate how we should think about the notion of trafficking in women that routinely connotes mail-order brides, exploitation, interracial unions, and a high degree of cultural difference.

Second, and relatedly, these two scenarios of out-marriage within and beyond China's borders force questions about how we might think about the notion of alliance. In the classical form, of course, the exchange of women was to produce solidarity among affines, a broader network of social allies than patrilineal kin would be able to access among themselves. Does marriage at greater distances still stand to produce forms of alliance, albeit perhaps of different types? It would seem that one of the things that has shifted in the interprovincial marriages within China is that the claims that in-laws might make upon one another have been nullified. While daughters may take pains to keep in touch with their natal families, it is often despite the ruptures in communication and interchange that the grooms' families have instituted. Indeed, even a bride-price of cash or gifts paid to the bride's parents is routinely, though by no means always, circumvented since liaisons are contracted sometimes by the bride herself, sometimes by brokers who have swindled girls away. Indeed, it would seem that the only generalization one might make about alliances in interprovincial marriage arrangements is that there are no guarantees, no socially sanctioned avenues that relatives can count on should they wish to call upon their affines. In some ways, even if they were not originally arranged through the bride's volition, the interprovincial unions seem to have produced marriages that are much more conjugal, less structured by the inter-changes and obligations among a broad network of affinal kin.

Conversely, alliance very much informs the imaginings about transnational marriages that Hmong and Miao enter into across the Pacific. Acutely aware of their diasporic dispersal, such unions are seen as ways to reweld ties shattered by the tragedies of history. Importantly, this fantasy is strongest on the part of Hmong from the West who are afflicted with the experience of loss. Yet, according to their "kin" in China, the fantasy does not always translate into reality, as Hmong from the West betray what those in China feel should be their obligations toward their poor relations in the Asian countryside. Inversely, in practice it is those families of Hmong/Miao in China who would most like to keep the structures of alliance intact, for they hope that, through such channels, desperately needed economic support and other opportunities for transnational migration will flow. Indeed, money *has* flowed to families in China, and in some cases even to needy villages, but it is with bitterness that many Hmong/Miao assess these tokens as not nearly enough. Even as they dream of transnational alliance, it seems, in the eyes of kin in Asia, that Hmong from the West have shattered the institution of alliance in its full socioeconomic sense.

Finally, we return to the issue of patrilocality, so commonly analyzed as a source of women's disempowerment. What complicates this formulation in both of these instances is not only that the brides regularly quest to move away through marriage, but also that the greater distances their marriages entail may shift the calculus in terms of their social standing. From the perspective of China's southwestern provinces where Miao reside and of China's impoverished interior as a whole, marrying to a wealthier part of China—to the extent that it improves brides' material circumstances—may be a much sought-after form of social mobility. The question of distance, then, can only be read in terms of a double valence: it 1) produces a greater isolation and potentially cuts the bride off from social supports, diminishing her power within her marital family, but 2) gives such a woman access to a more comfortable and more prestigious life within the Chinese social hierarchy and sometimes to economic power vis-à-vis her natal home. For those few women who are able to move abroad, they have in effect "jumped scales" (N. Smith 1992), repositioning themselves near the top of a global spatial hierarchy that shapes the aspirations of so many, even Han urbanites, who seek to exit China altogether.[8]

We must return, however, to the question of women's volition, since we cannot assume a uniform desire for long-distance or border-crossing marriages, nor is the actual experience always accompanied by commensurate forms of women's agency. To be sure, many of these marriages de facto involve some degree of coercion or deception of the brides, and others entail a high rate of frustrated expectations. One might ask to what extent the wishes and intentions of the brides, along with their degree of complicity in arranging the marriages, correlate with any assessment of their marital circumstances or their social power. The analysis of long-distance marriages cannot but demand a nuanced interweaving of structure and subjectivity, and of both the material and the prestige considerations that attach to certain locations within an increasingly global hierarchy.

Chapter 5
Marrying Up and Marrying Down: The Paradoxes of Marital Mobility for Chosŏnjok Brides in South Korea

Caren Freeman

The inability of rural bachelors to attract brides is an increasingly common problem in many rapidly industrializing countries, where educational, occupational, and marital opportunities are drawing large numbers of young women to the cities. In South Korea, the bride shortage in the countryside has reached the level of a national crisis, brought to the attention of the public by the media and, in some extreme cases, by the protest suicides of unmarried farmers (Kendall 1996:4, Park 1996:217). A 1997 Korean newspaper editorial emphasizes the gravity of the situation, warning that "the time is not far off when a 'home for bachelors' [*chonggak yangnowŏn*][1] will need to be established to care for the 400,000 rural bachelors who are past marriageable age" (*Tong'a Ilbo* [Na Chonggŭn] October 13, 1997).

After diplomatic and trade relations were established with China in 1992, the South Korean government saw a potential solution to the bride-shortage problem in China's population of nearly two million ethnic Koreans or Chosŏnjok (*Chaoxianzu*),[2] concentrated largely in the three northeastern provinces of Jilin, Liaoning, and Heilongjiang. Tens of thousands of Chosŏnjok women, lured by the wealth, middle-class lifestyle, and personal freedom that South Korea is imagined to hold, have stepped forward since the early 1990s to fill the vacancies in Korean households. What began as a government-led strategy to import brides to alleviate the farmer bachelor problem has expanded rapidly over the past decade into moneymaking "marriage tours" offered by licensed matchmakers (*kyŏrhon sangdamso*) and unlicensed traveling marriage brokers (*bŭrokkŏ*) working on both ends of the marriage migration stream. No longer destined exclusively for rural matrimony, Chinese Chosŏnjok brides can now be found in nearly every village and city throughout the South Korean peninsula.

The extensive reach of these migrant networks and the widely publicized failure of many of the resultant marriages have propelled transnational marriage into the realm of popular and academic debate. In this chapter, I examine a range of scholarly and popular understandings that alternatively depict Chosŏnjok brides as powerless victims of a government-sanctioned form of trafficking in women or, at the opposite end of the spectrum, as heartless opportunists who actively exploit the South Korean men they marry. While both of these competing representations capture aspects of reality, they are, in my view, more a reflection of the radically shifting political and economic relations in the region than an accurate indication of the degree of agency and control that Chosŏnjok brides actually possess in the process of marrying across national borders.

In this chapter, I hope to contribute to current understandings of the way power works in and through the movement of people across transnational space. Doreen Massey's frequently cited concept of the "power geometry" (1994:149) is particularly useful for analyzing issues of agency with respect to transnational processes. Massey takes the discussion of agency beyond the question of "who moves and who doesn't" to examine the differential positioning of social groups and individuals with respect to transnational flows and movement. She notes that it is not simply access to mobility that empowers people, but rather control over the mobility of others. As Massey points out, those who do the moving are often not "in charge" of the process and, as a result, do not stand to benefit from it the most (1994:149). These distinctions make it clear that any discussion of power and agency within a transnational context must take into consideration the differential social positioning of the various actors who initiate, control, or are otherwise affected by border-crossing practices.

The Chosŏnjok women in my study are not "in charge of" their mobility, in Massey's sense of the term. The South Korean government, eager to resuscitate the rural economy with a steady flow of brides from China, stands to gain, politically and economically, from the productive and reproductive labor of Chosŏnjok women. Marriage brokers on both sides are also crucial to the movement of brides across borders and make a sizable profit matching the supply of Chosŏnjok brides with the demand in South Korea.[3] Moreover, while it is important to note that the overwhelming majority of Chosŏnjok brides I met entered into their marriages of their own volition, the fact remains that these women depend upon South Korean men to achieve the mobility they desire.

Despite their seemingly disadvantaged social positioning, Chosŏnjok women make creative use of the limited opportunities available to them to enhance their social and economic status. Through a series of case studies, I illustrate the complexities of Chosŏnjok women's agency. I focus on the marital experiences of four individual brides in order to provide a nuanced depiction of the challenges that Chosŏnjok women encounter in their quest for upward mobility and the strategies they devise to overcome them. Then moving beyond their lived experiences of struggle and agency, I identify a number of paradoxes that complicate any straightforward analysis of the webs of power within which they are forced to operate. Specifically, in marrying across borders, Chosŏnjok brides traverse powerful and contradictory constructions of gender, nationality/race, and economic hierarchy that both constrain and promote their mobility in ways that Massey's "power geometry" framework might not predict.

Methodology: Mapping the Marriage Migration

The ethnographic data for this chapter are based on fieldwork I conducted while living in South Korea and northeastern China from 1998 to 2000. The project was carried out in three phases: ten months in South Korea, six months in northeastern China, and a return to South Korea for a final three-month period of follow-up research. The research methods I employed varied according to the vicissitudes of each particular field site. In South Korea, I had to craft a research strategy that would enable me to trace geographically dispersed marriage and migration patterns while at the same time allow me to enter into the daily lives of a significant number of transnationally married couples. I solved this dilemma by basing myself in Seoul and making periodic visits to rural areas to conduct structured interviews with Chosŏnjok brides, their marital families, and, on occasion, natal family members who had accompanied them. Living in Seoul enabled me to participate in a range of networks that cater to Chosŏnjok living in South Korea, including church-related organizations and private clubs and meetings. Through these channels, I developed close relationships with a handful of Chosŏnjok brides whose marital relationships I was able to follow over a two-year period.

Government-funded and private matchmaking bureaus were also crucial in providing me with introductions to couples in rural and urban areas across South Korea. I spent several months interviewing marriage brokers in Seoul. Nearly all of them were willing to put me in contact with farmers they had successfully matched with Chosŏnjok brides. Once contacted, the rural couples were equally willing to host me during overnight stays in their villages. While brief, these home stays were very informative and usually led to further introductions to friends and family living in both South Korea and China.

During the second period of my fieldwork, I lived in Heilongjiang Province in northeastern China to investigate how the exodus of young women from this region to South Korea was affecting kin and communities left behind. Heilongjiang was an ideal location because of the high rates of Korea-bound migration. I spent the first three months in the city of Harbin, living with a Chosŏnjok family whose daughter had married a Korean man. Aside from intimate glimpses into the social life of one particular family and their extended circle of friends and family, being located in the provincial capital allowed me access to media sources, especially local newspapers, which were useful in understanding the larger framework of public discourse surrounding the marital exodus to South Korea.

During the final three months of my research in Heilongjiang Province, I moved to a Chosŏnjok village just outside the city of Mudanjiang. There I was startled to discover that nearly all the daughters in this particular village had migrated out in search of employment or marriage partners. So pervasive was "Korea fever" (*han'guk yŏl*) that the question "When are you going to Korea?" was rapidly replacing the conventional greeting of "Have you eaten yet?" Most of the adults, young and old, who remained in the village had either been to Korea and back or were yearning to capitalize on their symbolic connections to South Korea and its labor market.[4] During the frigid springtime of 2000, the neighbors assembled on the fire-heated platform (*kang*) in our one-room house, with little to do apart from knit, play mahjong, and entertain the visiting anthropologist. It was an ideal setting in which to collect personal narratives of marriage, family life, and migration, while observing firsthand the ways in which local structures of marriage and family were being transformed in response to the newly emergent opportunities for outward migration.

I used the final three months of my fieldwork to return to South Korea to pay follow-up visits to rural and urban families I had interviewed during the first phase of the project and to pursue new contacts I had made during my stay in China. I found it very useful to experience reentry into the metropolis of Seoul after living for an extended period of time in northeastern China, following the route of the migrants I studied. It heightened my awareness of the extent to which uneven economic development can be viscerally and immediately experienced, even in the air one breathes. Adjusting physically to the move from northeastern China to Seoul also deepened my appreciation of the paradoxes of upward mobility that Chosŏnjok migrants experience when they make the journey themselves.

The Public Discourse: Trafficking in Women or By Women?

Focusing largely on state and mass-media discourses surrounding these marriages, anthropologist Heh-Rahn Park condemns the South Korean government for endorsing what she sees as part of an "international traffic in women" (1996:217–20). According to Park, the Korean government has strategically deployed Chosŏnjok women as a type of farm subsidy, doling them out to farmers to pacify their increasingly vociferous demands for economic security in an era of globalized markets. If the rigors of farm life had repelled local women from marrying Korean farmers in the 1980s, Park notes that the opening up of Korea's agricultural markets in the early 1990s only worsened the plight of unmarried farmers.[5] Instead of taking the political and economic action necessary to protect the agricultural sector against the volatility of the global market, the Korean government, according to Park, shifted its own responsibility for rural reform onto the backs of Chosŏnjok brides, whose productive and reproductive labor was expected to resuscitate the rural economy and repopulate the countryside (1996:219).

In contrast to Park's victim-oriented analysis, popular opinion in Korea displays much less sympathy for the brides from China. The public view has largely been shaped by the mass media, which have popularized an image of "runaway brides" who abandon their Korean husbands after obtaining citizenship. When the government first initiated its program of importing brides, the media portrayed Chosŏnjok women as saviors of the Korean countryside, "returning the sound of crying babies" to farming families and restoring "ethnic homogeneity" (*minjok t'ongjilsŏng*) to a divided people. It was not long, however, before the media changed their tune, and news coverage became heavily weighted toward stories of deception on the part of Chosŏnjok women.[6] The typical story features an ingenuous man (*sunbakhada*), often a farmer bachelor, who invests a small fortune in matchmaking fees, travel costs to China, and ceremonial gifts in order to bring home a wife who then disappears without a trace immediately after receiving her residence permit. If the farmer bachelor had been a tragic figure in the popular imagination, the brokenhearted farmer deserted by his Chinese wife engendered even more compassion. Indeed, the public perception when I arrived in Korea in the fall of 1998 was that the overwhelming majority of these marriages were "illegitimate" (*wijang kyŏrhon*)—in the sense that they were believed to be founded on the bride's interest in Korean citizenship rather than a sincere conjugal commitment.

Though the images are contradictory, both the depictions of Chosŏn-jok migrant brides as victims of the traffic in women and the portrayal of women as ruthless opportunists have some validity. Park's analysis points to a familiar pattern, one that is by no means exclusive to South Korea, of utilizing women's bodies to serve the goals of the state. It also draws attention to the broader structures of global inequality that chan-nel women in clear geographical directions, from economically and politically less powerful nations toward wealthier and stronger ones.

At the same time, there are undoubtedly many instances of Chosŏnjok women contracting marriages of convenience, with or without the knowledge and consent of the groom. Statistically, it is impossible to determine how many women enter marriages intending to divorce after they obtain citizenship. I met and interviewed half a dozen men who claimed to have suffered irreparable emotional damage and financial ruin when their Chosŏnjok wives unexpectedly deserted them, leaving behind, in a surprising number of the cases, a young child.[7] In other cases, however, desertion should be understood as a strategic response to the tensions and cultural disjunctures that Chosŏnjok brides encoun-ter in their marital households. Because of the uncertainties involved in traveling overseas to live with a family they have never met in a country they most likely have never visited, I found that cross-border marriages tend to appeal to especially ambitious women who are willing to take significant risks to better their futures. As the case histories below will illustrate, when Korean kinship norms and practices collide with their mobile outlook, some brides, as a last resort, take their Korean passports and search for new opportunities in the global economy.

The range of marital experiences and outcomes, as well as the perva-sive climate of suspicion in South Korea that casts these marriages in a largely illegitimate light, makes it difficult to generalize about the wom-en's motivations. However, it is important to place public concern about Chosŏnjok women and the purity of their motives in the broader socio-economic context in which they occur. The sensationalized images of "runaway brides," featured in the Korean mass media and circulating through informal channels of gossip, say as much about the wider ten-sions that have arisen in the course of increasing contact between the Chosŏnjok and South Koreans as they do about the immorality of Cho-sŏnjok women. In the next section, I will examine the transnational processes that have fueled the widespread desire among the Chosŏnjok to migrate to South Korea and the ambivalent manner in which they have been received by their Korean hosts once "they ventured into the everyday economic and social life of South Korea" (Moon 2000:159).

The Chosŏnjok: A People on the Move

The extensive and sudden mobility of the Chosŏnjok, both within and across the borders of China, is one consequence of the profound political and economic transformations that the Chinese people as a whole have experienced in the post-Mao era. Prior to economic reform, the Chinese state under Mao forcibly kept farmers in the fields and out of the cities with its household registration system (*hukou*). When the household responsibility system replaced collective farming in the early 1980s, agricultural productivity increased dramatically, revealing an immense surplus of labor in the countryside. Freed of the rural commune, many profit-minded peasants set off for the cities in search of new ways to put their labor to productive use (see Solinger 1999). The Chosŏnjok were no exception. By the mid-1980s, 20–30 percent of the Chosŏnjok rural workforce had left the countryside to seek urban employment in major cities throughout the northeast region of the country (Chŏng 1995:221). Over the next few years, Chosŏnjok followed the general coastward direction of China's rural population movement, venturing beyond the concentrated residential districts in the Northeast to Han-dominated cities along the eastern seaboard and southern coast.

The establishment of diplomatic and trade relations between China and South Korea in 1992 gave the Chosŏnjok an opportunity unavailable to other Chinese citizens to draw upon their ethnic/nationality and kinship connections and participate directly in South Korea's labor and marriage markets. Four decades of rapid economic development had culminated in the late 1980s in severe shortages in the most labor-intensive sectors of the Korean economy as well as bride shortages in the depopulated countryside. To the South Korean government, the Chosŏnjok represented an ideal source of workers for its factories and wives for its farmers, one that would presumably pose no challenge to Koreans' self-identity as a homogenous people. To the Chosŏnjok, who had watched from afar Korea's remarkable economic growth, rapprochement offered an opportunity to reap the benefits of Korea's comparatively high wages and standards of living.

Given the increasingly stringent entry regulations imposed by the Korean government, there are a limited number of ways Chosŏnjok migrants can legally cross the border into South Korea. Since the late 1980s, the Korean government has permitted (and in the early stages, aggressively encouraged) Chosŏnjok to enter the country for the purpose of reuniting with separated family members (*isan kajok*).[8] Although legally required to return to China upon the expiration of their three-month family-visitation visas, many Chosŏnjok find the temptation to overstay their visas and work illegally for a number of years irresistible. In the early 1990s, the Korean government implemented its industrial trainee (*yŏnsusaeng*) program to redress the shortage of workers in small and medium-size enterprises.[9] Under this initiative, Chosŏnjok men and women could apply for limited legal status as manual laborers in officially designated workplaces. After the Asian financial crisis of 1997, however, the government sought to localize the labor force and limit the number of industrial trainees from foreign countries (Moon 2000:165–66). As a result, Chosŏnjok without marital or verifiable kinship connections to South Korean citizens—including those who trace their ancestry to North Korean citizens—had few alternative means of entering South Korea apart from purchasing fictive kinship identities.

In response to the widespread desire to migrate by any means possible from China to South Korea, Chosŏnjok brokers with high-level political connections on both sides have set about manufacturing all manner of kinship, marital, and political connections, which they purchase and sell on a vast market in fictive identities. The arrangement of "paper marriages" to South Korean citizens is one of the most sought-after forms of commodified kinship because it offers the promise of South Korean citizenship and the associated privileges of working legally and moving freely back and forth across the South Korean border.[10]

As Chosŏnjok women scramble to cash in on their kinship and ethnic connections to South Korea, their claims to "Koreanness" are increasingly looked at with suspicion by South Koreans. Chosŏnjok migrants, and brides in particular, have become notorious for unscrupulous moneymaking schemes, considered at odds with their claims of patriotic attachment to South Korea. Chosŏnjok, at the same time, accuse South Koreans of similar acts of bad faith. Chosŏnjok migrants of all ages and backgrounds who had traveled to South Korea for various purposes, including marriage, work, study, and family visitation, recounted feeling discriminated against or looked down upon (*qiaobuqi*) while in South Korea. Painfully aware of the global inequalities that give rise to these attitudes and propel them into the South Korean labor and marriage markets, the Chosŏnjok deeply resent the bullying and condescension they encounter as a result of their Chinese origins. As the case studies below illustrate, it is within this context of mutual suspicion and conflict that Chosŏnjok brides must negotiate their relationships with their husbands and marital families. I will show how these tensions shape the strategies that Chosŏnjok brides devise to cope with their new marital situations.

Marriages to Korean Men

Of the myriad stories I collected, I selected the following case studies but make no claim that they represent an array of typical relationships. Given the wide diversity of marital experiences and outcomes, it is impossible to generalize about the character and quality of these transnational marriages. I chose the stories below because they show the range of ways that Chosŏnjok women and South Korean men meet and marry, the variety of obstacles migrant brides face in realizing their ambitions, and the degree of agency they possess in negotiating an improvement in their status.

Yŏnghwa: A Farmer's Bride

Yŏnghwa had refused many introductions to Chosŏnjok bachelors in China, pinning her hopes instead on a Korean husband. For years, the women in her village had been marrying to South Korea, and she, too, yearned for the good life that Korea was rumored to offer. When her father, after forty years of separation, visited his birthplace in South Korea's rural Kyŏngsang Province, he used his kinship connections there to locate for his daughter an eligible farmer bachelor by the name of Juno.

At thirty-five years of age, with elderly parents to care for and a family farm to manage, Juno said that finding a bride in Korea was more difficult than "plucking stars from the sky." In 1995, during the peak of the "China marriage boom" (*kyŏrhon ppum*), the government-funded Research Association for the Welfare of Farm and Fishing Villages (*han'-guk nongŏch'on pokji hoe*) was recruiting rural bachelors for its eighth marriage tour to China. Juno's father gave him money and urged him to go with the tour to Shenyang to meet Yŏnghwa, whose photograph he had seen and liked. While bringing home a bride from China presented a potential solution to Juno's dilemma, it also conjured up a host of reservations: Would he be able to communicate with his Chosŏnjok bride? Would she be too "strong" (*kanghada*) as a result of living under Communism, or worse, evil-hearted? Would she run away after getting Korean citizenship? "I was tempted to take my father's money and spend it in a karaoke bar," Juno recalls. But when two of his friends signed up for the marriage tour, Juno cast his doubts aside and joined them.

On the day the seven bachelors arrived in China, Yŏnghwa was notified to travel from her parents' home in the countryside to a hotel in Shenyang, along with thirteen other Chosŏnjok women. Though she had great difficulty understanding Juno's dialect, Yŏnghwa says a feeling inside told her that Juno was the man she should marry. Juno recalled with a chuckle, "I knew in my heart I would choose my wife in the end, but I wanted to enjoy myself first by talking with the other women." After lunch in a Chosŏnjok restaurant and a trip to a karaoke, the men and women were asked to match up if they had identified someone they liked.

The seven couples then had one week to explore their marital compatibility. They spent much of their time as a group, the Chinese-speaking women guiding their husbands-to-be by the hand on a tour of Shenyang's historic and entertainment attractions. At the week's end, six out of the seven men had secured promises to marry, visited the homes of their prospective brides, and begun the lengthy and politically complicated process of applying for a marriage visa.[11]

Looking back after five years of marriage to Juno, Yŏnghwa says she did not realize there was something lacking about men who go to China to find brides. She enumerates the potential detriments: "Either their jobs are unstable, or they are too poor, too short, or too ugly. Why else would they go all the way to China to get a bride?" She laughs when she thinks back to how naive she must have been to believe that "Korea was a paradise where machines cut the grain and tilled the land while the people sat back and relaxed." Nearly all the farmers' brides I met expressed their disillusionment with the same declaration: "Had I seen where I would be living, I would never have gotten married!"

As with many Chosŏnjok brides I interviewed, neither Yŏnghwa's upbringing nor her expectations had prepared her for the hard physical labor of running a farm,[12] the cultural imperative to serve her in-laws and husband, the isolation of living beyond the reach of public transportation, or the stigma of being treated as a foreigner in her father's homeland. In light of how much she claims to have suffered in the early years of her marriage, Yŏnghwa does not advise other Chosŏnjok women to marry to Korea. "If a [Chosŏnjok] woman is well educated and capable, she won't be able to endure [marriage to a Korean], especially if she sees she is not living as well as other people. Only if the man treats her very well will she be able to resist the temptation of running away."[13]

The story of Yŏnghwa highlights the gap between the fantasies that entice Chosŏnjok brides to South Korea and the constraints of their social and economic realties. The rural-bound brides I interviewed were shocked to discover that their marriages had destined them to live in remote villages nestled deep in the mountains where they were expected to serve as dutiful wives and daughters-in-law. Profound disillusionment has driven many Chosŏnjok brides to desert their husbands and, in some cases, their young children. Most farmers' wives whom I interviewed, however, were accepting of what they viewed as their marital fates (*inyŏn*).[14] While many believed they were no better off by marrying to South Korea—the work being too difficult, the standards of living too low, and the expectations of their husbands too high—they blamed themselves for their naive expectations and focused their energies on the hard physical labor of farming, household chores, and care of their children.

Yunok: A Marriage with Motives

Yunok entered her marriage to a Korean man with specific objectives she hoped to achieve. In contrast to Yŏnghwa, who expected marriage itself to deliver her into a life of material comfort, Yunok viewed marriage as a vehicle for carrying out her own agenda. Unlike Yŏnghwa, she had not been recruited to alleviate the bride shortage in the countryside, but instead arrived in Seoul under the South Korean government's industrial trainee program.

The pay in the Korean factory where Yunok had been assigned to work was so low that she was unable to pay the interest on the loans her family had taken out to enable her to travel to Korea, leaving her no other option but to break her contract with the factory and take up more lucrative employment: waiting tables in a restaurant. While many Chosŏnjok migrant laborers' work experiences followed a similar trajectory, Yunok was unusually ambitious. After three years of working in the restaurant, she saved up enough capital to open her own raw-fish house, using for legal purposes the name of a Korean citizen.

Though her business failed during the economic crisis of the late 1990s, Yunok was fond of talking about her success as an entrepreneur, the skillful way in which she managed her staff and earned their respect and affection, and her feelings of accomplishment in having "done something big." If she were to return to the village in China, she claimed she would be "wasting her life with nothing to do but crochet woolen booties and play mahjong." To remain in Korea as an illegal alien involved the risk of deportation and subjection to steep fines. Yunok explained that she could no longer bear the anxiety that swept over her every time she spotted a police officer. Marrying a Korean, she reasoned, would enable her to legalize her status in the country and pursue her entrepreneurial ambitions.

The opportunity to marry a Korean man arose when she received an introduction from a relative. Unlike the majority of women I interviewed, who, like Yŏnghwa, had met their husbands only once or twice on Chinese soil before agreeing to marry, Yunok moved in with her Korean fiancé, his mother, and his ten-year-old son from a previous marriage. She thus was intimately familiar with both the family and the country into which she would be marrying. She also knew she would have to overcome her husband's staunch opposition to her working outside the household. He had made it clear that he would marry her only on the condition that she stay at home, take responsibility for raising his son, and not go out to work. Yunok protested that her personality was not suited for domesticity, that she needed a job not for the money, but to feel as though she were leading an "active" life. Taking her at her word, her husband bought her an exercise machine. "He means well," she said. "He just doesn't understand."

Compared with the relative independence Yunok's entrepreneurial endeavors allowed her before marriage, she experienced an immediate decline in mobility and independence after marrying her South Korean husband. When I visited her in her home in Seoul shortly after she had returned from processing her marriage visa in China, she complained of feeling trapped and, with strong language, confessed her contempt for her domestic lifestyle and, in particular, the young boy in her charge. Yunok's disputes with her Korean husband-to-be over her desire to work outside the home had been a topic of frequent gossip among the villagers in her hometown during the long wait for her marriage visa. Many had speculated that her marriage would not last. Now just weeks after legalizing her marriage, I was taken aback to hear Yunok herself speak of divorce as a solution to her dilemma. While she believed that her husband sincerely loved her, she did not return the same degree of emotional attachment. She imagined that over time she would cultivate feelings of affection for him, but not if he continued to forbid her to work. Unless her husband yielded, Yunok vowed that she would divorce him after obtaining citizenship.[15]

One month later, Yunok was waiting tables in a restaurant. The threat of divorce, the only leverage she possessed, had been enough to chip away at her husband's opposition. For the time being, at least, Yunok had achieved what she desired through marriage—a legal entrée into the working world of a major metropolitan city. Yunok's relationship with her marital family members was secondary to this goal, by her frank admission. Chosŏnjok and South Koreans alike distinguished between the "purity" of rural-bound brides like Yŏnghwa, who naively believed that marriage would deliver them from poverty, versus the "cleverness" and opportunism of women like Yunok, for whom marriage was not an end in itself. These women were pejoratively spoken of as having married "with motives" (*you mudi de*).

Yŏnjae: A Love Marriage

Whether their motives were clearly defined or not, nearly all the Chosŏn-jok brides I met explained their marriages in terms of strategic upward mobility. Yŏnjae was unique in that she claimed to have married for love (*yŏnae kyŏrhon*). She met her husband, Jinwŏn, for the first time in a restaurant in Shenyang, China. Yŏnjae was visiting her older sister, who was working as a hostess in the restaurant. Jinwŏn managed the restaurant, which was owned by his father, a former taxi driver from South Korea. With the opening of Chinese markets to Korean investors, large numbers of South Korean petty entrepreneurs had opened small businesses (mostly restaurants and massage parlors) in northeastern China and staffed them with Korean-speaking Chosŏnjok workers. These business operations provide one of the primary contexts for Chosŏnjok women and South Korean men to meet each other "naturally," without the mediating influence of a marriage broker.

Yŏnjae remembers being unmoved by the initial encounter with Jinwŏn. A poised, well-spoken, and attractive twenty-six-year-old, Yŏnjae was accustomed to deflecting the unwanted attention of male suitors. But Jinwŏn was not easily dissuaded. He invited Yŏnjae and her sister to rent a room in his father's house, near the restaurant. The sisters accepted the offer, preferring the downtown location to that of their parents' home on the outskirts of the city. Living under the same roof, Yŏnjae and Jinwŏn established a friendship. Several months later, Jinwŏn asked Yŏnjae to marry him. "He and his father were both very good to me," she explained. "And I felt sorry for him because he grew up with a cruel stepmother. I thought if I treated him well I could make up for the pain he had suffered as a child." Motivated by a combination of kindness and pity, she agreed to marry him against the wishes of her own parents, who had higher marital aspirations for their college-educated daughter. In Yŏnjae's eyes, her husband's humble family background did not amount to a flaw. She professed to judge a man based on his character alone, not his money.

Yŏnjae may not have looked to her husband for monetary support, but, like Yunok, she sought to take advantage of the opportunities her Korean passport presented. Not long after her arrival in South Korea, Yŏnjae conducted Internet searches, circulated her résumé, and knocked on doors. In a matter of days, she found a job in a trading company as the in-house consultant on China-related commerce. What she lacked in training, she made up for in bilingualism, assertiveness, and charm. She worked extremely long hours, took frequent business trips to northeastern China, and earned a salary nearly twice that of her husband, an operations manager in a meatpacking company. She was exhilarated by her lucrative and fast-paced career. But her enthusiasm for her new life was severely dampened by her embattled relationship with her in-laws.

According to Yŏnjae, her parents-in-law had treated her well while she was dutifully caring for her husband's ailing grandfather in the final months before his death. The relationship became strained after Yŏnjae entered the workforce and her father-in-law asked her to hand over a portion of her monthly salary. She simmered in silence as Jinwŏn turned over his paycheck in full each month to his parents. Grudgingly, she complied with her in-laws' wishes. When her father-in-law refused to give her spending money for a business trip to Pusan, Yŏnjae retaliated by repossessing exclusive control over her purse strings. This incident marked the end of amicable household relations. Yŏnjae described the daily onslaught of insults and accusations she was forced to endure—pointed barbs regarding her ineffectualness as a daughter-in-law and her dirtiness and laziness as a "Chinese person" (*chungguk saram*).

To escape the constant fighting with her in-laws, Yŏnjae pressed her husband to establish a separate conjugal residence. Yŏnjae knew her husband was in a difficult position, caught between his desire to please his wife and a deep-seated fear of defying his father. "I feel sorry for my husband," she explained, "but I told him that if he doesn't stand up to his father and move out, I will divorce him and go to Japan or Hong Kong, as I've always dreamed of doing."

For both Yunok and Yŏnjae, the ultimatum of divorce was a remarkably effective strategy in bending the will of their husbands. One month after the above conversation, Yŏnjae called me to help her choose new kitchen appliances for the tiny one-room basement apartment she and her husband had rented with Yŏnjae's earnings. Yŏnjae was enjoying the freedom of her independent household and took a new interest in playing the role of homemaker. She took a leave of absence from work to set up the new household. While she busied herself in the kitchen, she talked of her plans for the future. She still intended to go to Japan or Hong Kong one day and pursue her studies. When I asked about her husband, she replied that he could follow her, if he desired.

Juju: A Runaway Bride

Juju, a thirty-four-year-old woman from Mudanjiang, married a Korean man after her first marriage in China ended in divorce. She joined her older sister, who had obtained Korean citizenship through a "fake marriage" to a South Korean man and was now working in Seoul with her "real" husband from China. Though Juju spoke no more than a few words of broken Korean, she had been continuously employed since she arrived in Seoul in 1996, first in a restaurant and then in a jewelry store that catered to Chinese tourists. When I met Juju, she was working long hours in the jewelry store and spending most of her evenings away from home, socializing with her older sister and other Chosŏnjok migrant workers she had befriended after arriving in Korea. Whereas many Cho-sŏnjok brides complained of being closely guarded and forbidden by their husbands to work, Juju seemed to enjoy an unusual amount of personal freedom in her marriage.

When I asked her about it, Juju voiced her dissatisfaction with her husband. "He is ten years older than I," she complained. "He is more like a father than a husband. We don't share any interests. He doesn't understand me at all, so he just lets me do as I please." Looking at the wedding portraits above their bed, I agreed that they seemed an unlikely match. She appeared radiant and beautiful. He looked weathered, sullen, and old by comparison. "If he had any abilities [*nengli*], I could overlook his personality flaws," Juju explained. "He works hard at his construction job, but he has no ambition, no skills, and no mind for business. Every day is the same—he goes to work, comes home, eats, watches television, and goes to bed."

Unlike her husband, Juju was continually brainstorming for ways to turn a profit. By her own admission, high wages had lured her to Korea in the first place. The numbers seemed high when she heard them in China, she explained, but she had not accounted for the high cost of living in Korea. She was exhausted by the long hours at work, frustrated by the slow pace of capital accumulation, and angered by her employer's discriminatory treatment toward Chinese Chosŏnjok. Like many Chosŏn-jok with Korean passports, she sought to make a faster profit by peddling goods back and forth across the Sino-Korean border. She enlisted my help in determining which sorts of consumer goods from Korea would find a ready market in China.

Juju told me in confidence that she often contemplated leaving her Korean husband. "I feel sorry for him," she said, "so it's very difficult to leave. It would be a much easier decision if he beat me or drank heavily. But I know that he really loves me and he's good to me. I guess I have *chŏng* for him."[16] As the months passed, however, I watched a restlessness brew inside her. Each time I saw her, she had devised a new scheme to relieve her unhappiness. In one plan, she considered going back to her first husband in China and their twelve-year-old daughter. Six months later, after I returned to Seoul from fieldwork in China, Juju had mustered the nerve to leave her Korean husband. She was living with a forty-something, heavyset Chosŏnjok migrant worker who had been courting her steadfastly throughout the course of my fieldwork. While she had earlier denied any romantic interest in this man, Juju now claimed to have discovered a great deal in common with him, not the least of which was his entrepreneurial spirit. Juju, it seemed, had found a partner in business, if not in romance. She proudly offered me one of her new business cards emblazoned with both their names and a picture of a rare breed of dog that she and her new mate would be exporting to China.

Complicating the Power Geometry

Perceptions of gender, nationality, and economic hierarchies are central factors fueling Chosŏnjok women's migration through marriage to South Korea. As the vignettes above reveal, however, the cultural assumptions that initially draw South Korean men and Chosŏnjok women into marital relationships take on different, even paradoxical, meanings in the course of their actual encounters. In the sections that follow, I will examine the contradictions contained within dominant understandings of ethnicity/nationality, gender, and economic development that at once promote the entry of women into South Korea and constrain their options for mobility once they arrive.

Paradoxes of Ethnicity/Nationality

The Korean government endorsed the program of sending farmer bachelors on marriage tours to China with the anticipation that these marriages would not only restore family life in the countryside but also, as quoted throughout the mass media, contribute to the sacred national goal of restoring ethnic homogeneity (*minjok t'ongjilsŏng*) to a divided people. The concept of ethnic homogeneity invoked here draws upon an idealized vision of the Korean "people," or *minjok*, as a racially and culturally homogeneous entity, which extends beyond the boundaries of the nation-state to unite Koreans throughout the diaspora on the basis of blood ties. The myth of ethnic homogeneity—the belief that Chosŏnjok and South Koreans belong to the same people *(kat'ŭn minjok)* and therefore are culturally one and the same—also leads South Korean men to imagine that incorporating a Chosŏnjok bride into their household will be a culturally seamless process.[17]

Contrary to these expectations, Chosŏnjok brides discover immediately upon arrival in South Korea that they do not blend easily with the local population. Readily identified by their style of dress, their patterns of speech and pronunciation, and their unfamiliarity with Korean linguistic and behavioral codes of politeness, Chosŏnjok are for the most part unable to "pass" as South Koreans. Many Chosŏnjok brides told stories of the embarrassment they would feel in the market when they lacked the vocabulary to ask for common household items, the names of which are often English derivatives like "shampoo" and "stocking." Many women also expressed frustration that their husbands were unaware of the challenges they face in adapting to life in a new country.

Ethnic/racial connections conceived in terms of blood ties may make South Korean families reluctant to acknowledge the existence of cultural differences, but at the same time these symbolic constructions are mediated by perceptions of global inequalities. While South Koreans look at the Chosŏnjok as their long-lost relatives, they are just as importantly viewed as poor ones. This double-edged tendency to elide cultural differences while highlighting economic ones places Chosŏnjok brides in a particularly vulnerable position. As Yŏnjae observed, the tolerance that is extended to the foreign anthropologist, whose best efforts to communicate and interact with Koreans understandably fall short of native, does not apply to the Chosŏnjok, who are instead criticized for their cultural incompetence. About her mother-in-law, she says, "If I do something well, she thinks it's to be expected. But if I do something wrong, she thinks it's because I'm from China. If I come home late from work and don't have time to do the laundry, she will say, 'Is it because you're Chinese that you're dirty?'" While not all the Chosŏnjok women I met experienced such baldly offensive comments from their in-laws, most reported feelings of defensiveness or sensitivity to the occasional disparaging comments made by family members or friends of their husbands.

Some Chosŏnjok academics argue that tensions that have arisen from contacts between South Koreans and Chosŏnjok migrants, including laborers, brides, businesspeople, and students, have served to foster a sense of "Chinese consciousness" (*zhongguoren zhi yishi*) among the Chosŏnjok (Zheng 1998:80). While most migrants I interviewed expressed ambivalence about belonging to any nation-state (more than one person invoked the metaphor of an orphan rejected by both "parents," China and Korea), they did indicate a reworking of their attitudes after arriving in South Korea. It was common for Chosŏnjok brides I interviewed to express this transformation in terms of the teams they rooted for while watching televised soccer matches. Many claimed that for the first time in their lives, they found themselves cheering for China's soccer team over the Korean one. Chosŏnjok migrants were also fond of comparing what they saw as lacking in Korea with certain abundances found in China, especially food, leisure time, close interpersonal relations (*renqing wei*), and hospitality toward guests (*haoke*). As one older migrant who had returned to China after working for several years in Korea commented, "[Koreans] think Chinese people are so desperately poor. They don't realize how well we eat here. It's true we lack money, but we have an abundance of food. The rice they eat in Korea is what we would use here for pig feed!"

These incidents resonate with larger questions about the tensions that potentially arise in response to increasing contact among diasporic peoples under transnationalism. Chosŏnjok migrant laborers, discriminated against in terms of pay, treatment, and immigration rights and benefits, are among the most vociferous in protesting the discrepancies between their supposed connections of blood and kinship to South Korea and their exclusion from legal participation in its capital and labor markets. Chosŏnjok brides are one of the few types of migrants from China that enjoy the protection of Korean citizenship, but, as suggested above, this does not lead to their acceptance as "Koreans." Ultimately, the ambiguities and contradictions surrounding the notion of ethnic homogeneity not only call into question official discourses that celebrate these transnational marriages in metaphors of national reunification, but also provoke Chosŏnjok and South Koreans to reevaluate their own conceptions of national belonging.

Paradoxes of Gender

As the stories above demonstrate, Chosŏnjok brides are motivated to leave their villages and marry into South Korea out of a sense of independence, adventure, entrepreneurialism, and a longing to lead a "modern" life in a "developed country." If cross-border marriages appeal to women who possess the will and strength of purpose to try to change their lives, their dreams are often immediately fettered by Korean kinship norms that bind them physically to the house and morally to the demands of their in-laws. In the case of Yunok, Korean kinship norms conspire with her husband's fear of abandonment to prevent her from working outside the household, while Yŏnjae's desire to manage her own finances collided with her in-laws' expectations of how a daughter-in-law should behave.

The pressure to keep a wife at home and out of the workforce is exacerbated by fears that a Chosŏnjok bride might run away. No matter how trustworthy their wives might seem, South Korean men tend to view the workplace as full of hidden dangers and temptations to which Chosŏnjok women are imagined to be particularly susceptible. Director No of the Research Association for the Welfare of Farm and Fishing Villages likened the anxious state of a man married to a Chosŏnjok woman to a person whose front door has no lock. "You know the security that most people feel when they lock up their homes when they are away? Well, the man who marries a Chosŏnjok woman feels as though his door is always unlocked and there's nothing he can do about it."

Ironically, the rigid gendered dichotomization of work and domesticity that presumably upholds the safety and stability of a wife's place within the home was one of the most common sources of dissatisfaction among brides I interviewed, and a leading cause of divorce or desertion. The stories of Yunok and Yŏnjae bring into sharp relief the gendered

conflicts and contradictions with which upwardly mobile, entrepreneur-
ial-minded Chosŏnjok brides must contend within the Korean kinship
system. Both of these women used the threat of divorce to negotiate a
favorable outcome for themselves. Their successes illustrate the potential for Chosŏnjok women to resist and, to some degree, overcome the
gendered inequalities that circumscribe their activities and impinge on
their sense of personal freedom and mobility.[18] Moreover, the story of
Juju points to the fact that, despite attempts to discipline and domesti-
cate them as wives within the realm of the Korean kinship system, Chosŏnjok women still have the choice of picking up and going elsewhere when
they become dissatisfied with their marriages—a choice not always open
to the men they marry or their male counterparts in China.[19]

Paradoxes of Geographic Positioning

While Chosŏnjok women might appear privileged in marrying up the
geoeconomic hierarchy, power disparities between nations do not automatically translate into differences between good and bad marital prospects, as Yŏnghwa learned. In the eyes of the villagers they leave behind
in China, these women have succeeded in marrying up. In reality, however, they have moved from one disadvantaged geographic location to
another. What is more, as shown above, Chosŏnjok women's disappointment is compounded by Korean constructions of gender and nationality
that reinforce their marginal status and "otherize" them as foreigners.

Over time, the Chosŏnjok have begun not only to have misgivings
about the type of Korean man who travels all the way to China to find a
bride, but also to question the wealth and power of the Korean nation
itself. In 1997, the Asian financial crisis sent a message to the Chosŏnjok
of the seeming fragility of South Korea's standing in the economic world
order. In response, large numbers of Chosŏnjok women began seeking
out what they considered more stable parts of the world, such as Japan,
to find husbands. Many Chosŏnjok I spoke with also expressed an awareness of China's potential to surpass South Korea some time in the not-
too-distant future, and many fantasize about a day when South Koreans
will be compelled to seek employment opportunities as well as husbands
in China.[20]

Conclusion

Having read Heh-Rahn Park's analysis of Chosŏnjok brides before
embarking on my fieldwork, I was predisposed to viewing Chosŏnjok
brides as unwitting victims in a transnational marriage racket that moves
brides, much like commodities, from less developed regions and nations

to wealthier ones. Given the Korean government's strategic recruitment of these women to fill its demand for foreign workers and wives for rural bachelors, this victim-oriented perspective is not entirely without validity. Though most women enter into their marriages voluntarily, the youth, inexperience, and utter lack of knowledge about Korea and their husbands-to-be, as in the case of many brides like Yŏnghwa, make them easy targets of political exploitation.

But at the same time, we must reconcile feminist critiques of trafficking in women with popular portrayals of Chosŏnjok brides in South Korea as heartless instrumentalists who marry for citizenship and their own material gain. Rather than interpret the media-influenced stigmatization of Chosŏnjok brides in South Korea as further evidence of their victimization, as Park has done, I have argued that the discourse on "runaway brides" is linked to broader socioeconomic tensions between Chosŏnjok migrants and their South Korean hosts as they encounter one another for the first time after nearly fifty years of separation. Specifically, I have treated transnational marriage as a dynamic cultural arena in which migrant brides actively struggle with their marital families over what it means to be members of the same *minjok,* or nationality, while finding ways to cope with the economic and gender inequalities they also experience in the process of moving between Chinese and Korean settings.

Contrary to studies that emphasize the intensification of male privileges and the exacerbation of gender inequality through transnational mobility (Brennan 2001, Clark 2001, Gilmartin and Tan 2002, Mahler 2001), the vignettes I presented above suggest that Chosŏnjok women are often well poised to use cross-border marriages to their own advantage. In comparison with their male counterparts in China and their South Korean husbands who hail from the poorest and least mobile sectors of South Korean society, Chosŏnjok women not only appear to have greater access to channels of transnational mobility, but the movement of Chosŏnjok women sometimes has immobilizing effects on the men they leave behind. A Chosŏnjok man whose wife had divorced him in order to marry a Korean man expressed frustration over the lack of opportunities for Chosŏnjok men to travel to South Korea. He explained, "The god of wealth has presented the Chosŏnjok with an opportunity to make money in the form of South Korea. To be female is a form of capital since it is through marriage that women are able to take advantage of this gift." Once they arrive in South Korea, Chosŏnjok women are also able to use their transnational mobility to refashion the gendered inequalities within their marital families.

Doreen Massey's concept of the "power geometry" provides a useful framework for analyzing the ways that differential access to mobility and control over mobility enhance the power of some while diminishing that of others. However, as I have tried to show here, the geometries of power cannot always be clearly delineated. In the case of Chosŏnjok brides who marry to South Korea, the complex and conflicting ways in which constructions of nationality, gender, and geography intersect in these marriages make it difficult to distinguish those "in charge" of migratory processes from those who are not, those who benefit from those who are deprived. It is equally difficult to determine to what degree mobility through marriage offers liberating returns for the women who pursue these strategies. Some Chosŏnjok brides succeed in using their marital potential in South Korea (and beyond) to expand their opportunities for social mobility, while others experience downward mobility and disappointment. No matter what the outcome, their stories highlight the paradoxes and contradictions with which women must contend as they maneuver between and across the shifting boundaries of the global economy.

Chapter 6
A Failed Attempt at Transnational Marriage: Maternal Citizenship in a Globalizing South Korea

Nancy Abelmann and Hyunhee Kim

This chapter considers a rural and poor South Korean mother's valiant, and ultimately failed, attempts at marrying her only son, who is disabled, to a Filipina woman through the Unification Church. Understanding that the prospect of this marriage—that of the son of a poor farming family to a Southeast Asian woman—is a very recent prospect in South Korea, one facilitated by both transnational geopolitical developments and local transformations in the late 1990s, we ask what this case can tell us about changing social and cultural formations into the new millennium in South Korea. We consider how it is that family is being imagined anew such that foreign, non-Korean brides are rendered viable marriage partners. We take up this mother's story in the broader social field of transnational marriage in South Korea, and more broadly still in the changing landscape of South Korean discourses of its place in the world.

The story we discuss in this chapter diverges from many in this volume because it does not draw on the voices or perspectives of those directly involved in the prospect of transnational marriage; indeed, we had no direct communication with the bachelor in question about this marriage attempt, and only a seconds-long phone encounter with the fiancée. As such, we offer no commentary on a critical debate on transnational marriage: the agency of the parties involved (see, for example, Constable and Freeman in this volume). We do, however, take up questions of gender and agency through the mother's story. Although we understand that ours is a very specific tale—that of the mother of a disabled son—we think that this story speaks to a larger truth: that men and women most often do what they do in concert and consult with a range of other consociates (for example, family members). A number of contributors in this volume argue for a nuanced appreciation of the play of structural forces and personal agency; to this we contribute consideration of what we might call "dispersed agency,"—in this case, along the lines of family. With this contribution, we echo a large literature on emigration generally in its family nexus (for example, attention to remittance economy) (see Schein 2000, Small 1997).

This mother's story—its strategies and narration—reflects both old and new projects: the valiant attempts of a farming woman from a relatively underdeveloped region to reproduce her husband's patrilineage and in so doing to care for her son; and her own struggles to achieve a particular maternal subjectivity or "maternal citizenship" in a transforming and globalizing South Korea. This mother's efforts for her son cannot be parsed as either/or (that is, old or new). Rather, the very acts that reflect highly traditional maternal efforts can also be seen as new because of their transnational nature. We hope to sustain precisely such an analytical edge as we interpret the mother's words and acts. The term "maternal citizenship" suggests that a constellation of maternal efforts (e.g., securing a child's marriage partner) can produce what Ann Anagnost describes as "a measure of value, self-worth, and citizenship" or "becoming a fully realized subject" (2000:392). Renato Rosaldo similarly describes "cultural citizenship" in terms of "notion[s] of dignity, thriving, and well-being" (1994:410). Although the constructs of maternal and cultural citizenship appreciate the importance of state and national affiliation, they highlight membership that exceeds legal status (legal citizenship, voting rights, and so on). The maternal project in this story is distinguished for having extra-local (beyond the mother's local world) and transnational coordinates (transnational communication and travel abroad) (see Anagnost 2000:412 on "cosmopolitan subjecthood"). The mother's marriage efforts afforded her participation in—albeit very partial—some acts of transnational consumption and movement that evoke middle-class or mainstream belonging in South Korea (see Berdahl 1999 on consumption and cultural citizenship). We do not claim that the mother had any real sense of significant upward mobility due to the transnational arrangements that afford the possibility of an international marriage. Rather, these practices, precisely because of their middle-class and transnational nature, offered the mother an enhanced sense of belonging in modern South Korea—namely, in a South Korea that is increasingly prosperous and global. While appreciating the ways in which her travel and arrangements reflect a sense of mainstream participation, we will also underscore the palpable ways in which her travel was of a quite different variety from that of the urban middle class. It is critical not to lose sight of hers as the story of a poor farming woman, however transnational some of its coordinates might be.

Precisely because this marriage attempt reveals multiple and competing meanings, we understand it as an instance of "transnationalism from below" (Smith and Guarnizo 1998). With Luis Eduardo Guarnizo and Michael Peter Smith, we see the " 'local' specificity of various socio-spatial transformations"—the "micro-dimension of transnationalism" (Guarnizo and Smith 1998:25, 26). In our consideration of maternal citizenship in this woman's story, we see the most local site of the story—namely, a village of about fifty households where the mother resides—while appreciating the transnational "imaging, planning, and strategizing" (Pessar and Mahler 2001:8) that enabled her efforts toward her son's marriage.

We begin with our own encounter with this failed marriage so as to introduce the story, key events, and persons. We then consider transnational marriage and hypergamy (with a focus on U.S. military men, Korean Chinese women, Southeast Asian men, and Southeast Asian women) in the final years of the twentieth century in South Korea. We consider the discursive coordinates of transnational marriage in the broader social field of South Korea's sense of its global membership. Next, we return to this chapter's marriage story to consider the mother's strategies, actions, and narratives both in terms of South Korea's global yearnings and her own project for maternal citizenship in the context of her considerable social marginalization in South Korea. This mother's case and narrative are particularly rich for analysis because of the ways in which her son's disability—a severe speech impediment and some mental impairment—both reveals and masks the coordinates of her marginalization (poverty, regional underdevelopment, social isolation, lack of cultural capital): on the one hand, the course of her son's disability speaks to that marginalization; on the other hand, the disability can be seen as a parameter that operates independent of economic circumstance. Finally, we turn to the narratives of two of the bachelor son's sisters on their brother's failed marriage. The sisters' distinct narratives deploy quite different transnational marriage imaginaries from that of their mother, imaginaries that speak to generational transformations and to the specificities of their life experiences. We conclude with thoughts on family, class, and transnationalism in South Korea, highlighting how South Korea's poorer men and women entertain international marriages in ways quite foreign to their more privileged brethren in South Korea's ever globalizing present.

A Village Evening

It is 2000, a late May evening in a farming village in South Korea's southwestern North Chŏlla Province. Like most villages in the southwestern part of South Korea, this village has long been poor. It comprises some fifty houses of agriculturalists, many of them elderly. In a country that is now less than 15 percent rural (Koo 2001), it is widely understood that villages such as this one can hardly reproduce themselves. For decades, South Koreans have been hearing about the marriage problem of rural bachelors (*nongch'on ch'onggak*). Most South Koreans could easily recite the basis of the problem: young South Korean women are reluctant to marry farmers because of the labor, social, and cultural demands of rural life. After many generations of rural exodus, the dramatic story of South Korea's rapid social transformation, South Koreans have left the countryside behind. To marry a farmer is, in a sense, to run against the historical grain of the times: hardly a desirable option for a young woman in South Korea's ever more prosperous and global times. The city—Seoul—beckons.

We traveled to the farming village on a social visit to the bachelor's mother featured in this chapter, whom we call here, as would be customary in South Korea, "Min's Mother." Nancy has known Min's Mother since the late 1980s, when Nancy resided in her village conducting dissertation field research on a farmers' land struggle that had enveloped a cluster of villages in the region (see Abelmann 1996). Min's Mother had been among the most active women participants in that struggle and Nancy has been in touch with her ever since. Our visit in May 2000 was not well-timed: the rice planting was not yet over, and that evening Min's Mother had to host her husband's elder sister and her brother-in-law for ancestral services (*chesa*). Moreover, one of Min's five sisters, Yun-a, had recently left her husband and was now living at home with her mother, her three-year-old daughter in tow. Yun-a had planned to leave her daughter with her mother while she went to Seoul to live temporarily with one of her married sisters until she could secure a job and a room of her own.

During our two-day visit, Yun-a asked us many questions about life in the United States—most specifically, she wanted to know about monthly costs and student and work visas. Although she never said so directly, it seemed as if she had entertained the prospect of emigration. She also told us quite a bit about one of her friends who would soon emigrate after marrying the U.S. serviceman with whom she already had a child. Yun-a did not mince words about her friend's likely prospects in the United States. The days in which South Koreans imagined the "American dream" that would meet the emigrant wives of U.S. servicemen are long gone, shattered by the popular understanding of the often social and economic marginalization of U.S. servicemen (for being poor, black, and so on). Thus, the "United States" in our conversations with Yun-a was an ambivalent United States (J. Kim 2001). At the margins of her imagination, Yun-a seemed to be entertaining the remote possibility of making her way abroad (while fully understanding the logistical barriers), but she was also keenly interested in reaffirming with her American (Nancy) and student-abroad (Hyunhee) audience that her friend's future in the United States would not likely be rosy.

We had caught Yun-a at a difficult juncture in her life: a marriage gone awry and considerable worries about the future of her daughter, whose father was threatening to take her away to be raised by his parents (this is not atypical in the case of marriage dissolution in South Korea, even though it is no longer the legally sanctioned solution) or even to place her in an orphanage. Min's Mother insisted that she would fight tooth and nail for her granddaughter—that at all costs, she would raise this little girl so as to help her daughter begin anew in Seoul (later, however, Yun-a did lose custody of the child). There was much to be said that first evening together. Min's Mother told Nancy the latest news about her then late-twenties son, whom Nancy had known in the village a dozen years earlier: she had secured his marriage with a Filipina woman through the Unification Church in the subprovincial capital (an hour or so away by bus); she had accompanied her son to the Philippines (a very costly venture for a poor farming family) because his disability had precluded his going alone (she had been the only mother to tag along with the group of farmer bachelors); her son had become engaged in the Philippines; and he had been "stood up" at a mass wedding in Seoul. In the meanwhile (nearly a year had passed), the fiancée had not come to South Korea, and it was becoming less and less clear whether she would ever come. For Min's Mother, the trip to the Philippines had been particularly burdensome (about 500,0000 won, or $4,167) because two people were traveling. In addition to the airfare were presents—cosmetics, clothes, a ring, and even dollars—for the bride-to-be and her family. Although these expenditures can be counted as transnational signs of Min's Mother's economic achievement, they were hard-earned.

Needless to say, the failed marriage had disastrous consequences: that the money, effort, and time had likely come to naught was no small matter for Min's Mother. At the time of our summer visit, she continued to hold a glimmer of hope that the Filipina fiancée might still come. Min's Mother had been able to speak with the fiancée by phone (although the fiancée had no phone, she could be reached via a church in her remote rural area in the Philippines), and she had proclaimed her love for Min and her steadfast plans to join him. Coincidentally, the Filipina fiancée called the first evening we were staying with Min's Mother. Knowing that the fiancée had more command of English than Korean, Min's Mother put Nancy on the phone. Indeed, in accordance with the story's telling, the fiancée proclaimed her love, referred to Min's Mother as *ŏmŏni* ("mother" in Korean), and indicated her desire to join them in South Korea.

Later that evening, Min's Mother's husband's elder sister and her husband arrived. With their arrival, Min's Mother placed the suspended marriage of her son in its familial history (parts of the story were already familiar to Nancy). Min is a so-called *samdae tokcha*, a third-generation only son. In Korean patrilineal logic, third-generation only sons are uniquely valuable and vulnerable: nothing short of the continuity of the "family" (patrilineage) hangs on their getting married and bearing a son. Although the significance of this kinship niche is waning in South Korea today, it remains secure by public measures, including the provision that *samdae tokcha* can fulfill their mandatory military duty by commuting to safer posts close to home. In the course of our conversation, Min's Mother turned the clock back one generation, to the trials of her deceased mother-in-law and father-in-law to secure the future of the patrilineage. Not only had her mother-in-law gone to great lengths to bear another child, but another woman had been brought in to bear a child (neither effort produced a second son). Unspoken in these stories was the fact of Min's father's disability (both Min and his father are disabled); Min's paternal grandparents had wanted a "normal" child to continue the family line. In South Korea, there is considerable social prejudice against those with disabilities that are classified as in any way biological; that disability is a debit in marriage is a South Korean commonsense.[1] Min's father's unnamed disability is a severe speech impediment that makes him all but incomprehensible to anyone who is not accustomed to his communication; although marginalized in the village for the disability, villagers were nonetheless at ease communicating with him. Amplifying the speech impediment are the husband's drinking habit and untoward manner. Min's own disability is an uncanny double of his father's; likely this has strengthened the local sense of the hereditary nature of the disability. Growing up with the identical speech impediment as his father, Min remained almost entirely unschooled and illiterate. Less clear was the matter of Min's intelligence—or, for that matter, his father's—or the more exact etiology of the disability.

In her village, it is well known that Min's Mother's marital life has been hard and that the family's economic gains (modest though they are, even in the context of a relatively poor village of small farmers) are all the fruits of Min's Mother's hard work, savvy, and intelligence. Min's Mother offered that her father-in-law (the honored "guest" at the ancestral services later that evening) had been eternally grateful to her for having married his son. Over a decade earlier, Nancy had heard the story of the marriage deception that had brought Min's Mother as a very young woman to marry Min's father (whom she had never met): Min's Mother had not known that he was disabled and property-less (see Kendall 1988 on marriage deception). Against this family history, and in the flurry of the food preparation required of an ancestral service, the efforts of Min's Mother to secure a wife for her son and male progeny for her husband's (and late father-in-law's) patrilineage echoed the efforts of her mother-in-law before her and spoke to pervasive Korean cultural and familial logics; how could anyone be surprised? To this story, however, we will add other skeins of meaning because of the particular transnational character of the marriage that Min's mother imagined and sought to realize.

South Korea's Fin-de-Siècle Marriage-Scape

In this section, we consider the broader social field of South Korean transnational marriage in the context of the changing landscape of South Korean policy debates on ethnicity, citizenship, and rights. Within this field, we consider marriages to American servicemen, Korean Chinese women, non-American foreign men, and, most recently, Southeast Asian women. We end with a discussion of hypergamy, considering how various international marriages are conceptualized in terms of social mobility.

Several contemporary policy issues index the question of South Korean global or cosmopolitan membership, including: the rights of (and South Korean responsibility for) Korean ethnics abroad (for example, in China); the voting rights of South Korean citizens residing abroad; and the naturalization policies for foreign residents and spouses in South Korea. Each of these issues is enlivened by competing conceptions of South Korea's place in a global community of nations. Broadly, we consider two visions of global membership—both similarly nationalistic. First is a homogeneous ethnic vision that imagines a "Korean" transnation that is centered in South Korea. Second is a multi-ethnic vision that calls for diversity in South Korea as an index of its stature among nations. We argue that the prevailing approach to national or ethnic difference in South Korea has been assimilationist such that some foreigners are permitted to become "Korean." Whether multi-ethnic or assimilationist, the idea that South Korea can in some fashion deal with racial or ethnic difference also serves to qualify South Korea as a modern state in a global state system in which internal difference of states is an international norm. Both visions, South Koreans abroad and foreigners at home, reveal a parallel nationalism in which either a "Korean" transnation or an assimilable foreigner speak to South Korea's global stature. It is precisely the strivings of this stature that are implicated in Min's Mother's own transnational marriage attempts, as we detail below.

A number of legal and policy issues concerning Koreans abroad and foreigners in South Korea reveal the tension between multi-ethnic or cosmopolitan yearnings and deep-seated nationalism. The 1990s witnessed the enormous expansion of the labor and marriage immigration of Korean Chinese to South Korea. Some argued that these Korean Chinese (as well as other Koreans displaced during the colonial period, for example, to the former Soviet Union and Japan) should be accorded citizenship precisely because of the colonial histories implicated in their dispersion—namely, their status as the former patriotic subjects of the colonial-period provisional government (JoongAng Ilbo editorial 2002:53). Revealing of the times, however, an editorial (originally printed in 2001) was quick to point out that "embracing Koreans worldwide" by granting citizenship should not be understood as the "revival of narrow-minded nationalism" (JoongAng Ilbo editorial 2002:54). The voting and citizenship rights of long-term foreign residents and foreign spouses in South Korea also reveal ambivalent consideration of South Korea's global membership. In a multi-ethnic or cosmopolitan vein, one recent editorial argued that the voting rights of long-term foreign residents can be taken as a "yardstick for measuring a country's maturity" in a world of nations (Ha 2002). In a nationalistic vein, the same editorial went on to assert that the voting rights of Korean ethnics abroad are the far more pressing issue. On the matter of regulating national membership, a key issue has been the naturalization rights of non-Korean spouses. Important here is the gendered history reflecting patrilineal kinship logics. Although it was only in 1998 that non-Korean husbands gained legal rights to naturalize, non-Korean wives on the other hand have been able to do so for decades. Implicit in this history is that non-Korean women have been assimilable into South Korean families, while non-Korean men have been understood to produce non-Korean households.[2]

We turn now to the primary instances of transnational or so-called international marriage (typically referring only to interracial marriage) in the South Korean marriage-scape. With the exception of marriages to non-American foreign men, the primary transnational marriage possibilities are all implicated in Min's Mother's management of her son's marriage prospects, including those to American servicemen, Korean Chinese women, and, most recently, Southeast Asian women.

Marriages of South Korean women to American servicemen, like that of the friend of Min's sister Yun-a mentioned above, run parallel to the entire course of South Korean history, beginning with the American military occupation in the immediate postliberation period (after 1945) (see Yuh 2002). These marriages are largely understood to be the unions of poor women, some of them tainted by images of the sexual-service industry (for example, the *yangkongju*, or "Western princess," a derogatory term for South Korean women serving American military men) (Cumings 1992; H. Kim 1998). These marital unions have not been understood to secure the continuity of Korean families; rather, it can be argued that their contours are off the Korean map entirely. Moreover, these women hardly figure on the map of the Korean diaspora, the diaspora having been largely imagined as populated by struggling co-ethnics in China (and other places of colonial dispersion) and by middle-class immigrants in the United States and other countries in Europe and the Americas (Abelmann and Lie 1995).

In contrast, the marriages of South Korean men, primarily bachelor farmers, to Korean ethnics from China (Chosŏnjok) have been signified both in terms of the maintenance or reproduction of South Korean families and in terms of the assertion of a global Korean ethnic community uniting the South Korean homeland and its diasporas (see Freeman in this volume). The romance of ethnic brotherhood, however, has been marred by images of ruggedly individualist Korean Chinese women who forsake their newlywed families in what has been imagined as the instrumental pursuit of their own private ambition (see Freeman in this volume). A partial counter-discourse (with feminist overtones) asserts that the patriarchal excesses of South Korean farmer husbands have driven these co-ethnic women away. Although critical of the vilification of the Korean Chinese women, this feminist call similarly engages the nationalistic imperative for South Korea's "modern membership": namely, they argue that South Korean patriarchal excesses must be curbed to allow for membership in a global community of modern advanced states. A recent progressive weekly magazine report on the high incidence of violence against international brides reveals that a feminist position does not preclude an assimilationist perspective. The article offered that, given the situation in which many farmers will need to marry non-Koreans, it is imperative that Korean patriarchy be curbed and that the South Korean state tend to the needs of these women. The article ended with a description of the group of foreign brides who had gathered to discuss their plight: the writer, the director of the Yŏngkwang hotline for women, observed that these foreign women brought to mind the image of a circle of Korean farming women gathered at the village corner to pick through red peppers for traditional Korean food preparation (T. Yi 2002). On the one hand, this article speaks to the special circumstances of these women, marking their exclusion and difficulties, but on the other hand, it easily assimilates them into an old-fashioned image of the feminine, subservient, rural wife. These images and this gendered contest aside, these marriages have been fraught with considerable marriage fraud and domestic violence, high divorce rates, and cultural tension (see Chŏng 2003 for a media report on domestic violence in the case of Filipina and Vietnamese brides).

In the late 1990s, Southeast Asian women began arriving in South Korea for work in the sex industries and as rural brides. We surmise that Min's Mother in 2002 was not familiar with the by-then pervasive image of the Filipina hostess or sex worker (Cheng 2002). But the term "foreign brides" has now taken on new meaning because of the growing awareness of a marriage market for those who can pay and because of the prominence of foreign prostitution rings (particularly tainting the image of Filipina women). But in the time in which Min's Mother was making her calculations, Filipina brides could still easily be posited as traditional women to answer to the call of family continuity.

In the 1990s, the ethnic/racial landscape of South Korean cities (and, more recently, of farming villages) was transformed with the entry of foreign laboring men. They married South Korean working-class women—another case of marriages outside the prerogative of Korean patrilineage, but inside the South Korean polity. Little research exists to suggest the cultural logics of these marriages.

To address this book's focus on global hypergamy, we briefly consider the above transnational marriages in relation to social mobility. The marriages of the daughters of farmers to American GIs could be—at least in the early years—considered ambivalently hypergamous: on the one hand, they offered a way out to a presumed more prosperous country and living situation; on the other hand, the marriages were considered disgraceful for being interracial and were tainted by their association with sexual services and the sex industry. In addition to the negative connotations of these marriages over time, and with the growing awareness of the often poor backgrounds of U.S. servicemen, even this ambivalent confidence in some sort of class mobility has been called into question. In the case of the rural bachelors in the recent past and into the present, the imagined hypergamy is rather that of the brides who are from less developed countries, and presumed to be from less prosperous families. Caren Freeman (in this volume) documents that some Korean Chinese women have hardly found their dreams of hypergamy satisfied in the South Korean countryside (see also Thai in this volume on parallel disappointments of Vietnamese men marrying émigré Vietnamese women in the United States). In the case of non-Korean women from Southeast Asia, it appears that the South Korean presumption of their hypergamy is even greater, obscuring again the specificities of the women's backgrounds independent of national GDP and GNP figures (see Constable in this volume for the case of highly educated, prosperous Chinese brides). Likewise, the often marginalized position of the South Korean farmer in relation to those national figures is obscured.

That Min's Mother and other women like her can claim membership in that national community of relative prosperity is precisely what allows her to sustain the possible fiction of the Filipina's presumed hypergamy. And it is the sense of that hypergamy in conjunction with her claim on South Korean prosperity that contributes to her strivings for maternal citizenship. Min's hypergamy is complicated by his disability: the presumed hypergamy of the Filipina fiancée must be considered alongside Min's hypergamy for the chance to marry an able-bodied woman (the imagined South Korean partner would have been, it had been implied, a disabled woman).[3] However, even for nondisabled farmers, their low marriage prospects in South Korea challenge any simple calculation of the foreign brides' upward mobility. Also, if we consider the presumed traditional feminine assets of women from less developed Asian countries (their gendered capital), the directionality of the hypergamy for South Korean farmers and Southeast Asian women is not entirely clear.

To return to Min's Mother, her calculations for Min speak to the assimilationism of international marriages reviewed above and to the nationalism implicated in the imagined hypergamy of foreign women. Min's Mother was optimistic about the prospects for her son's and her own life after marriage. She figured that in any case, her son would not be alone. She had heard that after about two years in South Korea, Filipinas were usually comfortable with the Korean language. Min's Mother was determined to be good to her future daughter-in-law; she resolved to teach her Korean and many other things about life in South Korea. Min's Mother was entirely satisfied with Min's Filipina fiancée, even wondering if Min was deserving of her. Of course, she realized that she could not know "the girl's true character," but based on what she had seen, she determined that the fiancée was a "fine girl." Min's Mother did acknowledge, however, that it was not ideal for husband and wife not to share a language. But she stressed that the fiancée seemed pure and lovable. Critical to this marriage imaginary is Min's Mother's sense of South Korea's economic achievements vis-à-vis the Philippines: she described the Filipina fiancée as "pure" for having lived in a less developed social reality that maps easily onto South Korea's (and, more particularly, Min's Mother's) past. Noticeably absent was any talk about a second generation of biracial children.

We turn now to Min's Mother's marriage activities and extend our discussion of both her traditional labor and her transnational efforts at a maternal citizenship in which South Korea's ascendance in the world of nations is implicated.

A Mother's Struggle for Her Family, Her Son, and Her Own Maternal Citizenship

Having reviewed the ambivalence about transnational marriage and other new membership in South Korea, we reassert that Min's Mother's ability to envision—and indeed, her tireless efforts to secure—a foreign bride for her son must be understood as combining long-standing and new social projects. What does it mean that Min's Mother could think about recruiting a foreign bride for her son, and yet imagine that the bride could become a Korean wife (a married rural woman, an *ajumma* or *sigol anak*) who could secure the future of the patrilineage and serve as a daily partner for Min? With these imaginaries, Min's Mother is realizing a very local and traditional project, while partaking partially of membership of a transnational nature that is a feature of fuller participation in a modern South Korea. This is not to say that with these activities, Min's Mother has illusions of upward mobility, but rather that in spite of her situation as a poor farmer from a marginal area, she has mobilized her resources in a purposeful and meaningful way. The marriage that Min's Mother was securing was an arranged group marriage, a mass wedding organized by the vilified Unification Church. These mass weddings are familiar to most South Koreans, although the Unification Church has been less successful in South Korea than in many other countries.

The attempted recruitment of a Filipina wife to be assimilated into the South Korean countryside is hardly a transnational project; rather, it can be seen as the fulfillment of a socially and culturally conservative project—the continuity of the Korean patrilineage. In this sense, the irony is that it is the "foreign" bride who can redress this local problem. The fact that Min's Mother set her sights on a Filipina bride, rather than a Korean Chinese bride—the more common solution—can be similarly understood as the contingency of strategy rather than an attempt to exceed the national or ethnic. Min's Mother calculated that a Filipina bride was more likely to fulfill her local project. In her cultural imaginary, a pure, "traditional" rural Filipina girl is posed in contradistinction to a scheming Korean Chinese girl. With these calculations, Min's Mother echoed the prevailing South Korean understanding of Southeast Asia as less developed than South Korea and as culturally legible. She presumed that the Filipina would be like South Korea's yesteryear brides, perhaps like she herself was as a young bride who married into difficult circumstances. Unfortunately for the case of this failed marriage, we know nothing about the Filipina in question other than that she is from a remote area where she did not have direct access to telephones, the sort of detail that impressed Min's Mother of her unfortunate circumstances. It was Min's Mother's sense of the fiancée's hard life and extreme isolation that perhaps sustained her conviction about the young woman's purity and good intentions. That a personal telephone was hardly on Min's Mother's horizon fifteen years ago does not change the calculation. Furthermore, with these calculations, Min's Mother drew upon long-standing Korean gendered understandings of marriage mobility, in which men can marry up on account of their personal assets (beyond family background, educational achievement) while women can marry up on account of their feminine assets (see Abelmann 2003). Beyond the former image of a woman securing a patrilineage, Min's Mother's project was also about arranging an attractive daily life for her son, one including a partner—a project that exceeds her interest in her own social standing or future social security. The efforts for a daily life partner speak to economic and practical imperatives, intensified by Min's disability, and perhaps to Min's Mother's own burgeoning sense (in step with the times) of the integrity of the conjugal unit itself (something that was stressed by Min's two sisters).

Min's Mother's efforts, activities, and narratives also reflect changing geopolitical circumstances (South Korea's economic ascendance, legal changes, and so on) that have made it possible for a poor and even disabled bachelor farmer to contemplate marriage to a foreigner who is imagined to be a feminine woman willing to sacrifice for the family (the image of the traditional Korean bride). Cosmopolitan membership in a global community as a cornerstone of maternal citizenship (in the village and national community) is at work in Min's Mother's story, independent of her son's marriage prospects and eventual failure. Min's Mother's story must also be understood as her own story, albeit inextricable from that of her son. Min's Mother is mobilizing capital with cosmopolitan and middle-class or mainstream characteristics (movement, travel, and consumption): in each task entailed in her management of this marriage, Min's Mother was exercising her savvy, knowledge, and confidence. What is new in Min's Mother's story is not the possibility of a Filipina bride per se, but rather Min's Mother's social and cultural membership which relies on the possibility of a foreign bride and the necessary international arrangements, including travel, to secure one. Although Min's Mother had no pretenses of full-fledged middle-class membership—as an unschooled poor farming woman, how could she?—nonetheless, this marriage story reveals her attempts at belonging and respectability, what we have called "maternal citizenship."

Min's Mother's marriage strategies for her son took her to a larger stage beyond her village—first to the subprovincial capital, and then to the Philippines—and extended her horizons and her participation in South Korea's rapidly transforming modernity. The significance of the eventual failure of the marriage must be seen in relation to these expansive efforts. In Min's Mother's narration of the course and causes of this failure, more is at stake than simply her son's failed marriage or the loss of her economic resources. At stake is her own stature in the village as well as her sense of belonging in South Korea. We will argue below that Min's Mother's placement of blame on the Unification Church—in spite of the many variables and contingencies of the story—is an effort at face-saving that speaks to the humiliation she suffered in her project toward maternal citizenship.

We turn now to the chronology of events and decisions that constitute Min's Mother's marriage plan for her son. Min's Mother's consideration of a Filipina wife for her son began with her visit to the Koch'ang Punyŏn-hoe, or Women's Club, where she had been a member, a quasi-governmental group organized at the subprovincial level that typically gathered at a quasi-governmental building. Min's Mother had first attended the Women's Club hoping to participate in a paper-flower-making course. As it turned out, because those classes were held quite far from her village—and because they met during the day and thus competed with her agricultural and supplementary work duties—Min's Mother had to give up the course. Nonetheless, it was through her attendance there that Min's Mother had learned that the umbrella organization of the Women's Club, the Nongch'on Chidoso (Farming Village Association), could facilitate her son's marriage prospects. Specifically, she had learned that the head of the Farming Village Association had contacts with the Unification Church, which could help bachelor farmers meet Filipina women. Apparently, the head of the Farming Village Association facilitated these unions by providing a meeting space. This could have given Min's Mother the impression that these unions were officially sanctioned by a South Korean quasi-governmental organization. Min's Mother had been drawn to the flower-making classes to assert her membership in a wider world beyond the confines of her village, and it was there that she would begin to mobilize her new social capital: namely, the knowledge of new extra-local networks (via the head of the Farming Village Association) that might help her address her local problem, her unmarried only son.

By 1998, the possibility of a foreign wife was a fixture in the rural imagination. There were many stories of foreign wives, and indeed, the nearby South Chŏlla Province had by then the highest number of émigré brides in the country. Min's Mother was already familiar with the stories of several Filipina brides in the nearby subprovincial capital. The possibility of a Filipina bride must be understood against the widespread images of Korean Chinese brides: images of instrumental "ethnic" brides who were motivated to use poor farmers as stepping-stones to more gainful employment and prosperous lives in the city, and who were strong-willed and willing to stand up to their husbands (T. Yi 2002). Drawing upon her new extra-local resources, Min's Mother decided to go to the Philippines with her son who was about twenty-nine. In the company of many other farmer bachelors, her son was the only one who traveled with a family member. She had never been abroad so a trip to the Philippines promised a big adventure; to some extent, it secured Min's Mother a place—if fleeting—in the company of women with the time and money to travel (Abelmann 2003). However, by this time there was a boom in onetime group travel abroad of villages (*tanch'e kwan-kwang* or group tourism). Although it is not inconceivable that some women from Min's Mother's village might have taken such a trip, it is unlikely, given the prosperity of the village; it is less likely still that Min's Mother would have joined them. In any case her independent travel for Min's marriage was different from such a village trip. Although Min's Mother understood that the trip used all her savings, that it was made solely for the purpose of her son's marriage, and that it proved a dismal failure, it still reflected her savvy and afforded her an international experience and thus offered her a heightened sense of cultural membership or belonging in South Korea. Min's Mother's narration suggested that her own hard life and achievements had given her the necessary resolve to prepare for the challenges of such a trip. A trip from one nation's periphery to another nation's periphery, Min's Mother's travel was hardly a conventional tour.

Min's disability complicates this story. On one occasion, Min's Mother said that she decided to accompany her son to the Philippines because he is not "normal." Min's Mother referred to Min's disability variously—as "not smart," not "able-bodied" (*sŏnghan*), and mentally "five years behind" his age-mates. As for his speech impediment, she said that, like her husband, her son has difficulty communicating with people—specifically, that he could not finish sentences (*mal i ttokttok ttŏrŏjiji annŭn*). We suggest that Min's Mother's variance on her son's disability indexes her conflicted estimations of the articulation between Min's marriage prospects and his disability. In thinking about Min's inability to marry in South Korea and about his failed marriage to the Filipina woman, Min's Mother left open the question as to whether it was his disability that had mattered or simply his position as a farmer's son, as a really poor farmer's son, and as an illiterate and largely unschooled young man. Indeed, it is hard for the listener to sort out the characteristics of her son's marginalization: biological, social, and economic. Min's Mother was aware that Min's disability as a marred speaking subject could render him invisible in a transnational marriage across the boundaries of language and nation. Min's Mother did recognize his disability in her assessment that he would never be able to secure a bride had he traveled to the Philippines alone. When she elaborated upon this situation, she spoke more vaguely about Min "having no mind of his own" and about "only succumbing to the will of others." That Min's disability and other disadvantages were not distinct in Min's Mother's narration of his failed marriage speaks to their inextricable articulation in her mind. Min's disabilities took on social life in relation to the family's poverty: if not for their poverty—Min's Mother seemed to be saying—Min could perhaps have become better educated and literate. The able-bodied Filipina bride would symbolically redress the very marginalization that rendered Min's marriage prospects so weak in South Korea. She would thus answer to Min's fine character and person, independent of his social and economic fate in South Korea.

In light of Min's disability, Min's Mother had gone against the grain to persist with her transnational marriage plan. Two of her daughters (discussed below) had recommended against it: because of misgivings about the Unification Church and because of the calculation that a South Korean disabled bride would make much more sense for Min. To her decriers (including several village relatives), Min's Mother was steadfast that hers was a "mother's heart"—going to great lengths to secure an able-bodied marriage partner for her son. Min's Mother repeatedly claimed that no one can stop a mother from doing as much. For Min's Mother, travel to the Philippines was charged with emotions about the exercise of maternal responsibility. It was as if opposition to her actions did not matter because she understood that one strain of cultural logic would allow for the celebration of her heroic actions. Min's Mother's evocation of a "mother's heart" is all the more convincing in the context of her own poverty and her suffering from an abusive husband. She described her life as one continual sacrifice for her family, explaining that seven people's well-being relied on her suffering (her children's and husband's).

Min's Mother spent three days in the Philippines, staying at the Unification Church quarters in the area. In the Philippines, Min's Mother was struck most of all by the life circumstances that recalled the South Korea of decades earlier; these were the sorts of observations that fueled her sense of the traditional Filipina fiancée and correspondingly of her own stature for traveling there. The Filipina women and South Korean bachelor couples exchanged words through two translators, one for Korean and the other for the local dialect. Min's Mother said that all the couples spent most of the three days together, except when they slept. They visited the local museum and took walks together. The couples' engagements were celebrated with the exchange of rings.

Reckoning the Marriage Failure

Min's Mother's narration of the failure of Min's marriage was simpler than her account of all she had done to secure its possibility. This reduced narrative of the failure is revealing: namely, it speaks to her unwillingness to erase her considerable accomplishments. By placing blame on one cog in a considerably more complicated wheel, Min's Mother sustains the narrative and hope of the sort of maternal citizenship we have been describing here. While Min's Mother evoked the authority of the Farming Village Association in narrating the first chapter of her marriage attempt, based on her (mis)understanding that the association had played a formal role, by the time she was describing the disastrous failure of her arduous efforts, Min's Mother laid the full blame on the intervening Unification Church. Similarly, in her narration of her trip to the Philippines, it was as if the Unification Church, like the Farming Village Association, was simply a stepping-stone in her own skillful management of her son's marriage. It was thus only from the perspective of the eventual failure that Min's Mother reinscribed her path to the Philippines as wholly a church matter.

Min's Mother spoke of having been deceived by the church. She described a church that is interested only in extracting money from poor South Korean farmers and in its own proselytizing efforts for which the Unification Church is particularly notorious in South Korea. She described, for example, having been forced to present a sack of rice when she attended the church—something that she resented deeply. Min's Mother drew upon what appeared to be her own long-standing feelings about rural churches as useless organizations that merely extort funds from poor farmers. On the other hand, she dismissed rural churches for being poor and hence of little use to rural people; in talking about the rural church on an unpaved path near her home, she did note that the church has offered food to the elderly and managed to hold small parties, but criticized the pastor and his family for being dirt-poor themselves. Min's Mother had come to think of the entire trip to the Philippines as the church's moneymaking stunt. As evidence, she noted that over the years the Unification Church keeps changing the country from which it recruits brides—proof, she thought, that the church was evading authorities. She insisted that she should be reimbursed for the cost of her travel, since the marriage had not truly come to pass.

Min's Mother understands that her son returned to South Korea alone, in spite of having become engaged in the Philippines, because the church had wanted more time to further proselytize the bride; this is a sticking point for Min's Mother because she is confident that she could have brought the fiancée back herself and secured the marriage. To make matters worse, when Min's Mother complained about the missing bride at the collective marriage ceremony, the Unification Church said that Min could travel to the Korean autonomous province in China, Yŏnbyŏn, to meet an ethnic Korean woman. A church representative told her that this time she need not join Min because they would tend to him. She was outraged: if the marriage had not worked when she had accompanied him, how could it ever work if she did not go? She saw this as yet another attempt on the part of the church to extract money from her—for her son's travel, which would lead to nothing. Min's Mother was also offended at the callousness of the Unification Church; its disregard for Min's engagement and for the very real attachment—in her opinion—of Min and his fiancée.

For Min's Mother, the bride was similarly the victim of the Unification Church—thus leaving the narrative of courtship, engagement, and the promise of marriage and a particular imaginary of transnational romance unsullied. Nonetheless, Min's Mother complained about Filipina fiancées in terms of the remittances that the South Korean husbands are expected to pay to their extended families back home. But Min's Mother held fast to her positive impressions of Min's fiancée and even to her romantic dream of her union with Min. It is perhaps because Min's Mother has sustained an untainted image of the Filipina fiancée that she could continue to preserve some hope of the young woman's eventual marital union with Min, keeping alive the romantic narrative of the trip and engagement, and preserving some measure of pride in her own deft arrangement and abilities.

Min's Mother's anger at the Unification Church aside, the marriage fiasco registers both as her own failure and her son's misfortune. It signals her inability to enact the membership that the promise of her son's marriage had seemed to offer: namely, membership in the company of women who fashion their family futures; of women who travel in wider social circles, with requisite networks; and of women who can travel internationally. Furthermore, the failed marriage halted the more local village project; Min's Mother imagined that such a marriage would have literally and metaphorically "normalized" her son and her stature. Were Min to marry and constitute a household, her precarious position between a disabled husband and disabled son would have been altered. Despite the eventual failure (the no-show bride), Min's Mother retains her having exercised a maternal cultural citizenship with this marriage plan (and activities) and its narration. As for her son, Min's Mother felt sorry for him. Min had traveled to Seoul for the marriage ceremony where the cohort of bachelor farmers who had visited the Philippines together would all marry in the same mass ceremony. It was only Min's fiancée who did not appear there; Min stood by alone, with a bouquet for his no-show bride.

Did Min's Mother wonder about his disability in relation to the no-show bride? This is not something that she mentioned overtly. Certainly, the thought must have crossed her mind: as far as we know, she was the only mother to need to accompany her son, and his was the only no-show bride. But we take her silence as a defiant refusal to blame her son's deficiencies. Or her silence could reflect her understanding of her son's disabilities as standing metonymically for his (and her) larger marginalization. Her laments about her and her son's failures index this broader social stage. In reflecting on the whole process, she matter-of-factly said that she had merely tried to find a partner for her twenty-nine-year-old son. She had figured that she would start this endeavor early and work hard at it, but, as she put it, "Even though I've been working hard since then to find a bride, I have not been able to find a girl." She reflected on her situation as doubly frustrating because it indexes the general situation of bachelor farmers. As she put it, "If even the smart ones among them could not find a marriage partner in South Korea, what chance would the likes of my son have?" In spite of it all, Min's Mother remains committed to the project of making a "normal" life for Min, a cornerstone of her claim to maternal citizenship.

In 2000, as we noted, Min's Mother still retained her affection for the Filipina fiancée. In 2001, she recalled the phone calls from the fiancée—like the one we had witnessed during our village visit—as indications of the woman's commitment to Min and her desire to come to South Korea. During one of her phone conversations with the fiancée, she told her, "I will go myself and bring you here." But she wondered aloud to Hyunhee whether she could make good on her word: there was likely little economic backing to the bravado of her words. With this narration, Min's Mother asserted that it was imperfect communication, transportation snafus, and financial limits that had thwarted the fiancée's travel—snafus that she thought to cut through. Min's Mother had indeed mobilized a transnational imaginary as well as a transnational network, but only partially, imperfectly, and at one moment in time. We cannot completely erase the significance of her work, in part because of the healthy and spirited way in which (at least in 2000 and 2001) she was still narrating the story. When Nancy met her in 2003, however, Min's Mother did not mention this past and Nancy decided not to ask.

Alternative Takes: The Sisters' Narratives

Min's above-mentioned older sister, Yun-a, who had been living with her mother at the time of our visit, understood her brother's failed marriage somewhat differently from her mother. Yun-a reckoned that the Filipina fiancée simply had not wanted to come to South Korea. Yun-a identified with the fiancée—imagining the position of a young woman contemplating a transnational marriage; recall that Yun-a herself had seemed interested in emigration and thus reflected on the difficult situation of South Koreans married to American servicemen. Yun-a's thoughts about the Filipina fiancée extend beyond the particulars of her brother's case (his disability, poverty, and so on) while still being mindful of them. For Yun-a, her brother's marriage was an instance of a so-called international marriage (*kukche kyŏrhon*), which also implies interracial marriage. Yun-a thinks of international marriages as difficult for the person displaced from his or her country. That the Filipina fiancée would have thought not to come made good sense to Yun-a, knowing that the marriage would have depended on the fiancée's sacrifices. Yun-a was well aware of how hard it is for a woman to be separated from her natal family and to live in an unfamiliar setting. In the case of Min's fiancée, Yun-a decided that it was probably also the case that her parents in the Philippines had forbidden her to come. Yun-a admitted that she had no real evidence for this, but was nonetheless convinced that this must have been the case.

Yun-a's thoughts on her brother's failed marriage draw on broader images and representations than those of her mother. While Min's Mother seemed to rely chiefly on local stories—for example, on the successful cases of marriages to Filipinas in the nearby city—Yun-a spoke about media sources, including a television documentary about Russian brides in South Korea, that had made a big impression on her. The documentary revealed that Russian brides often suffer from homesickness and depression. In the case of the documented families, all parties suffered: the mothers-in-law for not being able to communicate with their daughters-in-law; the brides, as well, because of language barriers; and the husbands for trying in vain to make the relationship work.

Yun-a's thinking on international marriage was informed by her own familiarity with the marriages or unions of a number of her friends with American servicemen—and more generally by her own experience of patriarchal excess in the case of her in-laws, and by her friend's encounter with domestic abuse. Yun-a was well aware of the often short life of international marriages. She said that international marriages dissolve after two or three years because the women "can no longer stand it." When Yun-a spoke about the perils and trials of international marriage, it was clear that her thoughts were refracted through the lens of her own situation as a young divorcée for whom international marriage did not seem to offer a way out. Yun-a was armed with many stories of South Korean women who had married foreigners. She spoke about one case in which a South Korean woman married to an American had been unable to see her parents for over thirty years. As for the friend she spoke of during our 2000 countryside visit (Hyunhee met Yun-a a second time in Seoul in 2001), Yun-a said that the friend had been too frightened to move to the United States; it was likely that this account prompted Yun-a to imagine the Filipina fiancée's position and probable reticence to come to South Korea. These sorts of real and mediated stories wrested international marriage from any romantic notions of love that easily transcends borders. Although Min's Mother's narratives did not dwell on this sort of romantic vision, she was more optimistic about the possibility of success. For Yun-a and her mother, international marriage is mediated by class—be it the case of Min and the Filipina bride or Yun-a's friends and American servicemen. These cases are both distinct from another sort of international marriage, that of elites operating in a transcultural, transnational sphere (for example, students studying or teaching abroad and professionals working abroad for foreign companies) quite distant from Yun-a and her mother—a sphere in which romantic visions of love transcending borders make more sense.

Although Min's Mother and Yun-a were aware that their stories were those on the borderlands of other people's cosmopolitan lives, both of them felt pained at the way in which the turn of events had hurt Min. Both blamed the insensitivity of the Unification Church. Yun-a was particularly incensed that the church had so casually thought to substitute another bride.

Min's youngest sister, an early-twenties single worker in a small factory in Seoul who had not completed high school, understood the failed marriage differently from both her mother and sister. This youngest sister is clear that she has no intentions of returning to her village, but can still imagine her brother's future there. This sister had warned her mother from the beginning of the folly of such an arrangement, particularly through the Unification Church. She could not understand why her mother had not simply recruited a disabled South Korean woman for Min's partner. Interestingly, it was this youngest sister who seemed to feel saddest about the humiliation and suffering that Min had endured on account of this failed marriage. She is one of the so-called new generation" (*sinsedae*), known for its discourses of love, happiness, and desire, so it is not surprising that she would feel this way most strongly (S. Lee 2002, Lett 1998, Y. Shim 2001 and 2002). She told her mother that there is a partner (*jjak*) out there for everyone in the world and that her brother, too, would find his mate. Although a laborer in Seoul whose life circumstances would be enviable to few in South Korea, this sister was somehow able to speak beyond contingency, to remove her brother's situation—or anyone's, for that matter—from any structural consideration of economy, nation, ethnicity, and so on. Of course, we should remember that this sister was unmarried, a recent arrival in Seoul, and unfettered by any difficult past romantic or marital history. As for her thoughts on her own future marriage, she asserted that she would only marry when she was financially secure. She stressed that she would not marry out of any necessity; in this way, she wrested marriage from instrumental calculation, delivering it to the province of love and romance.

Consider Min's Mother's maternal citizenship project in relation to the narratives of these two daughters. Although Min's Mother reserved some hope for an amorous marriage for her son, she was not shy about thinking in more instrumental terms: a successful living arrangement in which her son could more easily manage life. This logic runs against the grain of other logics in which the intimate sphere is necessarily limited to intimate matters such that instrumental calculation defies a discourse of pure and uninterested love. Such was the grist of the youngest daughter's criticisms of her mother's project: she wondered why her mother had taken what could have been an intimate local matter and delivered it to a nasty transnational plot. Yun-a is perhaps less optimistic than her younger sister, but nonetheless was quick to see the contradictions between transnational marriage and the intimate sphere. We suggest this possibility: while Min's Mother is able to sustain or at least narrate some hope of maternal citizenship, at the very least in her own small village, Yun-a has been made painfully aware of her own marginalization and is cynical about her brother's prospects and her mother's ability to navigate a larger world. The youngest sister, on the other hand, yet to have suffered in the ways her sister has and partaking of new cultural streams, recognizes her mother's limits (her vulnerability at the hands of the Unification Church) and sustains the hope of a local romance for her brother.

Conclusion: Transnational Marriage in a Global Era

This chapter has discussed the failed marriage of one poor and disabled son of South Korean farmers and a rural Filipina young woman—a case of transnationalism from below. This chapter is not the result of sustained empirical research on transnational marriage in South Korea generally or among rural men and women particularly. Nonetheless, we hope that the analysis of Min's Mother's narration and Min's story (and the thoughts of Min's sisters) reveals something about transnational marriage as it articulates with South Korean membership in a global community of nations and with maternal citizenship. Although Min's Mother's marriage prospects for Min could not have been set on a Filipina woman without a host of recent transformations—among them, Min's Mother's sense of South Korea's stature in a global community of nations, her confidence in her ability to fashion the Filipina fiancée's assimilation in the South Korean countryside, and the financial where-withal to take the trip to the Philippines—it would be problematic to argue that Min's Mother's marriage calculations are uniformly signs of a new borderless world and social imagination (Smith and Guarnizo 1998). Similarly, we have cautioned that Min's Mother's transnational participation is entirely classed. Her travel from a South Korean rural village and relatively underdeveloped area to a remote village in the Philippines must be differentiated from the middle-class travel of urban-ites to global hot spots and centers of cosmopolitan capital. Similarly, the nature of the international marriage that Min's Mother attempted to realize for Min is far from the international marriages of the mobile upper-middle and upper classes. While Min's was an arranged group marriage in the margins, theirs are the fulfillment of individual romances at global centers.

Min's Mother's story must also be registered as the story of a marginal-ized woman's valiant efforts to achieve a gendered belonging or mater-nal citizenship. For Min's Mother, belonging begins with her village, where she has been marginalized as the wife and mother of disabled men. Min's Mother is keenly aware of how differently she would be treated in the village if she had a "smart" (*ttokttokhan*) son—never, she thinks, would she be snubbed by a passerby. The project of belonging extends in turn to her status as a poor farming woman in a national com-munity in which poor farmers are a veritable vanishing minority. The savvy, knowledge, networks, and resources that Min's Mother mobilized in envisioning and attempting to realize a transnational marriage—efforts that took her to the subprovincial capital, enabled her first travel abroad, and posed her as a woman from a relatively developed country bringing goods and the vision of a better life to the Philippines—can all be seen as efforts to secure maternal citizenship in a rapidly transform-ing South Korea. In thinking about transnational marriage, Min's Moth-er's story emphasizes that we cannot presume the meanings of such arrangements without considerable investigation. With this, we echo the ethnographic methods and findings of most of the chapters in this vol-ume. In a sense, Min's Mother was enacting a profoundly local project, one "embodied in specific social relations, established between specific people, situated in unequivocal localities, at historically determined times" (Guarnizo and Smith 1998:11). As Nicole Constable argues per-suasively in this volume and elsewhere (2003a), the meanings entailed in spatial, social, or marital mobility need to be locally and ethnographi-cally researched, not assumed (see also Small 1997, Manalansan 2003).

Chapter 7
Tripartite Desires: Filipina-Japanese Marriages and Fantasies of Transnational Traversal

Nobue Suzuki

In July 1998, a television documentary entitled *Regī no Futoude Hanjōki* (Prosperous stories of dependable Reggie), which portrayed the ambivalence in the life of a Filipina living in Tokyo, was aired in Japan. Reggie, the widow of a Japanese karaoke pub owner, raises her Filipino-Japanese daughter and toddler son alone by running the pub at night. She opens the pub at eight in the evening and closes it at one in the morning. Then she drives two hostesses home, and only after that can she eat her dinner and sleep. In the morning, Reggie's first-grade daughter eats and dresses by herself and announces to her sleeping mother that she is leaving for school. Reggie finally gets up at nine and, while attending to her tot, spends the morning doing piecework, tanning shoe leather for twenty yen (eighteen cents) per pair to augment her income. Although she is the sole breadwinner for her family of procreation, for years Reggie has also been a chief provider for her natal family in the Philippines, remitting 50,000–100,000 yen ($450–900) monthly. Her mother, who lives in the Philippines in a comfortable home built by her overseas daughters, comments on Reggie's life in Japan: "Of course, I'd love to live with them, but she is stable [in Japan]. Even if she works a little, she has money. Here in the Philippines, life is hard."

In the contemporary Philippines, where overseas employment has been a vital part of the state machinery to defuse political-economic problems, countless families have sustained themselves through material contributions made by overseas family members. By supporting their families, some migrants gain much respect from family members left behind and feel satisfied by fulfilling their familial obligations. On the other hand, Reggie's case shows one way in which Filipinas abroad try to assume multiple familial responsibilities in both Japan and the Philippines. Although she has to bear a tremendous burden, Reggie's hardship is barely recognized in her mother's words. Rather, by containing the Philippines within geoeconomic boundary through the use of such common markers as "here in the Philippines" (*dito sa Pilipinas*), the nouveau-riche mother engages in the popular Filipino imagining that those who live abroad are enjoying a good and leisurely life. This "stability" abroad, which is juxtaposed with the "hard life" in the Philippines, encodes the mother's imagination that Reggie, though a widow, has attained upward mobility through marriage, or hypergamy, as well as through her location outside of Philippine national borders.

This chapter examines the tensions between the lived realities of Filipinas married to Japanese and their Filipino families' fantasies about the women's presumed upward mobility through transnational marriage. These tensions and desires are further complicated by the imagined possibilities that the women's Japanese husbands project onto their marriages. The clash between lived realities and imaginations illustrated here is not merely psychological. Rather, it is situated in the processes of social reproduction and globalization, in which national and familial political economies, gender, and family values are undergoing transformation. Emerging values and fantasies of particular family arrangements in global economic contexts engender power relations within the family as "simultaneously kin relations of solidarity and capitalist relations of exploitation" (Creed 2000:344).

These paradoxical kin relations and fantasies arising from the uneven political-economic powers between Japan and the Philippines may have further impacts on the lives of Filipina wives and their Japanese partners in Japan, especially when time is taken into account. Navigating through the multiply intertwined yet disjunctive familial affections and economic conditions over time, some wives and couples begin to reconfigure alternative lifestyles for their futures that are unimaginable in Japan but that increasingly appear imaginable in the Philippines. Sustained by the women's affective-cum-material relations with their natal families, the women and their husbands differentially fantasize highly attractive and gendered retirement options of becoming "señoritas" in comfortable homes and "lords of their own castles" and of various businesses in their later years in the Philippines. Thus, Filipinas, who crossed national borders to realize varied degrees of upward mobility through marriage to Japanese for themselves and their natal families, find themselves, as in the case of Reggie, somewhat "down-marrying" in Japan, wrought by unexpected hardship. They subsequently plan, with their husbands, to recross national and class borders to return to the Philippines in search of comfortable lives in their old age.

Below, using data most intensively collected between 1995 and 1996 and in 1998, I ethnographically document how marriage migration and Filipina women's material power, or the lack thereof, have variously inflected upon themselves and their transnational families over time, greatly altering the ties among family members. I begin with a discussion of the idea of the Filipino family as a site of contestation among differentially positioned members who attempt to accumulate capital for personal, social, and economic purposes. These negotiations are simultaneously part of the processes of the formation of the postindustrial family and of social reproduction in the transnational terrain. Then I describe their consequences, focusing on the workings of imaginations among family members left in the Philippines in their relations to their female kin abroad. I also introduce ways in which Japanese husbands express their personal dreams in terms of gender, class, and national hierarchies. Their masculine fantasies often resonate with their Filipina wives' and in-laws' personal and familial desires. Subsequently, I delineate the apparent and nuanced ways in which imagined "up" and "down" positionings of intermarriage become sources of familial tensions and the ways in which they are accepted and negotiated by family members situated in different social and geoeconomic settings.

Persistent Values and the Transnational Filipino Family

In the Philippines, the family has been commonly identified as "a sacred entity" (Aganon 1994:79) and "the most important, the most cherished and the most durable institution" (Asis 1994:16). Medina describes such a family as sharing "financial and emotional aid, pooling of resources and sharing of responsibilities [to] keep the bond strong" (1991:17). Ideally, Filipino "strong family ties" are "reciprocal" and not "parasitic" (Castillo 1977:424), and family members enjoy "mutual love and respect" (Medina 1991:16). Within this structure, the family is a source of emotional gratification and psychological security (Medina 1991:51). Eldest daughters are considered to perform their roles as "second parents" most faithfully and to be satisfied by their contributions. Such relations assume geographical proximity so as to provide mutual and necessary task-based and affective support. Responding to this cultural ideal, the phrase "for the sake of the family" has been entrenched in Filipino migrants' vocabulary as one legitimate reason for overseas work or arranged marriage (F. Aguilar 1999; Pertierra 1992).

Scholars of contemporary families have complicated the notions of "durability" and localized arrangements of the family. Their questioning reflects the emergence of family relations that do not follow the ideals of form, content, lifestyle, or geographical proximity. This is especially true for people who live under great economic and monetary instability, social inequality, urbanization, and migration (Rebhun 1999). As the global economy increasingly disregards state borders, families originally located in economically weak countries have begun to maintain themselves transnationally (Basch et al. 1994). Amid these global capitalist relations, the Philippine state has, since the 1970s, facilitated labor migration of skilled and unskilled workers to help fill these economic needs. For "brain drain" professionals and other economically displaced Filipinos, overseas work has become a vital means of familial subsistence. By 2000, one-eleventh of the Filipino population (seventy-eight million) lived abroad and remitted $6 billion back home (Migration News 2002). Thus, the "durability" of the family needs to be re-situated in relation to these global political economic transformations.

The rise in transnational Filipino families, whose ties stretch to over 160 countries worldwide (Tyner 2002:65), has greatly altered the form and content of family ties among variously positioned members whose relationships have now become shaped by various social orders (see Collier and Yanagisako 1987, Stacey 1991). Parreñas (2001) suggests that these families undergo not only physical but emotional dislocation. Such difficulties often develop alongside discrepant gender expectations as women and men migrants may experience emotional dislocation differently. While gender ideologies construct men as providers, women, even if family providers, can hardly escape from their caring roles. Daughters and older sisters may continue to receive gender-based expectations from families back home. Such expectations tend to render manipulation culturally acceptable (Creed 2000:340). As women's earning power increases, their new role of family provider ironically incorporates material care into their maternal care. Parreñas (2001:chap. 5) thus identifies one of the serious consequences of the transnationalization of family life as the clash between new forms of family maintenance and the legacy of traditional family values. In the process, migrants are compelled to rework traditional ideologies of family life.

As Reggie's story exemplifies, rapidly de-territorialized family relations have engendered sites of competing values that are reinforced and negotiated between family members in different geoeconomic locations. Such competitions emerge in the gap between the under-expressed lived realities in Japan and fantasies about mobility abroad and about disadvantages inside the Philippines. In the next section, I discuss ways in which numerous Filipinos fantasize the concept of "abroad."

Global Fantasies

As the capital of economic globalization penetrates into all areas of the globe, the cultures of the modern and powerful also permeate individual lives everywhere. According to Appadurai, the process of cultural globalization "takes media and migration as its two major and interconnected diacritics and explores their joint effect on the work of the imagination as a constitutive feature of modern subjectivity" (1996:3). This is because images and information about faraway worlds offer a rich, ever-changing showcase of possible lifestyles (Appadurai 1996). As migrants' remittance money, gift packages, photos, and stories about their experiences—the negative side commonly downplayed—fill these showcases, they further stimulate imaginations about what happens in global urban centers (Basch et al. 1994, Hannerz 1996). As a result, those who stay behind may begin to see migrant family members as immediate and available resources for materializing their own imaginings of the possible improvised dispositions. Such fantasies take on political implications that come under negotiation between the "haves" and "have-nots" within the transnational family.

As noted above, Filipinos are no exception here. Especially since the 1970s (im)migrants have sent enormous amounts of money and goods to families in the Philippines out of their sense of actual economic needs and because of familial obligation, sacrifice, and guilt for being absent from everyday exchanges (Parreñas 2001). This prolonged practice of a transnationally sustained lifestyle has expanded the phantasms of Filipinos left behind about the good life to be had beyond Philippine national borders. This practice has been compounded by the visibility of foreign capital and symbols of modernity inside the Philippines.

Following the Filipino cultural logic of "abroad," marriage to foreigners may be considered an easy and secure entry to wealth, stability, and mobility. Marriage is "safe" because spouses' legal status, unlike that of contract workers, is guaranteed for a longer term and can potentially become a permanent form of transnational relocation. Compared with other types of labor migration such as domestic and entertainment work, women's marriage migration is, as del Rosario (1994) asserts, "moral" and "less risky" sexually, mentally, and physically, and it is consistent with gender and family ideologies and role assignments. Under Catholicism, it is also meant to last until death do they part. Although marriage in the Philippines, as elsewhere, is not always as secure or lasting as it is hoped to be (Chant and McIlwaine 1995:13, Constable 2003a, Suzuki 2002), this ideologically framed view radiates a rosy aura. Colored by the image of the foreigner as rich, even underprivileged Filipino men fantasize about becoming mail-order bridegrooms in America, although this route is available primarily to women (see Margold 1995:284). I now turn to how real and assumed ups and downs in marriage fluctuate in interactions between and in the desires of Filipino families in the Philippines, Filipina wives of Japanese, and Japanese husbands in Japan.

Filipino Families Imagining Japan and the Japanese

Although Philippine-Japan relations cannot be summarized in simple terms, Filipino images of Japan and the Japanese reflect inter- and postwar Philippine-Japan relations of militarism, neocolonialism, dictatorship, and the sexual subjection of Filipinas by Japanese men (Constantino 1989, Fujieda 2001:101). Since the 1970s, capitalist interests on both sides have formed a particularly important ground for Filipino imaginings of Japan. Japan is also the primary donor of official development assistance to the Philippines, providing billions of dollars through international financial and cooperation agencies (JICA 2001). Such aid has resulted in a commonly held idea about Japan, expressed by the mother of a Filipina married to a Japanese: "Japan has provided a huge amount of aid and built a gigantic bridge on the island of Leyte [central Philippines]. Japan is rich and accumulates so much wealth that they don't know what to do with it. So they'd dispose a ton of money [in a foreign country]" (Nakano 1999:154).

The movement of Japanese capital, tourists, and material goods also stimulates Filipinos' fantasies about Japan and the Japanese. Dinah, a twenty-year-old Filipina entertainer described her imagined "Japan" before working there in the mid-1980s: "There were lots of Japanese coming to Manila. I got used to seeing them. Cassette radios, cameras, color TVs and those things [are my "Japan/ese"]. . . . I thought there were money-bearing trees in Japan. . . . When you go to the black market, . . . the dollar and yen are really strong. America is far away. So naturally Japan is the place [to go for work]" (Jowan 1986:114). Dinah equates Japanese people with the Japanese state, currency, and goods. Prior to working in Japan, she also saw her sister bringing back a significant amount of money that she had earned there. Other Filipino families in the Philippines may as well imagine their daughters' and sisters' associations with Japan and the Japanese through these lenses.

Of course, Filipino families' understandings of the mobility of their female kin abroad cannot be uniform, especially when class is taken into account. As one of my wealthy Filipino friends in Manila commented, rich Filipinos would not want to give up privileges, such as having servants, by going abroad (see also F. Aguilar 1996, Vergara 1996). Many Filipina wives in Tokyo who come from better-off families in the Philippines have been materially supported by their families rather than the other way around. Yet Filipino imaginings today inevitably often revolve around the material mobility and wealth that are available abroad. When (felt) class differences between family members widen, those who identify themselves as "have-nots" desire more from those who are linked to "Japan." This is one point where family members and overseas members have come to grapple with the cultural notions such as *pakiki-sama* (mutual cooperation or familism) and "for luck to continue, good fortune must be shared" (Castillo 1977:430).

In the summer of 1998, I spent time with Belle's family in Manila. Belle was the joint owner with her husband of a small trading company in Tokyo and Manila. On various occasions, they hired her natal family members at these two locations, though not without considering their personal merits. Some of her siblings expressed bitterness about the tough decisions that their business-owner sister had made. For example, Belle's younger sister complained to me in exasperation, "If Belle had taken me to Japan, I would've been rich already! But she didn't give me the chance to work there!" Belle's youngest brother, Mike, was also unhappy about the "lack of support" from Belle. In 1993, Belle thought that Mike was not mature enough to run a business by himself and refused to provide the capital that Mike wanted to borrow from her. Five years later, when Belle saw that he had finally developed a sense of responsibility and shared his business connections with her, she hired him as the manager of her office in Manila. However, Mike claimed, "But I am only a caretaker and not the [real] manager [even though] I have the capability to run this business here! When I asked her for capital to start my own business, she turned me down. She has everything and wants more by keeping me under her!" A few years later, a frustrated Mike suddenly disappeared, leaving the office unattended.

Belle's siblings and relatives in the Philippines felt that Belle had breached the Filipino practice of mutual assistance and sharing of one's fortune. Belle's other more economically stable siblings did not seem to request favors from her, especially since they knew how hard she actually works to achieve her own financial stability. Yet the view of wealthy Japan/ese has been so pervasive that many Filipina wives of Japanese have to negotiate what they can actually offer and what their family members imagine about their marriages.

These cultural logics and fantasies about Japan and Japanese as well as the imagined deprivation and disparagement held by Filipino families in the Philippines underlie the hardships experienced by Filipinas in Japan described above. In some cases, the tensions have led to serious spousal and familial discord and (threats of) divorce among Filipina-Japanese couples.

Filipina Wives

As of 2002, Filipino registered residents numbered 169,359 in Japan, of which 141,557 (84 percent) were women (Ministry of Justice 2003). During the 1990s, Filipina-Japanese marriages constituted the second-largest group after Chinese in Japan among intermarriages in Japan where husbands are Japanese. In 2002, 45,510 Filipinos in Japan (27 percent) held "spouse-or-child" visas (treated as one category). Although the statistics do not give breakdowns by sex or spouse/child, over 90 percent of the holders of this visa are surmised to be wives.[1] Together with the holders of permanent and long-term visas, the number of Filipina spouses or former spouses in Japan is estimated to be around 87,000.[2]

As noted above, familial expectations spawn gaps between Filipino ideas about traditional gender roles and about the upwardly mobile life abroad, including marriage to a foreigner, on the one hand, and the lived realities of Filipina wives overseas, on the other. The two sides are not necessarily mutually exclusive but rather create coterminous zones of negotiation. The women's struggles are further complicated by their own desires, which move between their actual situations and their senses of caregiving and obligation. While they may feel burdened by the normative expectations of their families, the women themselves may also endorse ideologically sanctioned reciprocity from their families. This is especially so upon the women's homecoming visits and in their future plans, which are conversely affected by how well they can keep up with their assumed mobility by marriage.

Stories of Filipinas in Japan show the intricate consequences of these conflicting projects and prospects among family members. The consequences of the discrepant desires are not shared among all Filipina wives and are more real for those whose natal families are in working- and middle-socioeconomic strata than those in the upper strata in the Philippines. Hence, what follows are largely the experiences of Filipina wives in the former economic standings.

Jennifer

Jennifer, in her early forties in the late 1990s, is the eldest child of a working-class couple in rural Pangasinan. At age fourteen, despite her wish to continue her education, she was sent to Manila to work as a live-in maid, as her father had become unable to work because of an accident. Although there are Filipinas who almost completely embody the social construction of the eldest daughter as, in the words of another Filipina wife, "the one who always thinks and helps my parents," Jennifer has been ambivalent about her situation. By the late 1990s, she felt exhausted by her ascribed duties. Her relationship with her Japanese husband has also been constrained by her filial role.

In the early 1980s, Jennifer met her freelance engineer husband, Kishida, while working at a souvenir shop near the Manila International Airport. Prior to their marriage, Jennifer made her role in her natal family clear to him, insisting that marriage could not prevent her from supporting her family. Accepting her family role, Kishida and Jennifer married and moved to Japan. He initially remitted 50,000 yen monthly (approximately $170 in the early 1980s). A few years later, however, he felt as if he were married not to Jennifer but to her family. He was also annoyed by Jennifer's family's attitude toward his earnings. He told them that he was making 500,000 yen ($4,500) monthly, but that he and Jennifer really needed 600,000 yen ($5,400) to pay various expenses for their household and for his business. But Jennifer's family, he added, "stops listening at the point when they hear my income. They convert it into pesos and think that I'm rich. Really, our finances are in the red!" Kishida decided to terminate the remittances to his in-laws. Consequently, Jennifer began working as a babysitter and house cleaner so that she could send monthly remittance back home.

Jennifer has two sisters and two brothers, all of whom she sent to school, while suppressing her own educational aspirations. Three of her siblings became economically independent. Her brother Jes, for example, became a successful factory owner in Manila, with six employees and two maids. Jennifer felt ambivalent about her contribution to Jes's success: on the one hand, she was happy to see Jes doing well and repaying his financial debts to her; on the other hand, she lived in a small two-bedroom apartment in Tokyo, where her daughter and son shared a room. Sitting on a couch at Jes's home in Manila, Jennifer said, "he lives in a nice home and has two maids. Me, I'm working so hard, but we could never afford this kind of house in Japan."

Unlike the siblings who achieved financial independence, Jennifer's youngest brother, Butch, and their parents have not tried to earn an income and have continued to ask her for support. In 1992, aware of their hardship, Jennifer bought a piece of land near her parents' house where she let her parents and Butch plant rice with the hope that they would generate an income by themselves. Jennifer covered all the related expenses. Despite Jennifer's hopes, they consumed all the rice harvested instead of selling any of it at the market. Frustrated, Jennifer converted the paddy into an orchard a few years later for her personal investment and hired a nonrelative, Jose, to tend the farm. This act angered her parents and Butch and they had a serious dispute over Jennifer's land that lasted several years. Denied access to the land, an outraged Butch pointed a gun at Jose in 1997. In front of Kishida, Butch said that Jennifer and Jose were having an affair and that she had hired him for that reason. Fortunately, Butch did not shoot anybody, though he deeply hurt and enraged his sister and brother-in-law. In the same year, Butch also borrowed 10,000 pesos ($400) from Jennifer to start a *sarisari* (general) store in the front yard of their parents' house. However, in Jennifer's observation, none of the family members seemed to stay around to run the store. When I was there in 1998, I served as a messenger to Butch's wife, who often sat in the kitchen, far from the shop.

In 1998, while meeting to settle the land dispute, Jennifer's parents and Butch insisted that the traditional values of providing support for one's family be observed, saying, "If you're a family member, why don't you help your family? You are no longer a Filipino!" Butch also said that his siblings "are having a good life and only I live in this rural province. You must be looking down on me!" Although she receives little appreciation from her parents or Butch for her contributions, and although, unlike Jes, she has not achieved significant material success in Tokyo, Jennifer with "rich" Kishida is nonetheless imagined to be enjoying a good life in an urban center in Japan. Bitter about contributions she has made since childhood and reflecting on her marriage to Kishida, Jennifer stated that "once you are in Japan, then you can get a job. You also think in that way. By nature, eldest daughters are pitiful. Filipinos in the Philippines think that once we're abroad, we become rich. When I was a child, my mother did not even allow me to continue high school and made me a maid. I'm still a maid! I'm not picking gold up off the street!"

Other Filipina wives in Tokyo may express similar reasons for marital decisions and sentiments for their families. On occasion, they are caught between rival expectations of natal and affinal families. Noticing their wives' commitment to their natal familial duties, many husbands refuse to give their entire salaries to their wives because some women remit any "excess" in the family budget. Neneng, a Filipina wife in her mid-thirties in Tokyo, suffered her husband's wrath and threat of divorce because of the overuse of credit cards to support her natal family. For her parents, her siblings, and their twenty-three children, Neneng squeezed money out of her affinal family budget and personal allowance: she bought two passenger cars and a passenger tricycle for her natal family's subsistence. They later had to sell the vehicles and continued to rely on her, with little effort on their own part. Neneng says that her natal family assumes that she does not mind giving money to them because she is married to a Japanese. Many other Filipina women have also undergone serious spousal discord or divorce because of similar circumstances. Even under such pressure and unrealistic imaginings about their lives abroad, these

women's struggles bounce between their ambivalent feelings of obligation and constraint. As expressed by Neneng: "Where will they get
money if it's not from me? I hate myself. I can't say no. . . . I really can't
give up until when? Until I die!"

Millie

Millie, in her mid-thirties, was the child of a constabulary officer and his
mistress and lived separately from her maternal half-siblings. Stifled by
paternal overprotection, she sought freedom in her maternal brother's
home when she reached her mid-teens. Later, she had a boyfriend and
became a single mother (see Suzuki 2002:105–6 for details). In the mid-
1980s, in order to provide for her child, Millie went to Japan to work as a
dancer, leaving her child with her mother. There, she met her husband,
Sasaki, the owner of a booming real-estate firm, whom she married in
1989. According to Millie, he is, "nice and understanding. For instance,
I want to remit money regularly to my family in the Philippines. He
understands it really well and never complains about it. Even if I don't
mention it, he says, 'Oh, it's time to send the money.' He loves me, so
he loves my family."

Although she stopped working when she got married, when I interviewed her in 1996 Millie still remitted to her family in the Philippines
150,000 yen ($1,350) monthly, which she received from her husband. In
addition, her husband also gave her the same amount of money as a
personal monthly allowance that she could decide how to dispose of.
When Millie returns for visits to the Philippines, Sasaki gives her 500,000
yen ($4,500) as a cash gift in addition to money to buy souvenirs, which
constitute an important part of Filipino homecoming. These gifts have
significantly changed her status within her natal family. In the early
1990s, she built an imposing home in an exclusive subdivision in Manila
and housed her child, mother, and single-father brother, Bait, and his
children.

Though she is the youngest child, Millie has acquired much influence
over her family. After her family moved into the new house, Millie asked
Bait to stay at home, for security purposes, without working, even
though he could work as an engineer. When he has to work on the
house, he always consults Millie. When I was at her home in 1995 and
1998, Millie always sat at the head of the dining table and ate only with
the children and me, her guest, while her mother and Bait stayed
behind the kitchen wall watching to see if we would need anything. Clar-
ifying their relationship, Millie said: "Now, Bait lives in my house. Everything is mine. I respect him, of course. But about the house, I'm the
boss because the house is mine. . . . His earnings? He helps. He pays for

food. He also gives allowances to the children, including my child. . . .
In this house, everyone listens to me. Even if he says no, as long as I okay
it, that's it. So, for example, when the kids want to go to the disco and
Bait says no, they phone me [in Japan]. When I say, 'fine,' he can't say
anything." Indeed, after she started contributing to her natal family,
they began treating her differently: "They changed. When I come back
to the Philippines, they treat me well. While in Japan, I have to do everything. But if I need to get something done, they do it for me. I don't
have to do anything. I don't have to touch the water. It's like I'm the
president!"

In 1998, Millie gave birth to her second child. During the postpartum
period in the Philippines, if mothers can afford it they refrain from chill-
ing their bodies by doing dishes, laundry, and the like and instead have
female kin help. To increase what she calls her "presidential" comfort,
she had more helpers that year than I had previously seen. Prior to her
return, she phoned her own nursemaid Lou to come from a nearby
province to straighten up the house. Millie's cousin volunteered to baby-
sit the newborn. This cousin's teenage son was also at Millie's home in
case her teenage nieces needed a chaperone on social outings. These
helpers were well aware that Millie would respond generously to their
services. Lou, for example, enjoys a large weekly compensation of 1,300
pesos ($52) plus transportation fees for five days of work, whereas Mil-
lie's regular maids receive 1,500 pesos ($60) a month. The boy indeed
accompanied us to a posh disco, a middle-class treat that neither he nor
his mother could themselves afford.

Millie's popularity thus reflects her economic magnanimity and faith
in sharing. Millie and Sasaki have also brought her natal family a sense
of honor and pride among their relatives by serving as godparents for
ten children and couples at christening and wedding ceremonies. When
talking about Lou's son's recent wedding, where the couple also served
as godparents, a smiling Bait told me, "In the Philippines, the groom is
expected to pay for the wedding—the dresses, ceremony, and reception." With pride, he was implying that his sister had provided the necessary funds to honor the groom and, by extension, Millie's family, of
which he is a member. Conversely, Millie's contributions have been
reciprocated with signs of kin solidarity: her nieces now call her
"Mommy," rather than "Auntie," as their stated acknowledgment of
her support (see Parreñas 2001:111).

Having satisfied her natal family's material and cultural desires, Millie's marriage to a Japanese has now stirred more distant relatives' imaginations about her wealth and generosity. Prior to her homecoming,
Millie receives numerous letters from her relatives. Upon her return,
they may also visit Millie in their attempt to get her to "share" her for-

tune with them. In 1995, learning about Millie's arrival, one distant relative traveled for several hours to ask for money. Millie was visibly annoyed but the woman continued to try to pursuade Millie to give her several hundred pesos. After a few hours of negotiation, Millie finally rejected this request. She later complained, "Everyone thinks that because I'm married to a Japanese, I'm rich. No, I'm not! Japan's rich, but not the Japanese. Besides, everything costs so much in Japan, the housing, the food. . . . No, we aren't rich!" But there is no question whether or not she is not rich. She is.

Millie's altered financial status through her marriage to a Japanese is both a source of joy and a nuisance. It is a nuisance because candidate beneficiaries fantasize about Millie's bottomless wealth and benevolence. Millie comments on letters from her relatives: "I'm happy to read the first half of their letters, but I don't want to see the second half because it's usually a list of items that they want me to get from Japan." She also expressed her ambivalence; she actually enjoys all these guests—including neighbors and distant relatives—"fifty-fifty."

Millie's "presidential" comfort in the Philippines contrasts sharply with her life in Tokyo as an isolated urban housewife who is the sole caretaker of the home and a newborn and who receives practically no help or support from her husband's female kin or younger family members. Sasaki spends many hours outside their home for his business, with the telephone as the closest link to Millie. Under such circumstances, Millie feels that "I am only a maid as long as I am in Tokyo!" and so she finds occasions to return to the Philippines three or four times a year, which alternately offers a "presidential" paradise and an aggravating struggle over traditional values.

These Filipinas' lives are full of contradictions born of the discrepancies between imagined and real living arrangements that emerge in the trans-border terrain of intermarriage. Many Japanese husbands have been perturbed by their wives' natal family relations. Interestingly, other Japanese husbands seem to hold less conflicted ideas about their lives with Filipinas and about their in-laws in the Philippines. How, then, do these Japanese men situate themselves amid Filipino family values as well as in relation to their own personal desires? What conditions allow them to enjoy such values and relations?

Japanese Husbands and Family Ties

Because of their border-crossing nature, intermarriages everywhere tend to place intermarried individuals on the social margins. Men from the First World who marry women from the Third World are popularly considered to be nonelite, divorced, unattractive, violent males living in the "empty North" (Holt 1996). Similar stereotypes surround Japanese men married to Filipinas, and they are often considered to be farmers, blue-collar workers, and the like located in the bottom ranks of a masculine hierarchy and desirability (Suzuki 2003c). Otherwise, they are often assumed to have picked up Filipina prostitutes in the sex industry or to have purchased the women as their brides only to satisfy their sexual and social needs.

The prevailing views of the husbands and their intermarriages have largely ignored the men's individual situations within culturally and historically specific contexts as well as their personal desires for and in marriage.[3] For example, in Japan's body politic, though gradually thinning, heterosexual marriage (and subsequent procreation) continues to be the ticket to full-fledged adulthood, which grants men patriarchal privileges as well as "correct" male citizenship (Roberson and Suzuki 2003). This is because through marriage, men become legitimate procreators of the nation and supporters of their families and the state. However, when one's marriage is not "normative," this legitimacy crumbles. Some men seem to respond to this downgrading by trying to make their marriages appear as "conventional" as possible. They remain indifferent to their wives' and Filipino in-laws' desires for financial assistance, which can undermine the economic foundation of their nuclear families, where the men are the expected main pillars. Conversely, at the personal level, being able to help their wives' natal families may elevate other husbands' discursively lowered sense of masculinity.

In speaking of the reasons for being attracted to Filipinas, one man bragged, with an imperialist tone, about his imagined power: "If it is the Philippines, I can save the country!" Another man expressed patronizing desires to assist his wife, who "is so young, but supporting her entire family by sending remittances monthly. I've got to help her!" And another said, "Marrying a Filipina means taking care of her family in the Philippines! That's the way Filipinos think of their families!" At this moment, these men's and their wives' and in-laws' desires, though different in content, articulate with one another. When the men give support directly or indirectly to their Filipina wives and in-laws, their value increases within their respective Filipino families. If this is so, under what conditions can the men achieve this? An inquiry into Japanese men's family relations provides us with clues as to what situations enable, or are imaginable for, the men to participate in Filipino family romances.

As I discussed elsewhere (Suzuki 2003c), one dominant view of Japanese husbands of Filipinas has identified the men as being the eldest sons of their households, especially in rural farm communities. In order to sustain their households, communities, and, by extension, the nation, their gender and sibling rank have nailed them down to the culturally scripted roles of heirs (Suzuki 2003b:especially n. 71). Many of their urban counterparts, however, seem to have different notions about and relations with their natal families. Although studies of Japanese men's intimate ties with kin and friends, as well as studies of male gender performances as part of the transformation of Japanese families deserve serious academic attention in their own right, I briefly sketch out certain natal family relations among the Japanese men I interviewed, as these relate to possibilities for the men to develop their own global fantasies and desires. I start out with the men's sibling ranks and their expected role performances in family political economies and ancestor rituals.

Of the forty-three Japanese husbands whose sibling ranks were known to me, a majority were, as their stereotype describes them, the eldest sons of their respective families, and the remaining were second sons or below.[4] In spite of their familial position, only three men were the primary providers of a home and financial assistance to their (widowed) mothers. Ten other men gave partial assistance to parents living in separate homes or may assume this role in the future. Thus, most of the urban men I interviewed had no present need to support their parents financially on a regular basis. Their parents either had gainful employment or sufficient assets to support themselves.

In addition to family finances, successor sons in Japan are supposed to be responsible for their natal families' Buddhist altars and graveyards. Despite their traditional role, a small number of husbands had become devoted Christians. These men and all other husbands I talked with regarding these filial duties said that these are more ritualistic than mandatory and that they would perform them "ethically" while their elders are still alive. Some of the husbands, including one heir of the main house, added that "after all the elders' passing no one would know [how much care they are getting]." These men planned to spend much time in the Philippines in their later years.

The urban men's other family relations did not seem to be very close. Ogawa was antagonistic to his older and single brother, who did not accept his Filipina sister-in-law, Bea. Ogawa said that this was due to the pervasive negative images of Filipinas in Japan, although his parents were quite helpful to Bea. Mitarai, in his late forties, supports his mother but meets her only once or twice a year, even though she lives alone in an adjacent house.[5] Sasaki had not introduced his wife, Millie, to his widowed mother until seven years after their wedding, though Millie interacts with her stepchildren and some of Sasaki's siblings. Umezu did not seem to be close to his siblings. He felt particularly bitter about his younger brother, whom he sent to university and who, with this symbolic capital, became a manager of a leading company. Despite his social and economic ascendancy, the brother had not reciprocated Umezu's help. Instead, he relegated care of their mother to his eldest-son brother. Miura was one of the few husbands I knew who spent much time with his natal family and relatives living in close proximity. He and his wife and their children frequently visited Miura's natal family and took trips together.

A large majority of the Japanese husbands associated with their parents and siblings only during seasonal events—New Year holidays and Buddhist rituals—while physical and psychological distances and work seemed to keep them apart. Moreover, middle-aged and older people in Japan today, when asked in surveys, say that they try to live by themselves in later years. Otherwise, they enter nursing homes or ask their daughters—and not sons or daughters-in-law—for care (see Suzuki 2003a:chap. 7). To reduce its responsibilities for citizens' welfare, the Japanese state has recently been promoting "individual independence within the family" (see Ishii-Kuntz 2003). Although survey responses and state provisions are only ideals, this still relates to the situations of the Japanese men I interviewed who give care mostly to widowed mothers. Following this trend, these men's parents may not designate their sons, even if they are the eldest, and their Filipina wives to take care of them if they can afford an alternative mode of living.

All these situations enable urban men to enjoy greater freedom and spatial mobility. When their husbands are less bound to or defy their gendered, familial duties, the women's transnational wishes for their natal families may more easily come true. Their wishes are also often joined by their husbands' masculine imaginings and desires. How do such desires resonate with these women's embattled lives and into their futures? In the next section, I discuss how these family romances project into Filipina-Japanese couples' retirement plans.

Future Outlook: "Señorita Life" and "Lord of One's Castle"

Intermarried Filipinas have been rewarded for their contributions to their families by various degrees of respect from their natal family members. However, they still have to grapple transnationally with everyday hardships, contradictory consequences, and continuing (unreasonable) expectations if they want to retain their future kin solidarity. In the case of migrant Filipina domestic workers, they try to overcome such paradoxes through what Parreñas (2001:172–74) calls the "fantasy of reversal," in which they hope for an increased class status upon their return to the homeland. Thus, domestic helpers in Rome aspire to dislocate their downward class mobility abroad by relegating all the dirty work to their maids upon return to the Philippines. They say, "I will not lift my finger and I will be the signora" (Parreñas 2001:173). Millie's "presidential" life at her spacious home in Manila represents this fantasy among Filipina wives from Japan.

Likewise in Japan, Grace, a Filipina wife of a Japanese, exhausted by the double burden of running both home and a branch of her affinal family's meat shop on her own for six or seven days a week, longs for "a comfortable life. I want to enjoy a señorita's life (*senyorīta no seikatsu*)." This is especially true for women like Grace who were petit señoritas coming from asset-owning families or who had prestigious occupations before bartering socially downgrading jobs abroad for upward economic mobility and for other reasons. Grace's use of the term "señorita" rather than "señora" (or signora, in Parreñas's study) reflects her awareness of a lost youth, spent frying croquettes and scraping off excess meat and fat from the pig bones that she sells to noodle shops. Under what circumstances can these women envision a "señorita life" as a form of the fantasy of reversal?

Unlike Millie, who leads a double life in geographically separated homes, many Filipina wives in Japan fantasize that the improvement of their lives in Japan will happen in the Philippines after they have prepared their children for independent lives and during their retirement. They expect the undisturbed practice of the traditional cultural norm in the Philippines whereby the elderly are well taken care of by their children (Medina 1991). Millie describes how her grandmother was treated: "Everyone took care of her. So we never send grandmas to the nursing home." With her strong influence on her natal home, Millie expects to permanently resettle in the Philippines after her husband retires and to enjoy her "presidential" life until her death, as her grandmother did. Although she is sometimes critical of Filipino relationships where people are always asking for help—and paradoxically because of such relationships, where she invests in her kin's sense of indebtedness (*utang na loob*) to her—Millie, as an acknowledged "mommy," can more easily anticipate traditional elderly care.

Yet when the women's resources have been constantly siphoned off or when they lead an unexpectedly hard life through migration, they may have to project a different future for themselves. As described above, Neneng agonizes that she will contribute to her natal family "until I die!" instead of enjoying a "señorita" life. How are Neneng and other women preparing for their old age? Many Filipina wives in Tokyo predict that their children, growing up in Japanese social and economic environments where children cannot or will not easily provide care for their parents, will eventually leave them. Observing their husbands' relations with their own natal families, many women can project only a gloomy picture about what they can expect in their later years. If that happens, will the women's natal families reciprocate with their sisters by faithfully observing traditional cultural tenets?

For Jennifer and Neneng, marriages to Japanese and struggles to satisfy their families' imaginings bring them only dim futures in spite of the persistent Filipino ideal about old age. Neneng flatly rejects such an idea: "If you have money in the Philippines, all your relatives will take care of you. Don't go home if you don't have money!" Jennifer, on the other hand, now sometimes skips visiting her natal home when returning to the Philippines. For their preparation for retirement, she seeks land outside her province, but still on the island of Luzon, in order to keep some distance from her natal family. For these women, the traditional value of mutual sharing has drained too many resources from their hard work. Even though Jennifer enabled her brother to enjoy upward mobility, her parents and Butch felt that she was not doing enough for them. These women have been "unwilling" to keep up with their families' fantasies about the "true" Filipina daughter/sister and upward mobility through intermarriage. Ironically, another cultural value—of elderly care—seems to discipline Jennifer and Neneng. For them, the effects of this familial imagination constrain and nullify the women's fantasies of reversal.

As in Parreñas's notion of the fantasy of reversal, transnational traversals of men are highly gendered and classed (Margold 1995, Nonini 1997). Some Japanese husbands imagine different futures from their wives in their relations to their in-laws and the Philippines. The lure of family romances for these men may begin with their relative power fantasized through their gender and nationality and through new patterns of consumption and desire in the Philippines. To be men in Japan means to be family providers first to their nuclear families and possibly to their extended families. If they provide assistance to their in-laws, they may also invest in their wives' relationships with their natal families. As seen in Millie's case, this enables the women to gain much power in family politics and restore the practice of elderly care in the Philippines. Through their assistance to their in-laws, Japanese husbands fantasize about their increased value within Filipino families. Thus, one husband stated some merits of marrying a Filipina and retirement in the Philippines: "I can live in leisure in the Philippines with the interest of my savings in Japan for the rest of my life. When I permanently settle there, I will enjoy feeling like a lord for the rest of my life. . . . Even when I become an ugly old man [*jijī*], my Filipino family will take care of me. In Japan, I only have my pension money to depend on" (Tamagaki 1995:102).

Thus, a leisurely life is imaginable in the Philippines—but not among

Filipinos abroad—for working-class, and even middle-class Japanese men now living under Japan's troubled economy and deteriorating welfare schemes; a lordly retirement appears to be possible in a developing country. As one husband put it, "We can't afford 'my home' [*mai hōmu*] in Japan and so we buy a house [in the Philippines]. Prices of land and goods are one-tenth [of the cost]. We can enjoy a dream that we can't achieve otherwise." Marriage to Filipinas incites Japanese masculine imaginaries of being the "lords of their own castles" (*ikkoku ichijōno aruji*), receiving their Filipino in-laws' caregiving during their old age but outside their original national boundary. Furthermore, aside from the examples of successful Filipina wives, such "traditional" family values and lifestyles are guaranteed by the Philippine Retirement Authority (PRA). One PRA brochure states that Japanese retirees will be welcomed with the Filipino "natural national character, respectful of the elderly" and that for foreigners, the Philippines will require only "low living costs and medical fees, and excellent services."

Besides homeownership and comfortable retirement, Japanese men fantasize futures that upgrade their social standing through business ownership and philanthropic activities. For example, after retiring in the Philippines, Kurama hopes to open a jazz club and to obtain a soccer field where neighborhood children can play this still-unfamiliar sport for free. Umezu plans to operate a supermarket, restaurant, and rice-threshing house to supplement his Japanese pension while in Pampanga. Toyoda spoke passionately of his plan to establish casino and bar businesses targeting Japanese tourists. These men are aware that many Japanese have failed and lost all of their capital as well as their relationships in the Philippines (see Hama 1997), where land and business ownership by foreigners alone is not legally permitted. Nevertheless, for them the Philippines is still a place in which to materialize their dreams, especially when the fantasy of reversal is not easily achievable in high-cost Japan. Hence, popular and ethnic magazines as well as Web sites circulate information about various opportunities in the Philippines for Japanese men stirring up their fantasies of becoming owners of homes and businesses in this developing country.

Through Japanese men's desires for economic, social, and masculine capital in the Philippines, their wives and in-laws can also imagine upward mobility and secure lives. This suggests that as long as there is a huge discrepancy in political-economic power between Japan and the Philippines such inequalities will continue to influence the differentially deployed dreams of Filipinas, Filipino families, and Japanese men. As long as this is the case, such desires will continue to circulate and compete. Prospective Filipina brides hope that Japanese men will be rich, potential candidates for upwardly mobile marriages while their families fantasize that these women as daughters and sisters will provide a good life once they arrive in the "money-bearing" country.

Conclusion

I have illustrated the ways in which Filipina wives and their Japanese husbands and Filipino families each in discrete geoeconomic and gendered positionings imagine and desire one another's contributions and commitments to affinal and natal families over time. Treating the Filipino family and its values as unchanging entities eclipses the fact that their existence articulates with processes of global social reproduction and forecloses internal divisions, contradictions, and power relations. Discrepant conceptualizations of members within a family spawn tensions and felt differences in class standing, especially in families now sustained through material and affective exchanges situated within the rapid expansion of global capitalism and consumerism. Familial solidarity possibly metamorphoses into the exploitation of family values and family members' material and affective contributions.

In this context, the Filipino cultural logic of "abroad," characterized by its affluence and leisure, feeds internal struggles. Filipina-Japanese marriages imagined as a fast lane to upward mobility articulate with the Filipino fantasy of life abroad and with the women's initial and continuing desires for the welfare of their natal families. Upon marriage, these improvised visions of imagined possibilities quickly clash with the discipline of traditional values such as family cooperation and the daughter/sister role. The economic value of family commitments and of success that the women are assumed to embody over time further reinforces and expands family-focused sentiments among natal extended family members. The women's material power gained through marriage, or the lack of it, seriously affects their roles and status within their natal families as well as their future fantasies of reversal in old age.

Significantly, Japanese husbands' national, gendered, and classed desires and fantasies about their marriages play an important role. Taking advantage of the huge discrepancies in the value of the Philippine and Japanese currencies, the men's masculine desires to help their wives and, by extension, their in-laws resonate with the Filipino imaginaries. The men's dreams of and success in becoming "lords of their own castles" or business owners potentially spur desires for and fantasies about Filipina-Japanese marriages among both Filipina women and Japanese, as well as inciting the family struggles and negotiations.

Given all this, we must ask for whom the marriages discussed here are "hypergamous." The Filipinas? Their Japanese husbands? Or the Filipino families? I hope my ethnographic descriptions have shown that the interconnected locations of intermarriage and individual positions therein must be seen in the process of their formations and within particular personal, familial, national, and global contexts. Neither one's gender, generational or sibling rank, class, nationality, or geoeconomic location serves as a clear indicator of "up" or "down" within the context of the transnationalization of family relations and in marriage across national borders.

Chapter 8
Clashing Dreams in the Vietnamese Diaspora: Highly Educated Overseas Brides and Low-Wage U.S. Husbands

Hung Cam Thai

Hours before her husband's plane was due, Thanh Nguyen[1] and about thirty of her family members and kin anxiously waited outside of Tan Son Nhut, Saigon's international airport.[2] Thanh's family was understandably excited. For many families expecting a relative or close friend from the Vietnamese diaspora, the waiting is an event in itself. More often than not, they come to the airport long before the plane is due, creating such a commotion outside that it is difficult to follow any one conversation. As I watched and listened like a waiter at a busy restaurant, intently but discreetly, I could make out only fragments of conversations among people of a culture known for making sure: "Make sure you greet him properly," adults told young children. "Make sure the restaurant knows we are coming," men reminded women. And, of course, "Make sure you always show him love and respect," Thanh's parents reminded their thirty-two-year-old daughter.

The Nguyens were prudent people. Although they knew Thanh's husband, Minh, well—he had made the long journey across the Pacific from his home in Quincy, Washington, three times during the past year—they wanted him to feel welcome and important each time he visited. Their instinct was a good one: when I visited him in Quincy, ninety miles from Seattle, the thirty-seven-year-old Minh revealed to me that he often did not feel important or respected in the small suburban town where he lived. Seattle is one of the most heavily Vietnamese-populated cities outside of Vietnam. Thanh's husband is one of the more than two million Viet Kieus, or Vietnamese people living overseas, who make up an aging diaspora that largely began emigrating in the mid-1970s.[3] He is also one of over a million Viet Kieus who returned to visit family and friends during 2000, a dramatic increase from the 160,000 who did so in 1993 (Nhat 1999).

Thanh will soon join Minh in Quincy as one of over 200,000 women and men worldwide who come to the U.S. each year through legal marriage migration.[4] Women currently make up more than 65 percent of all marriage migrants. While male marriage migrants make up about a quarter of all men who enter the U.S. each year, female marriage migrants make up over 40 percent of all women who enter (USDOJ-INS 1999a, USDOJ-INS 1999b).[5] It is no news that females have dominated in U.S-bound migration since the 1930s (Houstoun et al. 1984) and that, historically, more women than men have migrated as spouses (Thornton 1992). However, despite the fact that marriage remains the number-one reason that people migrate to the U.S. (Rumbaut 1997), we know very little about specific contemporary marriage migration streams or about why women overwhelmingly dominate them.[6] What we do know about marriage migration is the highly publicized, and often sensationalized, phenomenon of commercialized mail-order brides (Foote 1991, Glodava and Onizuka 1994, Halualani 1995, Langevin and Belleau 2001, Robinson 1996, Tahmincioglu 2001); though an important part of the female international marriage migration puzzle, such women constitute at most 4 percent of all marriage migrants.[7]

During fourteen months of fieldwork done in phases in Vietnam and in the United States from 1997 to 2001, I got to know couples like Minh and Thanh. In addition to understanding their distinct national and local cultures, I paid particular attention to some of their most private matrimonial thoughts—thoughts that they have not yet disclosed to each other. For they are in a migration waiting period, a period in which the women are waiting to be united with their husbands through migration. In this distinct and emergent global marriage market, the immigrant Vietnamese men typically go to Vietnam to marry through arrangement and subsequently return to their places of residence in the Vietnamese diaspora (most are from the United States, Canada, France, and Australia) to initiate paperwork to sponsor their wives. During this waiting period, I came to know them by first entering the lives of the brides in Vietnam and later the U.S.-based grooms.[8]

The marriage of Minh and Thanh follows a global trend that has been gathering momentum over the past forty years: immigrant and immigrant-origin men are more and more frequently seeking wives in their countries of origin. An estimated two-thirds of all marriage migrants are of the same ethnicity, and among migrants who come to the United States married to noncitizen permanent residents (presumably immigrants), almost 90 percent are women (USDOJ-INS 1999a).[9] Like many international marriages between same-ethnic individuals, especially in Asia, the marriage of Minh and Thanh was arranged. Marriage arrangements come in many forms, and I have addressed this elsewhere (Thai 2003). What Minh and Thanh represent is a specific and fairly typical pattern: the marriages of the two "unmarriageables," namely, of highly educated women in Vietnam to overseas Vietnamese men who do low-wage work.[10]

Globalization and Marriage Squeezes Across the Vietnamese Diaspora

In this project, I attempt to capture dynamics of "globalization from below," an approach prompted by earlier research on "globalization from above" (Schiller et al. 1992, Constable 1997, 2003a, and 2003b, Guarnizo and Smith 1998, Portes, Guarnizo, and Landolt 1999). Before I began this study, I was fully aware that Vietnamese people worldwide are pressed by what demographer Daniel Goodkind (1997) calls the "double marriage squeeze," a unique situation in the worldwide marriage market for any ethnic or cultural group. A high male mortality rate during the Vietnam War, combined with the migration of a larger number of men than women during the past quarter of the twentieth century, has produced a low ratio of men to women in Vietnam, as well as an unusually high ratio of men to women in the Vietnamese diaspora, especially in Australia and in the United States. A shortage of one sex or the other in the age group in which marriage generally occurs is often termed a marriage squeeze (Guttentag and Secord 1983). The Vietnamese double marriage squeeze specifically refers to the low ratio of males to females in Vietnam and the unusually high ratio of males to females in the Vietnamese diaspora, especially in Australia and the United States. Of the fifteen most populous nations in 1989, Vietnam had the lowest ratio of men to women at the peak marrying ages. By 1999, there were approximately ninety-two men for every hundred women between the ages of thirty and thirty-four in Vietnam. The reverse situation prevails in the diaspora: in 2000, there were 129 Vietnamese-American men for every hundred women between the ages of twenty-four and twenty-nine. Among Vietnamese Americans aged thirty to thirty-four, there were about 135 men for every hundred women.[11]

These numbers are important. They tell us that, given the severely skewed sex ratios resulting in the dramatic shortage of marriageable women in the Vietnamese diaspora and, to a lesser extent, the shortage of marriageable men in Vietnam, there is a good reason that men would return to their home country for wives. But while the numbers are significant, they tell only part of the story. The link between demographic numbers, intensified transnational and global processes in Vietnam and worldwide, new contours of kinship, and the intersection of gender and class in marriage markets throughout the Vietnamese diaspora provides a much more in-depth look at social processes involved in the emergence of a Vietnamese transpacific marriage market.

Those who study marriage markets have long documented a nearly universal pattern, called the "marriage gradient," whereby women tend to marry men who are older, better educated, and higher earning than they are, while men tend to marry younger women who earn less money and have less education (Fitzgerald 1999). Men "marry down" economically and socially; women "marry up." Transnational couples like Minh and Thanh, however, seem to reverse the marriage gradient. But depending on the measure one uses in the marriages I studied, it is difficult to tell who is really marrying up, and who down. Thanh belongs to an emerging group of highly educated women in Vietnam who have delayed or avoided marriage with local men. These women have found that too few men in Vietnam are employed and successful relative to themselves. More important, in the eyes of many men influenced by traditional Asian and Confucian hierarchies of gender, age, and class, a highly educated woman like Thanh is unmarriageable. As with highly educated African American women in the United States, there is a surfeit of women like Thanh in Vietnam relative to their educated male counterparts. Minh, on the other hand, belongs to a surfeit group of Viet Kieu men, accumulated in part by the scattering of postwar Vietnamese migration, who are unable to find marriage partners partly because they are low-wage workers. Some of these men, though certainly not all, experienced tremendous downward mobility as they migrated overseas after the Vietnam War.

In my study of sixty-nine Vietnamese transpacific marriages, 80 percent of the men were low-wage earners like Minh. These men generally work for hourly wages, though some work in ethnic enterprises where salaries are negotiated "under the table." For the most part, they work long hours for low pay. In contrast, almost 70 percent of the brides are women like Thanh, who are college-educated, about 40 percent of whom have advanced degrees, which permit them to work as doctors, lawyers, computer programmers, and the like. Of my entire sample, about 55 percent were marriages between these two "unmarriageables."[12] They are unmarriageable along both gender and class lines. Statistically, because of the double marriage squeeze, there is simply a surfeit of women relative to men in Vietnam and a surfeit of Viet Kieu men relative to Viet Kieu women overseas. But their unmarriageability does not end there. If the demography of the double marriage squeeze is a structural condition propelling these transpacific marriages, the cultural belief in the marriage gradient is perhaps a more powerful force driving these marriages. Vietnamese women and men worldwide have not dared to break the marriage-gradient norm in their local marriage market. Many Vietnamese, including the unmarriageables themselves, believe that by making these unorthodox matches transnational ones, they somehow get around the discomfort of breaking the marriage-gradient norm. It is as though despite their relative incomes and education, if the man is from a First World country, he has the "up," while a woman from Third World Vietnam has the "down." And though it is no surprise that the economic divide between the First World and Third World deeply penetrates the private lives of Vietnamese transpacific couples, it is not always clear who has the Third World life in marriages of the two unmarriageables.

While reaching out overseas seems a perfect solution to the double marriage squeeze, it gives rise to an unanticipated collision of gender ideologies in 90 percent of these couples. The reason is that the dreams that led both partners into the arrangement often had as much to do with gender as with economic mobility. Educated women like Thanh hope that a man living overseas in a modern country will respect women more than men do at home, who may still be in the sway of ancient Vietnamese traditions. Low-wage workingmen like Minh, meanwhile, often look to women in Vietnam precisely because they wish to uphold those ancient traditions, which they believe have been eroded in modern industrialized countries like the United States, but which they expect a woman in Vietnam will maintain. In their search for spouses, both parties have relied to some extent on tradition, which leads them to agree to a marriage arranged by family members. But it is the new globalizing culture of Vietnam that makes the transnational match possible. In 1986, after having had no contact with the outside world for over a decade, the Vietnamese government adopted a new economic policy known as *doi moi*. It did not end state ownership, but encouraged private enterprise, free markets, and global engagement. In the 1990s, Saigon was reemerging as a major international city, first within the Asian landscape and soon to the rest of the world. At the time, Vietnam was in the news and was projected to be one of Asia's next "tigers" (Pierre 2000). Recognizing an enticing labor and consumer market of eighty million people, foreign companies were eager to move their factories there and make their products known.

Globalization rapidly opened impersonal markets of capital, goods, and labor, and in conjunction with these markets, it also opened a rather personal market of emotions and marriages. But unlike two-way flows of capital and goods, the divide between the First World economy of the West and the Third World economy of Vietnam makes it impossible for women in Vietnam to go abroad for grooms, but very easy for men to go to Vietnam for brides. There are related impediments, put forth by a global inequality rooted in historical, political, and economic relationships between nations-states, for Vietnamese and other migrants from developing countries who wish to seek employment overseas. Like global corporations and factories that recently moved to Vietnam because of its large supply of labor, Viet Kieu men go there for brides because there is a much larger selection of marriage partners. However, unlike locals who eagerly work at foreign factories mainly for the monetary rewards, Vietnamese transpacific brides have a wide range of reasons for choosing to marry Viet Kieu men.

The Highly Educated Bride

Twenty years ago, Thanh's father was a math teacher at Le Buon Phong, a prestigious high school in Saigon. After the war, Thanh's uncle, her mother's younger brother, and his family were among the thousands of Vietnamese who were airlifted out of Vietnam on April 30, 1975, when Saigon surrendered to North Vietnamese military troops. They eventually settled in Houston, one of the larger Vietnamese enclaves in the U.S., and started a successful restaurant business specializing in *pho*, the popular Vietnamese beef noodle soup. Remittances from Thanh's uncle helped her parents open a small candy factory in the late 1980s, which now has over forty employees. Thanh's parents belong to a small but visible class of Vietnamese families who enjoy access to overseas resources. They are part of a Viet Kieu economy that has grown from roughly $35 million in 1993 to an estimated $2 billion in 2000 (Pierre 2000).

Thanh was only seven years old when Saigon fell. She is not as old as Minh, whose memory of the war is very strong and formative; nor is she able to put that era completely behind her, like her peers born after the war, who are eager to move forward and to join the global economy. She embraces foreign influences and appreciates the access she has to them. Many of her friends work in foreign companies as translators, or in marketing or sales; some have become local branch supervisors of international corporate offices such as Citibank and IBM. Nevertheless, Thanh is conscious that her parents have sustained hidden injuries from accepting remittances from her uncle in Houston, and this saddens her. She observes:

My father is a very strong man; nobody ever tells him what to do with his life, like how to raise his children. But I think it is very hard for him when he has to deal with my uncle. My uncle is a very nice man, and he cares a lot for our family. But even though he's younger than my mother, his older sister, he doesn't respect my father. He thinks my father has to listen to him about everything, like how to run his business. When he comes back to Vietnam, he always tries to change the way my dad runs things. And my father always defers to him. He feels that because my uncle helped him financially to open up the candy factory, he has to do everything my uncle says. I know he feels very embarrassed and humiliated, but would never tell anyone about it.

Thanh's family is not alone in its discomfort with receiving money from abroad. Remittanceships create social inequality and stress between givers and receivers, and even greater inequalities between receivers and non-receivers in the same community. Nonetheless, Thanh knows that she owes the lifestyle she enjoys at least partly to her uncle's remittances. After all, the average salary for Saigonese lawyers, according to Thanh, is a little over two million Vietnamese dong (VND), or $150 per month, whereas the net profit of her father's candy factory averages close to VND 900 million a year. Thanh earns about VND 2.5 million a month as a part-time lawyer in a small firm that handles legal contracts of all sorts. Although her salary is six times the standard income of the average worker in Saigon, it is still low on a global scale. But the remittances that gave her parents' business an advantage have also enabled Thanh, an only child, to have a greater than average degree of educational and social mobility. She has been able to obtain a good high school education, to study law, and to take lessons at international English schools in Saigon.

Most of Thanh's peers married soon after high school, but Thanh and a small group of her female friends from Le Buon Phong high school decided to continue their schooling instead. Of her seven close female friends from high school, only one did not go to college, choosing instead to marry early. The rest, including Thanh, quietly built professional careers. Most went into fields traditionally reserved for women, including education and nursing. Two pursued advanced degrees. Thanh obtained a law degree, while her friend became a prestigious physician at Vinh Bien, a private hospital catering to Saigon's middle class. Four of the seven, now in their early thirties, remain single. At the time of this writing, there are no available data on the extent of delayed marriages across class and educational levels in Vietnam. But if the paths of Thanh and her four friends who chose singlehood are any indication, a quiet gender revolution is taking place among highly educated Vietnamese women. These women have opted for singlehood in a culture where marriage is not only presumed, but often coerced. Women and men who have not yet married at the "appropriate" age are often dismissively referred to as "*e,*" or unmarketable. In contrast, women (often young and beautiful) and men (often educated and financially secure) who fare well on the marriage market are considered "*dat,*" or scarce goods. As Thanh explained to me, "I am already *e* in Vietnam. You know, at thirty-two here, it's hard to find a decent husband. I knew that when I decided to get a good education that many men would be intimidated by me here. But it was important to me to get an education, even though I know that for women, marriage is more important. In Asian cultures, and maybe especially Vietnam, the men do not want their wives to be better than them. I think for me it's harder, too, because my parents are successful here, so on the outside [to the outsider] we are very successful."

In truth, Thanh is not completely *e*: several men, sometimes with their families, have come to propose marriage to her. Arranged marriages remain common in Vietnam, although they are more common in villages than in urban areas. Young couples who marry by arrangement are susceptible to significant difficulties if class differences divide their families (Belanger and Hong 1996, Hirschman and Loi 1996, Kibria 1993, D. Tran 1991, Wisensale 1999). Individual and family success can make a Vietnamese woman, particularly if she has passed the socially accepted marriageability age, unmarriageable. Thanh had several proposals for marriage arrangements when she was in her mid-twenties, before she got her law degree, from men who wanted to marry down. Now she is thirty-two and educated; she believes that marrying up is no longer an option, since there are few available men in that category. Although she has many suitors of lesser means and education than herself, Thanh explains that she does not find marrying down to be an appealing prospect: "When I look up, there are few men 'up there' whom I could see as suitable husbands. But those men, the few men I know who have more education and who are more successful than I am, usually want to marry young, beautiful women. To them, I am now too old. The backward thing about life is that the men below are very unappealing. And, of course, there are many of them! There are many, many non-quality men I could choose from, but that's what they are—non-quality."

Thanh's marriage procrastination was partially anchored in her confused class and gender status. Her upward mobility puts her at the top locally, but globally, she is at the bottom, since Vietnam has low status among nations. In a traditional marriage, her husband must be the household's provider; but given that she is marrying a low-wage worker, she may end up being the one to seek economic security through her own means. Yet marrying a low-wage worker overseas looks attractive to Thanh because she knows that in Vietnam, her high educational status will not help her escape the gender subordination of marital life. She can think of few men she knows in Vietnam who show respect to their wives. On our third and final interview, Thanh and I walked along the

Saigon River. It was early evening, and the city skyline loomed in the near distance, separated from us by the cacophony of countless motorcycles, cyclos, and taxis. Disconsolately, Thanh explained: "In Vietnam, it is hard being single, female, and old. People will criticize and laugh at you. People always ask me, 'Where are your husband and children?' And when I think about that, I realize that I have two choices. I can marry a man in Vietnam who is much less educated and less successful than I am, whom I will have to support and who will likely abuse me emotionally or physically or dominate me in every possible way. Or I can marry a Viet Kieu man. At least Viet Kieu men live in modern countries where they respect women."

Ultimately, what Thanh wants in a marriage partner is someone who will respect her and who will not seek to control her the way she sees so many Vietnamese men control their wives. As she told me: "If I found a nice man 'below' me whom I could marry, he wouldn't want to marry me because he's afraid that I'll take control of the house or that if anything goes wrong in the marriage, I could turn to my family for help. Most men in Vietnam want to control their wives, they want their wife to be subordinate even when she is more successful and educated. That leaves me with very few choices in Vietnam, you see, because I for sure don't want a man to take control of me."

The Low-Wage Working Groom

If Thanh's desire for respect stems from her upward mobility, her husband's parallel desire has everything to do with his downward mobility. Minh, whose hands, facial expressions, and graying hair make him seem older than his thirty-seven years, was the only member of his family to leave Vietnam during "Wave II" of the boat refugee exodus that took place after the war (Zhou and Bankston 1998). As the eldest son, he was vested with a special status and with a good deal of responsibility for his six siblings. Both of his parents were teachers of philosophy at Le Buon Phong, where they have known Thanh's parents for many years. Today, three of Minh's sisters are teachers, and his two brothers are successful merchants in Saigon.

In 1985, at the age of twenty-one, Minh was a man of intellectual ambition and curiosity. He had just completed his third year of engineering school when his parents asked him if he wanted to go to America. They didn't know anyone overseas at the time, but they knew of several people, among the many hundreds of thousands of "Boat People" who had fled and safely reached a Western country. Of those who successfully made the trip, over 90 percent eventually settled in France, Australia, Canada, or the U.S. (Merli 1997). Minh's parents also knew that as many as half of the refugees on any given boat did not succeed. They died along the way because of starvation, pirate attacks, and often, in the case of women and children, the combination of rape and murder en route to a refugee camp. Many were also caught by the Vietnamese government and severely punished with long prison sentences. Nevertheless, Minh's parents were confident that he would survive and find a better life abroad. They spent their entire life savings to put him on one of the safest and most reputable boats run by private individuals, to leave the Mekong Delta for Western lands of opportunity. Those boats and their routes via refugee camps in Southeast Asia were a carefully guarded secret in Vietnam, and they were accessible only to wealthy or well-connected families. Being caught by government officials could lead to severe punishment. Many who were not wealthy, like Minh's family, managed to pool resources so that one person, usually a son, could go. They saw this as an investment, which they made with the hope that it would yield high returns.

Today, Minh considers himself one of the lucky ones who left. After surviving two years—a lifetime to Minh—in a refugee camp in Malaysia, he was selected in 1987 for entry to the United States. Many people he met at the camp ended up in less desirable places, such as Finland, Belgium, or Hungary. Back then, as now, the United States was the top-choice destination, followed by Canada, France, and Australia. Minh arrived in rural Wyoming under the sponsorship of a local Catholic church. Like many of the American churches that sponsored Indochinese refugees from the late 1970s to the mid-1990s, Minh's church sponsored only one person (Zhou and Bankston 1998). He spent the first five years of his new life as the only person of color in a rural town in Wyoming, the name of which he doesn't even want to remember. Like many Vietnamese refugees of the past three decades, Minh decided to migrate a second time. He wanted to go to Little Saigon, the most highly concentrated Vietnamese enclave outside of Vietnam, located in a seemingly quiet Los Angeles suburb, though today plagued by urban problems reported regularly by the media (Leonard and Tran 2000a and 2000b, Marosi and Tran 2000). But he had little money and no connections in or around Los Angeles. Then one day, in one of the Vietnamese-produced newspapers in the U.S. that flourished following the influx of refugees, Minh read about a Chinese restaurant called the Panda Garden that needed dishwashers. Unfortunately, it was not in Los Angeles but in a small town called Quincy, ninety miles from Seattle. Minh heard that Seattle also had many Vietnamese people, and he thought a move there would bring him closer to other refugees.

Eleven years later, Minh still lives in Quincy and works at the Panda Garden. He is now a deep-fryer and an assistant cook, which is several steps up from the dishwashing position he was first given. Although to him, an assistant cook carries less stigma than a dishwasher, it is far from the engineering career he envisaged in his premigration years. His responsibilities include helping the main cook with various kitchen tasks and making sure that the restaurant has a constant supply of egg rolls and wontons. Though known as one of the best and most authentic ethnic restaurants in town, the Panda serves a mainly "white American" clientele that, according to the owners, probably wouldn't know the difference between authentic Chinese food and Sara Lee frozen dinners.

Quincy is similar to many suburban towns in Middle America: it is not quite rural, but far from urban. People who live there drive to Seattle to shop and eat if they have money, but stay in town if they want to see a movie. The town has two Chinese restaurants and a dozen other ethnic restaurants that, taken as a whole, symbolize small pockets of ethnic minorities located in many middle-American towns. Minh knows five other Vietnamese people in Quincy. They are all men, and three of them work with him at the restaurant. He shares a modest three-bedroom apartment with the barest of furnishings with these coworkers.

Like many Viet Kieu people, Minh sends remittances to Vietnam. But though remittances allow their receivers to enjoy First World consumption, givers only partake of these fruits when they return to their Third World homes. In the First World settings where they live and work, some givers, like Minh, are able to sustain only a Third World consumption pattern. Minh earns approximately $1,400 a month in Quincy and sends $500 of that back to his family. That amount is much higher than the average of $160 the grooms in my study remit to their wives and families on a monthly basis. At $900, his remaining budget would be considered far below the poverty level anywhere in the United States. But the stream of cash he sends his family permits them to stay connected in the small, though conspicuous, circles of families who have overseas kin networks.

In the meantime, however, Minh finds himself lacking not only in material comforts but in the kind of respect he had come to expect before he migrated. Minh remembers vividly that in his early twenties, his peers considered him a good catch. He came from a well-respected family, and he was headed for a career in engineering. Young men he knew had not one but several girlfriends at a time, and this was accepted and celebrated during those difficult postwar years. Minh was relatively fortunate: his parents were respected teachers with small but steady incomes. They could afford to spend small amounts of money on leisure activities and on materials that bought them some status in their pre-remittance circles. When we talked over beer and cigarettes in the hot kitchen where he worked, Minh told me:

Life here now is not like life in Vietnam back then. My younger brothers and sisters used to respect me a lot because I was going to college and I was about to get my degree. Many young women I met at the time liked me, too, because I came from a good family and I had status [*dia di*]. But now, because I don't have a good job here, people don't pay attention to me. That's the way my life has been since I came to the United States. And I don't know if I'm lucky or unlucky, but I think it's hard for a [Vietnamese] man to find a wife here if he doesn't make good money. If you have money, everyone will pay attention to you, but if you don't, you have to live by yourself.

For the most part, that's what Minh has done in the sixteen years since he arrived in the United States. Minh believes that money can, and often does, buy love, and that if you don't have much of it, you live by yourself. Although his yearly income puts him just above the poverty level for a single man, I discovered in a budget analysis of his expenditures that after remittances he falls well below the poverty level. The long hours that often accompany low-wage work have made it particularly difficult for him to meet and court marriage partners. If Minh worked long hours for a law firm or a corporation, he would not only get financial rewards but also the status and prestige that men often use as a trade-off in marriage markets. If he were a blue-collar white man in Quincy, he could go to church functions, bowling alleys, or bars to meet and court local women. For Minh, a single, immigrant man who does low-wage work in a low-status job with long hours in Middle America, the prospect of marriage has been, and remains, low. Even under slightly more favorable circumstances, Viet Kieu men complain of a lack of marriage partners. Men I interviewed in ethnic enclaves such as Little Saigon faced difficulties because, as one man told me, "Viet Kieu women know that there are many of us and few of them!"

Low-wage workers like Minh find it especially difficult to compete in intimate markets. Unlike women like Thanh, men like Minh are at the bottom locally, while globally they are at the top, since the United States enjoys high status among nations. That is one reason they turn to Vietnam. After all, men like Minh are in the market for more than just intimacy. They are in it for respect and for a kind of marital life that they believe they cannot obtain locally. For men in general, but especially for working-class men, as sociologist Lillian Rubin (1994) has argued in a compelling study, a worthy sense of self is deeply connected to the ability to provide economically for one's family. As Minh movingly explained to me,

I don't know if other men told you this, but I think the main reason that a lot of Viet Kieu men go back to Vietnam for a wife is because the women here [Viet Kieu] do not respect their husbands if the husbands cannot make a lot of money. I think that's why there are a lot of Viet Kieu women who marry white men, because the white men have better jobs than us. Many Viet Kieu women, even though they are not attractive and would not be worth much if there were a lot of them, would not even look at men like me because we can't buy them the fancy house or the nice cars. I need my wife to respect me as her husband. If your wife doesn't respect you, who will?

How They Meet

Although Minh was upwardly mobile in 1985 and would have become an engineer had he remained in Vietnam, he is now an assistant cook who has spent the bulk of his adult working life confined to a small Chinese restaurant in Middle America. He hasn't read a book in recent memory. In fact, he says little about what he does, except work, or what he owns, except a used Toyota Tercel he recently bought. Meanwhile, Thanh is a relatively successful lawyer in urban Saigon, where Chanel perfume and Ann Taylor shirts are components of her daily life. Thanh speaks very good English, the language we used when she and I met in Vietnam; Minh and I spoke Vietnamese when I interviewed him in Quincy. Thanh is currently working toward an English proficiency degree at an international adult English school, and her reading list includes F. Scott Fitzgerald's *The Great Gatsby*. She often prides herself that she is not as thin as the average woman in Vietnam, nor does she have the stereotypically Vietnamese long, straight black hair. Instead, Thanh has a perm with red highlights, and she spends a large part of her leisure time taking aerobics classes at the Saigonese Women's Union. She likes to joke, "Some people in Vietnam think that I'm a Viet Kieu woman."

Today Minh and Thanh live in seemingly separate worlds. The network of kin and acquaintanceship that unites them was riven by the war, but it still shares the history, memories, and connections of the prewar years. In 1997, when he was nearing his mid-thirties, Minh's family pressed him to find a suitable wife. In Vietnam, there is a strong cultural belief that one should marry in early adulthood, and most certainly before one turns thirty. In 1997, Minh, at thirty-four, was getting old in the eyes of married Vietnamese people. At twenty-eight, Thanh was considered even older as a woman, and both were very old according to Vietnamese notions of fertility. Most people are expected to have a first child, preferably a son, early to ensure patrilineal lineage. Although the average age of marriage has increased in Vietnam in the past few years, as it has worldwide (United Nations 2000), Vietnamese women are often stigmatized and considered unmarriageable at as young as twenty-five. In the villages, some women are considered unmarriageable at twenty.

Transpacific marriage arrangements are not always the idea of the

grooms or brides involved. More than 55 percent of the grooms I interviewed said the idea of a transpacific marriage did not occur to them
until a close friend or family member suggested it. The same was true of
only 27 percent of the brides. In other words, more brides than grooms
expressed an initial desire for an overseas spouse, while grooms were
somewhat hesitant until encouraged. The arrangement for Minh and
Thanh started when Minh's siblings expressed concern that their eldest
brother appeared lonely and needed a wife (though they never asked
him if this was the case). After all, he was the eldest sibling but the only
one who remained unmarried and childless. The average age of marriage for his three younger sisters was twenty-one and for his two brothers, twenty-four. While these ages seem lower than the current
Vietnamese average of twenty-four years for women and twenty-five years
for men (Minh 1997), they were not unusual at the time, since all five
siblings married in the late 1980s and early 1990s. Minh's next brother's
eldest child is now in her first year at Le Buon Phong high school. Minh
feels old when he thinks of this. He is often embarrassed when his family
asks him, "Why didn't you bring your lady friend back to visit us, too?"
Minh's long work hours, along with the scarcity of Vietnamese women
(relative to men) in the United States in general and Quincy in particular, were among the real reasons that the lady friend was generally "too
busy to come home this time."

Both Minh and Thanh faced structural and demographic limitations
in their local marriage markets, but in different and reversed ways. Minh
knew very few Vietnamese American women, and those he knew usually
earned the same amount or more than he did, which made him a less
attractive marriage candidate in the United States. Among Asian Americans, especially in California, women tend to get low-wage jobs more easily, to work longer hours, and to earn more money than men (Espiritu
1999). By contrast, Thanh knew many single men in Saigon, but they
were far below her in educational status and made much less money
than she did. Her economic and educational status made her a less
attractive marriage candidate in Vietnam, but the same qualities served
her well on the transpacific marriage market. As Thanh explained
to me:

Any Viet Kieu man can come here to find a wife. And he can surely find a beautiful woman if he wants because there are many beautiful young women willing to
marry anyone to go overseas. I think there is something different when you talk
about Viet Kieu men coming back here to marry. The women here who marry
for money, many of them will marry other foreign men, such as Taiwanese and
Korean, but they have sacrificed their lives for their families because they think
they can go off to another country and later send money back home. Those
[non-Viet Kieu] men seldom check the family backgrounds of the women they

marry, because they don't care. They, the women and the men, know it's something like prostitution, like selling oneself, even though they have weddings and
everything. But it's not really a marriage. If the brides are lucky, their foreign
husbands will love them and take care of them. But when it has to do with Vietnamese men, they are more selective. They look for a real marriage. And a marriage that will last forever. So it's important to them to check everything about
the woman they will marry and her background. These [Viet Kieu] men want a
woman who is educated and who comes from an educated family, because that
means she comes from a good family. And if her family has money, he knows
she just doesn't want to marry him to go overseas because she already has a comfortable life in Vietnam.

News of a split marriage market, one for foreign non-Viet Kieu men
and the other for Viet Kieu men who usually have family connections,
has circulated extensively throughout the Vietnamese diaspora. Men
who want "real" marriages are careful not to meet women on their own,
because they fear they will be used as passes for migration. When I visited Saigon nightclubs, cafés, and bars where overseas Vietnamese men
and local women converge, I found that both men and women
approached public courtship with a lack of trust. Like women in Taiwan,
Thailand, Singapore, Malaysia, Hong Kong, and other Asian countries
I've visited or studied, Vietnamese women who seek transpacific spouses
are so afraid of being seen as prostitutes that they rarely allow themselves
to be courted by foreign men in public. Some Viet Kieu men come back
and visit local bars and dance clubs in search of "one-night stands"
either with prostitutes or non-prostitutes, but they rarely marry women
they meet in these public spaces. My sample of marriages yielded only
one couple who met by any means other than kinship introduction or
arrangement. That couple had met through an international Vietnamese newspaper based in Sydney. Ninety percent of the couples had their
marriages arranged, and of the remaining 10 percent, the men had
returned to Vietnam to court old school friends or neighbors.

If women are afraid that they will be sexually exploited, Viet Kieu men
are wary of being used as a "bridge" to cross the Pacific (Ong 1999).
These concerns, combined with the availability of transnational networks, have propelled women in Vietnam and Vietnamese men who live
overseas to rely on marriage arrangements rather than engaging in individual courtship. As in the case of arranged marriages among other ethnic groups, marriage candidates in the Vietnamese diaspora believe that
family members make the best judgments in their interests when looking for a spouse (Batabyal 2001). Thanh explained the logic of marriage
arrangement, which may seem illogical to a foreigner:

It's very easy to trick people now. Both men and women can trick each other.
Women will pretend to love so they can go abroad and men will pretend to love

so they can get a one-night relationship. So that is why people will choose a family member who could investigate both sides for them. Most of the cases I know
are similar to mine. Usually a Viet Kieu man says he wants a wife, and then he
will call a family member here who will search for him. His family member will
try to contact friends, neighbors, whoever he can in search of a suitable wife who
happens to also be waiting for an overseas man to court her. There's always a lot
of women willing to marry a Viet Kieu man, even though she may never have
thought about it until someone asks them. If you have a family member choose
for you, as my uncle helped me get to know my husband, you will end up with a
real marriage. Otherwise, it can be risky for both people if they meet each other
on their own.

Minh's parents have known Thanh's family for more than two decades. Even though Thanh's father taught at Le Buon Phong two decades
ago and was a friend and colleague of Minh's parents, the current consumption gap between the two families has created a social distance over
the years. When Minh's siblings persuaded him to search for a wife in
Vietnam, he was hesitant at first, but later followed their advice when his
parents promised that they would invest time and care in finding the
most suitable spouse. According to Minh, however, they were surprised
to discover that arranging a marriage for a Viet Kieu was more complicated than they had anticipated:

I thought that it would be easy for them to find someone. I thought all they had
to do was mention a few things to their friends, and within days they could
describe a few possible people to me. But my parents told me that they were
afraid that women just wanted to use our family to go abroad. We had many
people get involved, many people wanted to be matchmakers for the family, and
they added so much anxiety and fear about people's intentions. But the first
goal for them was to find a woman from a wealthy family so that they were sure
she wasn't just interested in money, because if she has money she would already
be comfortable in Vietnam. And it would have been best if she had family in the
United States, because we would then know that they already have overseas people who help them out and they would not expect to become dependent on us.
In Vietnamese, there is a saying, "When you choose a spouse, you are choosing
his or her whole family."

Minh's parents finally contacted Thanh's parents, after the traditional
fashion in which the groom's parents represent him to propose, often
with rituals and a centuries-old ceremonial language. Like most brides
in my study, Thanh relied on an overseas relative—in this case, her
uncle, Tuan—for advice on Minh's situation in the United States. The
family discovered that Minh was a low-wage worker, but a full-time
worker nonetheless. During a walk that Thanh and I took through the
busy Ben Thanh market in the center of Saigon, she revealed that she
and her family were already prepared to support a reversed remittance
situation: "My father and mother didn't care about how much money

Minh has. They figured that they could help us out if Minh doesn't do so well; it sounds strange and hard to believe, but my parents said that they could help us open up a business in the United States later on if Minh wants us to do that. They liked the idea that he is a hardworking man and that he comes from a good family. . . . They know he comes from a good family because he sends money back to his parents. He knows how to take care of them."

Virtually all of the locals I met in Vietnam viewed overseas men as a two-tiered group: the "successful," who were educated or who succeeded in owning ethnic enterprises; and the "indolent," who lacked full-time jobs and were perceived as being welfare-dependent or as participating in underground economies, such as gambling. Some felt that the latter group had taken up valuable spots that others from Vietnam could have filled. "If I had gotten a chance to go, I would be so rich by now," I heard many local men say. Most people, however, could not explain a man like Minh, who is neither lazy nor extremely successful. Thanh's Uncle Tuan seemed to know more men in Houston who were not only unemployed but alcoholics and gamblers. Her parents were worried that their daughter was unmarriageable, because there was certainly no shortage of younger women in Vietnam for local men her age to marry. Thanh, too, was already convinced that she was *e*. Both her parents and her uncle worried that Thanh was facing a life of permanent singlehood. Finally, they all believed that marrying Thanh to Minh, a Viet Kieu man, would be more desirable than arranging her marriage to a local man in Vietnam. Thanh's parents were confident that Minh's status as a full-time worker who sent remittances back home to his family spoke well for him as a suitable husband. Most Viet Kieu single men her uncle knew belonged to an underclass of which Minh was not a part. For Thanh, Minh's geographical advantage translated into something socially priceless: a man living in a modern country, she was sure, would respect women.

A Clash of Dreams

Highly educated women like Thanh resist patriarchal arrangements by avoiding marriages with local men. They do not want to "marry down" economically and socially—though this seems to be their only choice—because they believe that marrying local men will only constrain them to domestic roles in a male-dominated culture. As Thanh told me, some women will endure the often painful stigma of singlehood and childlessness over the oppression they could face from dominating husbands. For some of these women, the transpacific marriage market holds out hope for a different kind of marriage—one in which Vietnamese women imagine that their husbands will believe in, and practice, gender equity. Many such women will instead find themselves back in the premodern family life they hoped to avoid. As Minh told me, "A woman's place is in the home to take care of her husband and his family."

All but three of the twenty-eight grooms I interviewed shared Minh's view. But this conflict in gender ideology between the two unmarriage-ables never seemed to come to the fore until it was too late. During the migration period, each expensive phone call and visit is an occasion for love, not for discussing the details of what life will be like when the woman joins the man abroad. Most couples shared only words of joy about being together in the future. And yet, as I interviewed the couples in their separate countries during this period, I found that the two par-ties usually held conflicting views of the life they would soon lead together. I did not interview all of the grooms, but I did ask all of the brides about their husbands' ideas about gender relations, and about how they envisioned the organization of their households after they joined their husbands abroad. Among other things, I asked about house-hold division of labor, about whether the couple would live with or with-out kin, and about whether the women expected to work outside the home. Although these concerns address only a small fraction of a mar-riage's potential promise or pitfalls, they can certainly help us under-stand the interplay between a husband's gender ideology and his wife's (Hochschild 1989).

Nearly 95 percent of the brides in Vietnam wanted to work for a wage when they joined their husbands abroad. Though wanting to work out-side the home is not the ultimate measure of a modernized woman in Vietnam, it does indicate these women's unwillingness to be confined to domestic work. Some women who wanted paid jobs were not averse to the idea of doing second-shift work as well (Hochschild 1989). However, most of the women, and virtually all of the educated ones—the unmar-riageables—wanted and expected to have egalitarian relationships with their husbands. In general, they objected to traditionally female tasks, although they did not fully embrace what we might call a peer marriage (Schwartz 1995). For the men and women I interviewed, as for main-stream dual-career American couples, marital life consists of much more than just household tasks. But these tasks are important symbols in the economy of gratitude among married people, "for how a person wants to identify himself or herself influences what, in the back and forth of a marriage, will seem like a gift and what will not" (Hochschild 1989:18). As Thanh explained when I asked her about the implications of a purely egalitarian marriage: "I don't want everything split fifty-fifty. For exam-ple, I like to cook. But it's important for me as an educated woman not to be controlled by my husband. I don't mind cooking for my husband, but I don't want it to be forced on me. That's how the men in Vietnam feel; they feel that their wives are like their domestic workers. Men in Vietnam never do anything in the house. I think they have to know how to respect educated women."

Women like Thanh want a respectful marriage based on principles of gender equality. According to these principles, women expect to work for a wage, to share in making social and economic decisions for their future households, and to have their husbands share in the household division of labor. Above all, they do not want to live in multigenerational households, serving as the dutiful daughter-in-law and housewife, the two often inseparable roles historically delegated to women in Vietnam. Many express that reluctance, because they know numerous Viet Kieu men who live with their parents or who plan to do so when their parents are old. In Vietnam, and more generally in Asia, elderly parents often live with their eldest sons. The daily caregiving work then falls to their sons' wives. Forty percent of the U.S.-based grooms and a third of all Vietnamese grooms live with their parents, most of whom are elderly and require care. Of all low-wage workingmen married to highly educated women, about 35 percent currently reside with their parents. Virtually all of the men in my study who resided with their parents wanted to continue to do so when their wives joined them abroad.

For Minh, the possibility that a wife will insist on an equal marriage is one of the anxieties of modern life:

Vietnamese women, they care for their husbands and they are more traditional. I think non-Vietnamese women and Viet Kieu women are too modern. They just want to be equal with their husbands, and I don't think that is the way husband and wife should be. . . . I mean that husband and wife should not be equal. The wife should listen to the husband most of the time. That is how they will have a happy life together. If the woman tries to be equal they will have problems. . . . I know many Vietnamese men here who abandon their parents because their wives refuse to live with their parents. If my parents were in America, I would definitely plan for them to live with me when they are old. But because they are in Vietnam, they are living with one of my brothers.

Instead of seeking peasant village women or uneducated ones, after the fashion of white men who pursue mail-order brides because they believe such women consent to subordination in marriage, men like Minh seek marriage arrangements with educated women. As Minh explains:

For me, I want to marry an educated woman, because she comes from a good, educated family. It's very hard to find a poor woman or an uneducated woman who comes from an uneducated family to teach their daughters about morals and values, because if they are uneducated they don't know how. I know many men, Viet Kieu and foreign men, who go to Vietnam to marry beautiful young women, but they don't ask why those women want to marry them. Those women only want to use their beauty to go overseas, and they will leave their husbands when they get the chance. They can use their beauty to find other men. I would never marry a beautiful girl from a poor, uneducated family. You see, the educated women, they know it's important to marry and stay married forever. As they say in Vietnam, "*Tram nam han phuc* [a hundred years of happiness]." Educated women must protect their family's reputation in Vietnam by having a happy marriage, not have it end in divorce.

The Inflated Market of Respect

At first glance, Minh and Thanh seem to come from two vastly different social worlds, assembled only by the complexity of Vietnamese history. But at a closer look, we learn that these two lonely faces of globalization are very much alike. Both of their parents were educated and middle-class. Both lack the emotional fulfillment and intimate partnership that adults of their social worlds enjoy. Both long for a kind of marital respect they perceive as scarce in their local marriage markets. Minh has experienced immense, swift downward mobility as a result of migration, and he is eager to regain the respect he has lost. Thanh has practically priced herself out of the local marriage market by acquiring an advanced degree, which she could not have obtained without her uncle's remittances. She wants a husband who respects her as an equal and who accepts that she is a modern woman. He wants to regain something he thinks men like him have lost; she wants to challenge the local marriage norm, including the very preindustrial Vietnamese family life Minh yearns for. Many men in Vietnam do live that life. As Minh told me: "My younger brothers have control over their homes. Their wives help them with their shops selling fabrics in Saigon, but their wives don't make any decisions. I think that if they lived in America and their wives were working, they would not let my brother make all the decisions in the house. . . . And I think that Vietnamese women, when they come to the United States, are influenced by a lot of different things. That is why there are a lot of divorces in America."

Minh believes that when he migrated to the United States, he left the respect he now craves behind him in Vietnam. Thanh imagines that the marital respect she craves is unobtainable in Vietnam, but awaits her in the United States. Each has inflated the true extent of the respect the other is willing to give. For though there is a quiet feminist revolution of sorts going on among highly educated women in Vietnam, that revolution has not entered the experience or expectations of the less educated, low-wage husbands living overseas. And while many of these Viet Kieu men seek reprieve from modern Western life, the women they marry have washed away those traditions during the long years that the men have been gone.

The Future of Transpacific Marriages

Surely, this clash of dreams and expectations will result in marital conflict when the couple is united overseas. Such conflicts have several potential outcomes. The happiest would have Minh joining the feminist revolution and abandoning his desire for the preindustrial, traditional family life he never had. Some men will go this route, but only a few. In other cases, such marriages may end in divorce—or worse, domestic battery. I believe the latter scenario is an unlikely one for the couples I studied. Many women like Thanh have considered the possibility and are careful to maintain contact with transnational networks that will look out for them. Seventy-five percent of the women in my study have at least one overseas relative. Virtually all the middle-class and college-educated women do.

Most likely, these marriages will resolve themselves with the men getting the respect they want and the women consenting to subordination in the name of family and kinship. Thanh will be going from the patriarchal frying pan into the patriarchal fire, but with one big difference: in the United States, her desire for gender equity will find more support, in a culture where women dare to leave their husbands if they aren't treated equally. But Thanh will still bear the burden of Vietnamese tradition, which will prevent her from leaving her husband. In Vietnam, divorce is stigmatized, and saving face is especially important to educated, middle-class families. If Thanh daringly divorces her husband, she will damage her family's reputation in Vietnam and overseas. She told me she would not be likely to take this risk. If she stays in the marriage, she will probably wind up serving as the traditional wife Minh desires.

Although globalization appears to offer some Vietnamese women an escape from local patriarchal marriages, it may in fact play more to the interests of certain Vietnamese men, offering them the opportunity to create the traditional life they've always wanted within the modern setting where they now live. Strong traditions back in Vietnam protect them against instability in their marriages. But the women they have married don't share their husbands' traditional vision of marital life. The only thing educated women like Thanh have to look forward to is more waiting—waiting for men like their husbands, who live in a modern country, simply to respect women.

Chapter 9
A Tale of Two Marriages: International Matchmaking and Gendered Mobility

Nicole Constable

During the summer of 2002, while I was in India working on this chapter, an episode of the U.S. television drama *Law and Order: Special Victims Unit* was aired on the Asian television network Star TV. The program caught my eye because it was about "mail-order brides" and introduction agencies. The episode encapsulated many of the most common negative stereotypes about so-called mail-order brides and international introduction agencies. Central to the show's story line was Euromatch, an agency that introduced U.S. men to Eastern European women, which turned out to be a front for a prostitution ring, trafficking in women, and immigration fraud. The Eastern European women were depicted as poor and therefore desperate to come to the United States, thus rendering them especially vulnerable to being "imported" by unscrupulous traffickers. The foreign women's character types ran the gamut from helpless innocent victims who had been deceived into marriage by the agency, to sly, devious, and heartless prostitutes who were desperate to emigrate at any cost. The U.S. husbands were portrayed in equally stereotypical terms as socially inept, innocent, and naive dupes, or as violent and deviant wife abusers. The owners of the agency were crooks who profited by selling poor and desperate foreign women, as wives and prostitutes, to provide sexual and domestic services to U.S. men. Such images caught my attention because they stood in sharp contrast to my own impressions of introduction agencies and international correspondence marriages based on several years of ethnographic research among Chinese women, Filipinas, and U.S. men.

In numerous popular sources as well as in many activist, feminist, and anti-trafficking sources, correspondence marriages involving U.S. men and foreign women are often depicted in similarly negative and stereotypical terms: poor and desperate and thus eager to marry Western men.[1] As illustrated by the words of the European teacher in the story of the Japanese "mail-order bride" in the story by Yoko Tawada (1998), women's presumed poverty is tied to the assumption that they are marrying up socially and geographically. Such stereotypes and generalities serve as a convenient jumping-off point from which to consider some actual experiences and motivations of women and men involved in correspondence. On the whole, the Chinese and Filipina women I knew did not appear to be passive victims, trafficked women, desperate gold diggers or green-card seekers; nor did the men fit the image of victimizers out to find subservient maids and sexual partners. The introduction agencies I studied, moreover, might be said to traffic in particular images of foreign women, but it would be difficult to conclude that they sell women or that men buy wives.[2]

One objective of this chapter is to provide an overview of the process of introduction and correspondence among Filipinas, Chinese women, and U.S. men, and to depict the men and women involved in such courtships as real people whose lives and experiences challenge many common stereotypes and images. Another objective, one that is shared with the other chapters in this volume, is to question the common assumption that such marriages are hypergamous—that they entail upward social and geographic mobility for the women, and to consider how such cross-border marriages are patterned in relation to gender. A gendered cultural logic is embedded in the practice of international introductions by correspondence, in the language and presentation of introduction-agency Web sites, as well as in the resulting marriages. This logic applies to relationships between Asian women and U.S. men, but not to those between Asian men and U.S. women.

In the first half of the chapter, I describe how cross-border correspondence marriages are initiated, arranged, and imagined in the early stages. I explore the role of various sorts of introduction agencies and highlight some of the mixed messages that introduction agencies convey about gender and nationality. In the second half of the chapter, I present the stories of two women and their marriages. I have written about Ping and Rosie elsewhere (Constable 2003a and 2003b); here I update their stories. The early stages of their courtships and engagements illustrate their initiative, their negotiation of the correspondence process, and their optimistic dreams of upward mobility and romance. The early stages of marriage and migration, by contrast, reveal a greater sense of personal difficulty, disappointment, loneliness, and adjustment to a social reality that often bears little resemblance to earlier imaginings. I conclude with a discussion of gendered geographies of marriage and global hypergamy.

Introduction Agencies and Correspondence Marriage

I use the term "correspondence marriage" to refer to marriages between men and women of different nationalities who meet through introduction services and whose courtships involve correspondence. A variety of labels are used to refer to the array of clubs, agencies, and businesses that facilitate marriage introductions between U.S. men and foreign women. In U.S. popular media and among certain advocacy groups that are critical of international introductions, they are often derogatorily referred to as "mail-order bride" businesses. As discussed below, this label promotes the unfortunate connotation that women are commodities, who are bought by male consumers.

More neutral terms, such as "introduction services," "international introduction agencies," and "international matchmaking organizations," are often used interchangeably (see USDOJ-INS 1999a, Simons 2001). Strictly speaking, however, "matchmaking" does not accurately convey the role of such clubs or agencies, since they do not make matches or arrange marriages, but rather provide individuals with the information to locate their own matches. The Chinese women, Filipinas, and U.S. men I knew located one another through Internet or print resources provided by international introduction agencies. They then communicated by mail, e-mail, or other forms of Internet communication, and also by telephone for anywhere from a few months to well over a year before actually meeting face-to-face, as is required by U.S. immigration law.

Men and women both cited numerous reasons for corresponding with foreigners, including their dissatisfaction with local prospects and their attraction to foreigners. U.S. men, many of whom were divorced, cited bad experiences with Western women, whom they often characterized as too feminist, career-oriented, or independent to make good wives. They cited physical attraction to Asian women and a desire for partners who had "traditional" family values, who took marriage seriously, and would not consider divorce an easy solution. Chinese women and Filipinas spoke in general about freedom and opportunities in the West. Filipinas often expressed the desire to provide economic assistance to their natal families, whereas Chinese women spoke of providing their children with a chance to emigrate to the West. Chinese and Filipinas spoke of bad experiences with and mistrust of local men. Many Chinese women I interviewed had been divorced and thought their prospects for remarriage were better in the West because of less negative attitudes toward divorce. In China, if a woman is unmarried at thirty, her chances of marriage are thought to be diminished and she becomes an object of social concern. In the Philippines, unwed mothers or women who have had previous sexual relations are not considered marriageable.

Contrary to many popular U.S. depictions of so-called mail-order brides, most Chinese women and Filipinas I met thought that U.S. men were more open and liberated than their own countrymen and that life abroad could offer a more egalitarian marriage. Lisa Simons's study of Filipina, Russian, and Ukrainian women reflected similar views. As Simons writes, "What so many of my respondents, male and female alike, said they wanted out of an international marriage (that they believed they could not achieve as easily by marrying within their culture) was a 'soulmate' and/or a 'partnership of equals,' meaning those with shared goals, values, and visions of family life" (2001:167). Among many Filipina-U.S. couples I met, this partnership referred to a complementarity of roles in which women do much of the housework and men provide economic support. Such a division of labor was not considered exploitative, as it might to some in the West, but as complementary and preferable to underpaid menial labor or the un/underemployment of educated professionals in China or the Philippines.

After corresponding for several months, many couples made plans to meet in person, and the men traveled abroad one or more times, for one or two weeks or longer.[3] At that point, some couples chose to discontinue the relationship, and others became engaged and made plans to marry. Correspondence usually continued for several more months as couples awaited permission for the woman to immigrate to the United States. Such courtships, it should be noted, allow couples to begin to get acquainted at a distance before they meet face-to-face. They differ from prearranged group tours in which men travel to another country where they are introduced either individually or through parties or mixers to numerous women.[4] Many men commented on the value of getting to know someone "before complicating things with a physical relationship." Besides this attention to personalities and compatibility, men also scrutinized photographs and paid attention to the potential for physical attraction and "good chemistry." Women also considered men's appearances, but they often framed their likes and dislikes less in terms of physical attractiveness than in terms of social ideals and good taste. Many Chinese women, for example, disliked tattoos and facial hair, which conveyed negative social messages, and preferred men who appeared neatly dressed and well-groomed.

Introduction-agency Web sites often disavow the term "mail-order bride," display an awareness of problematic negative representations of foreign brides in the popular media, and express a desire to create greater gender balance on their Web sites. Yet the term "mail-order bride" and the wider negative implications surrounding correspondence marriage still circulate widely. The Immigration and Naturalization Service report entitled "International Matchmaking Organizations:

A Report to Congress" (USDOJ-INS 1999a) openly describes its study as one of "mail-order marriages."[5] The Web site goodwife.com, cited in the appendix to the INS report, describes itself as the "Mail Order Bride Warehouse" and identifies several hundred Web sites devoted to introducing U.S. men to foreign brides. Goodwife.com states that it is "the single American man's best resource for finding love abroad via the mail order brides method." It provides links to Web sites "whose charter is helping to bring North American men together with beautiful, eligible, foreign women." As goodwife.com explains, such services are called "foreign matchmaking services, pen pal clubs, international introduction agencies, foreign marriage agencies, etc., but the one thing they have in common is that their business is getting western men married to foreign wives."

It is difficult to say how many U.S. men and foreign women meet through introduction clubs or how many of those couples actually marry. The U.S. Immigration and Naturalization Service does not keep records of how couples meet. Many introduction agencies brag of having introduced hundreds or thousands of successful couples. Cherry Blossoms, one of the oldest and best-known agencies, claims that since its founding in 1974, it has facilitated more than twenty thousand marriages, and that it attracts over a thousand new clients a year (http://www.blossoms.com). The INS report estimates four thousand to six thousand marriages a year resulting from "mail-order agencies" and that "mail-order marriages" account for 2.7 to 4.1 percent of all immigration involving female spouses (USDOJ-INS 1999a:12, see also Simons 2001:313). These estimates may be low. First, it is often difficult to ascertain how the couple met, and many couples are loath to identify their relationships as "mail-order marriages." Thus couples I knew, when interviewed for a visa, said that they had met informally or while traveling. Second, if the INS report includes "spouses," it does not include those who enter with K-1 "fiancée" visas and then adjust their status later on. Of the couples I knew, more than half entered the U.S. on K-1 visas.[6] The proportion of women who meet through correspondence who entered as fiancées and later marry is likely to be at least equal to those who entered as spouses, and possibly higher. The increased popularity of international introduction agencies would also seem to indicate an increase in such marriages.[7]

It is difficult to know exactly how many international introduction agencies exist, but their numbers have clearly mushroomed over the past several years. In an appendix to the INS report, Robert Scholes reported that in mid-March 1998 there were 153 international introduction services listed on goodwife.com, and by early May of the same year, 202 (Scholes 1999). As of August 2000, I found 350 listed—a 75 percent increase in two years. Under the category "Asian," the number had increased from fifty-five in May 1998 to eighty-nine in August 2000, with Filipinas the most commonly represented nationality. The "Soviet" category had increased from 105 in May 1998 to 164 in August 2000. I also located numerous clubs and agencies that were not listed on goodwife.com, so four hundred introduction Web sites in 2000 is a conservative estimate.[8]

There are various types of introduction services. Some are designed as formal profit-making businesses, with fees charged for services and membership. On the opposite extreme are those not run for profit, often presented as a hobby or personal interest of the person(s) who started the Web site. Many introduction services are run by couples who met through correspondence. Hundreds of agencies promote their services to U.S. and other English-speaking men as a means to meet more suitable, traditional, or devoted marriage partners from Asia and other parts of the world. Although many of these Web sites include some men's listings, and some agencies are involved in domestic matchmaking as well, the vast majority of the listings with international agencies are of non-Western women. Most agencies are geared almost entirely toward men searching for brides, but others have recently incorporated services for women searching for grooms as well.

Cherry Blossoms began in 1974 with a printed catalog that was sent by mail to male subscribers, but has since shifted to an electronic format that can be accessed privately via the Internet. Its Internet home page, easily accessible to non-subscribers, includes a button for "MEN seeking WOMEN" and one for "WOMEN seeking MEN." On the home page, it claims to have been "successfully helping men and women meet by publishing their personal ads." The Cherry Blossoms personal-ad database includes "single men and single women from all over the world." Yet despite an attempt at gender balance, it also stresses that there are over "5 times as many women" using its services as men. In summer 2002, the Cherry Blossoms home page featured six photographs, four of women (two who appeared to be Asian and two who were Caucasian and blond) and two of men (both Caucasian). The Web site describes how it "started the business of helping Asian, Russian and other women place their personal ads in our paper publication to meet men from the US and other countries" and how it has now expanded into electronic publication. Its personalized marriage and dating service, it notes, is "sometimes referred to as a *traditional mail order bride* service." Like China Doll (http://www.chinese-women.com) and several other agencies, Cherry Blossoms offers both introductions for correspondence, as well as tours for U.S. men (but not U.S. women) to meet potential marriage partners abroad. Cherry Blossoms facilitates tours for men to travel to China, the Philippines, Thailand, and Vietnam to meet prospective partners. The tours promise to introduce men to "as many [women] as needed within reason," assuring their customers that 90 percent of the men who go on such tours have become engaged or married as a result. Although the agency lists men and women of various nationalities, it is clear that the primary focus is on introducing Western men and non-Western women.

As mentioned above, goodwife.com describes itself as the "Mail Order Bride Warehouse," despite the fact that many of the agencies it lists criticize, distance themselves, or disavow the term "mail-order brides." Some introduction agencies, such as Sunshine International, are explicitly critical. On its Web site home page (http://sunshine-girls.com), Sunshine International describes itself as "one of the oldest and most reputable Asian Penpal International Dating Services for single men seeking nice, English-speaking Asian women (not so-called 'mail order brides' or 'Asian brides') for friendship or marriage." Moreover, its question-and-answer section, asked if it is a "mail order bride company" it explains that it is not, because it does not sell "marital slaves" but rather, provides correspondence/pen-pal services that promote friendship. It also insists that "in reality," there is no such thing as a "mail order bride company," since it is the women who choose which men with whom to correspond. Other agencies, such as Cherry Blossoms, only use the term "mail order bride" in italics or in quotes, thus indicating some qualification of their usage.

U.S. men and most Filipinas I spoke to took offense at the term "mail-order bride" because of the implication that men "buy" women—just as one might order an item of clothing or a music CD from a Web site or catalog—and that women are commodities to be bought and sold. U.S. who found the term "mail-order bride" offensive pointed out that they did not "buy" wives, and many Filipinas insisted that they were not mail-order brides because they had not been bought by men, but that they met as "pen pals" and that they had made their own decisions. In China, on the other hand, women had rarely heard the term, and when I mentioned it they laughed or frowned at the prospect that they could be bought like a commodity from an Internet catalog. As Rubie Watson observes, Chinese often attach "great importance to separating marriage from commercial transactions" (1991:359). Unaware of this conceptual separation, critics use the term "mail-order bride" to indicate a wider critique of an industry that profits from the commodification and "trafficking" of women (D. Aguilar 1987, Glodava and Onizuka 1994). Others (Julag-Ay 1997, Robinson 1996 and 2001, Simons 2001, Constable 2003a) caution against the use of this term to blur the line between actual commodities and women and men whose images can and are at times and in certain ways commodified.

The label "mail-order bride" obscures the degree of selectivity and choice exerted by most women. Women as well as men can choose not to respond to or communicate with particular individuals, and they decide whether to give out personal or contact information. Several women I originally contacted in 1999 remained unmarried four years later, and some had stopped seeking partners because they did not consider the men who had written to them suitable. The term "mail-order husband" is, to my knowledge, never used except facetiously or as a joke (see below, see also Margold 1995:284), and thus "mail-order bride" implies that men control the financial resources to "buy" a bride, whereas brides, like commodities, are devoid of agency. As Simons notes, "Women act as the supply to meet the male demand for wives. But likewise men act as the supply to meet the female demand for husbands" (2001:173). That women are often commodified, especially by the Web sites that are moneymaking businesses, is not in question, but the fact that their images are commodified does not make them commodities. The label "mail-order brides," moreover, blurs the boundaries between marriage, prostitution, sex tourism, and forced labor, implying that the distinctions are of little relevance and that all such women are similarly "trafficked" (see Tolentino 1996, D. Aguilar 1987).

Many men I encountered took it for granted that China and the Philippines are "poor" or "less developed" countries and that poverty is one underlying factor that encourages women to submit their names to an introduction agency. Yet they consciously sought women who were not among the poorest or most desperate, because they thought it would be more difficult to gauge their sincerity when it came to the prospect of marriage. The image of desperately poor women and prostitutes stands in contrast to the image of wives, mothers, and women with "traditional" family values that men pursue. Men shared the common assumption that poverty is associated with a lack of free will. As scholars have demonstrated, however, women who emigrate for work or marriage are not likely to be among the poorest. Following Portes and Rumbault (1996:12), Simons argues that "bride-sending countries are midlevel in terms of development, and the women within each sending country are not usually the very worst off" (2001:9). Portes and Rumbault argue that it is "*relative*, not absolute deprivation [that] lies at the core of most contemporary immigration" (1996:12, Simons 2001:9, see also Constable 1997).

A high degree of contradiction and ambivalence surrounds the issue of the relative poverty of the women listed on Web sites and catalogs. While some agencies convey an overall sense of women's poverty and seem to use this factor to explain why such beautiful young women would be willing to marry men who might not be attractive in the United States, others call such stereotypes into question. China Doll, for example, stresses that the women it lists are "educated" and "elite"; they are "not low class . . . bar girls or domestic helper[s], they are the top level ladies of China" (http://www.chinese-women.com). Leading one to assume that some women are motivated at least partly by financial concerns, Cherry Blossoms requires that women who register agree to the statement "I am here only to meet men for Friendship, Love and Marriage. I will not ask (or hint) for financial support for any reason." Men, on the other hand, are not required to submit an agreement of any sort. Despite an explicit criticism of the assumption of all Asian women's poverty, Sunshine International promotes the idea that women from poor families make good partners. As it explains with seeming ambivalence: "Most of Asia is very modern and the people enjoy a high standard of living. Granted, there are a few places of poverty such as the slum sections of Manila but these are the exception not the rule. Just because a person is poor does not mean that they are a thief. On the contrary, some of the nicest and most sincere ladies come from poor families."

One of the few existing surveys of men who seek to meet wives through international introductions indicates that, although a heterogeneous group in many ways, they tend to be mostly white and above average in education and income (Jedlicka 1988).[9] Sunshine International describes its male clients as mainly from the United States, with occupations ranging from white-collar professionals to policemen, farmers, and university students. China Doll aims its service toward men who are "professionals" and "gentlemen." While such Web sites say relatively little about the men, except that anyone can find a partner regardless of age or status, men's own discussions in chat groups serve to explicitly convince themselves and one another that most Filipinas and Chinese women would be happy to come to the United States, regardless of the specific circumstances, because of the "better opportunities." Men who are already married and whose wives live in the United States are more aware of some of the disappointments and difficulties that women may face.

"Fritzie's Filipina Pen Friends" home page is an example of the sort of Web site that does not charge fees for women's contact information and that does not use the term "mail-order brides." Fritzie describes the women listed on her Web site as "English speaking Filipina[s] looking for foreign men for correspondence, romance, love, and marriage." Yet she also makes a more explicit statement about the appeal of the West. Her home page states, "Filipinas are widely regarded as making wonderful wives and mothers. These women are seeking foreign marriages because they believe the quality of their lives, and their children's lives, will be improved. They feel that they can best help themselves and their families by marrying outside of the Philippines" (http://www.filipina penfriends.com). Fritzie explains her motivation for setting up the Web site as a way to offer her friends and neighbors "the same chance for happiness and economic opportunity" as she had. Her posted biography, along with a narrative of how she met her husband (a Florida electronics technician and part-time options trader), stresses her educational background, includes high school and college graduation photographs, a photograph of her in her "Citizen's Army Training" uniform and as a beauty contest winner. In contrast to some of the larger introduction businesses that seem to second-guess men's dissatisfaction with Western women and their desire to meet traditional and beautiful foreign brides, Web sites such as Fritzie's, despite their equally selective narration, come closer to representing women's own stories (Wilson 1988, Tsing 1993). As such, it strays furthest from the popular media images and comes closer to the views expressed by "real" women involved in correspondence.

Women's own stories, as many of the chapters in this volume suggest, call into question the idea that they are unilaterally poor, helpless, desperate, trafficked, or sold. While one might expect women to express hope and self-determination at the early stages when they contemplate submitting their names and photographs to an introduction agency, or when they first meet a prospective partner, a skeptic might suggest that such notions of agency diminish once the momentum of marriage and migration builds. As I argue below, although marriage and migration do present new obstacles and often disappointments, they also present women with new opportunities in which to shape their marriages, their lives, and their futures. Women maintain their claims to self-determination even if this means returning home or divorcing their husbands, decisions that may be very difficult and that are not taken lightly. Moreover, while critiques of trafficking and of so-called mail-order marriages often cast husbands as exploiters or potential victimizers, the decision to return home or divorce a husband suggests that women sometimes see the state or U.S. government as the adversary rather than the husband.

Two Tales

In 1998, my research began with a close examination of introduction catalogs and Web sites. The following year, I wrote to about forty women in China and forty in the Philippines. I explained that I was a woman researcher and that I hoped to meet some of them in person and talk to them about their ideas and experiences with pen pals. In 1999, 2000, and 2002, I met a number of these women in person, and continued to correspond with them. I also met with some of their partners, and with their friends and colleagues who were also writing to foreign men. Meanwhile I also joined a number of private chat groups for men who were corresponding with Filipinas or Chinese women.[10]

The following stories contribute to my wider critique of reductionist stereotypes of so-called mail-order marriages. Ping's and Rosie's stories suggest that we must question the one-dimensional depictions of women as either trafficked victims of Western men or of global economy, or as ruthless hyper-agents who instrumentally and single-mindedly attempt to marry men as a means to immigrate. Although such stereotypes saturate much U.S. discourse about brides of U.S. men, such images leave us with little more than caricatures that misrepresent actual life experiences and complex motivations. Instead of focusing on globalization as a grand homogenizing process and assuming that Western men have a monopoly on power over the women, these stories, like many others in this book, vex easy attempts to generalize about globalization and Western male dominance, and complicate simple assumptions about hypergamy.

These accounts update the stories I began to tell elsewhere.[11] Ping is from Beijing, the capital city of the People's Republic of China, and Rosie is from Mindanao, a largely rural island in the southern Philippines. They are two of the women I knew best of those I met in China or the Philippines in 1999 and 2000 who had submitted their names to international introduction agencies. Their stories are neither unique nor entirely representative of the wider collection of experiences of Chinese and Filipina brides I encountered. Both arrived in the United States in 2000, Rosie as the wife of a U.S. citizen, and Ping as a fiancée. Both had been in the United States for about two years when I caught up with them in the summer of 2002.

Ping

I first met Ping, a professional woman in her fifties, in Beijing in the summer of 2000. She was divorced and had an adult son. A decade or two earlier, she would not have thought it possible for Chinese women to meet foreign men over the Internet and marry them. During the Maoist period (1949–76), in contrast to earlier and later periods in Chinese history, it was almost unheard-of for Chinese women to marry foreigners, and even marrying overseas Chinese was uncommon and frowned upon. Not only were there few opportunities to meet foreigners or overseas Chinese during China's closed-door era, but foreigners were considered politically undesirable. In the post-Mao period, one in which new forms of consumer desire, sexual openness, and romantic yearnings appeared (Davis 2000, Farquhar 2002, Farrer 2002), foreigners came to symbolize new forms of openness, freedom, and independence, and they offered potential for material improvement.

As in the Philippines, Chinese women often spoke of foreign men— based on television images and popular culture more than actual experience—as more open-minded, romantic, and modern than local ones, and as a source of mobility and comfort. Many of the Chinese women I met were over thirty, divorced, and had good jobs. In contrast to a Chinese cultural preference for lateral or hypergamous marriages (Croll 1984, Fan and Huang 1998, Lavely 1991, Parish and Farrer 1993, Whyte and Parish 1984), they often complained that their local marriage prospects were "beneath them." Filipinas who had had a relationship or a child or who were known to have had sexual relations were not desirable marriage prospects.

Opportunities for Chinese and foreigners to meet and marry are thus linked to the post-Mao economic reforms, the economic and social "opening up" of the country during the 1980s and 1990s. By the early 1990s, building on culturally accepted local and domestic forms of matchmaking and introduction services that utilized advertisements and computer technology, introduction agencies expanded to include or came to specialize in international introductions of overseas Chinese and non-Chinese men with local Chinese women (Clark 2001).[12] The notion of urban elite women marrying foreigners can also be seen as a broad extension of a pre-reform pattern of patrilocal residence and of "spatial hypergamy," in which rural women married up into more desirable physical locations (Lavely 1991). As C. Cindy Fan and Youqin Huang suggest, the reform period version of spatial hypergamy entails greater geographical distances as women marry across provincial boundaries into more developed and desirable regions, even though their husbands are often the "socially and economically disadvantaged" of that region (1998:246, see also Chao, Oxfeld, and Schein, in this volume). International marriage migration involves a similar desire to attain a more favorable position in the spatial hierarchy and to benefit from the advantages of a better location.

Ping was introduced to me by two of her colleagues, whom I had met through one of the correspondence clubs I joined in 1998. Both colleagues were in their forties; both were divorced and corresponding with foreign men, but neither had yet met the "right" one.[13] Ping's colleagues had arranged that we meet, and enthusiastically introduced Ping as a "success story," because she had the opportunity to go to the United States on a K-1 fiancée visa. Ping, however, expressed ambivalence and had not made up her mind to marry Elvin, an American white-collar professional over ten years her senior, who was also divorced with adult children.

Ping and Elvin initially met through an Internet "friend finder" club, where both had signed up to chat and communicate via e-mail. Neither had to pay a fee to join. They communicated for several months, and then Elvin came to visit and asked her to come to the United States and marry him. Ping confided that she had reservations. Her main concerns involved the fact that he lived in a nudist colony and his unwillingness to discuss financial issues. At first, she was not as troubled by the prospect that he was not well-off, which she strongly suspected, as she was with his reluctance to discuss finances openly, a practice that was common among the couples she knew in China. Ping believed that a marriage should be an equal partnership of sorts and that she could be helpful in managing their finances, as do many women in China, but that in order to do so she had to understand the situation and they had to work together to improve it.

As Ping explained, Elvin had a very simple and frugal lifestyle, and he was attracted to Chinese women because he believed they were less materialistic and demanding than U.S. women. A left-leaning intellectual, he was attracted to the ideals of the Maoist socialist period. Seemingly less aware of the materialist boom in China, he was drawn to meeting a Chinese partner. Ping, on the other hand, was attracted to the idea of meeting a foreigner who shared her intellectual interests in books, art, and culture. Like many other professional women in their late thirties or forties whom I met in China, Ping had been interested in meeting a foreigner because she felt her local marriage prospects were not good, given her age and her status as a divorcée. Although divorce no longer held the stigma it had during the Maoist period, divorced women often still felt themselves to be at a disadvantage. Ping, and many other women commented on the low quality of the local men they met and also expressed concern that local men were attracted to them for the housing or economic benefits they could provide. Local Chinese men whom they considered more worthy prospects were attracted to much younger, very attractive, never-married women. Like many others, Ping also commented on the extreme "pickiness" of overseas Chinese men, who preferred young, beautiful, and never-married women.

In the summer of 2000, before the ninety-day stay in the United States that was permitted by her fiancée visa had expired, Ping decided to marry Elvin. Her worst fears about the nudist colony had been laid to rest. The people she met there, she said, were decent, respectable people who included doctors, lawyers, and ministers. Though still anxious because of the impossibility of having friends or relatives visit, she was relieved that she could remain clothed. She had gradually learned more about Elvin's personal and financial situation, and although struck by his lack of resources, she saw prospects for improvement. Over the coming months, we spoke several times and continued to communicate by e-mail. Many times she complained of Elvin's lack of flexibility, her feelings of isolation, and her thoughts of returning to China. She contrasted her U.S. lifestyle with that in Beijing, where she could meet friends, eat out, and socialize at minimal cost, and where health care was affordable. She often complained that the three months permitted by the fiancée visa was not enough to allow her to make a well-informed decision. She updated me about some of her friends in Beijing and the warnings she had issued to them about marrying foreign men and the difficulties of life abroad.

Other times, Ping reported improvements in their situation. She persuaded Elvin to move out of the nudist colony into a small apartment in a less isolated region. She had obtained a Social Security card and could apply for work. Eventually, she found a job in a day-care center. Although it was for minimum wage with no benefits, she enjoyed the work and managed to save some money. She obtained a learner's permit to drive. Her attitudes about Elvin continued to waver as he struck her as rigid, set in his ways, and lacking in empathy. She described to me one angry dispute in which she broke some dishes and left the apartment. Later they seemed to reconcile, although she became increasingly frustrated with his uncommunicativeness and his insensitivity to her isolation and loneliness. At one point she returned to China for a few months under the pretext that her necessary dental treatment would be cheaper there. Once there, she seriously contemplated remaining, but finally she decided to return to the United States and try again.

After a few more months, in June 2002, Ping phoned to tell me that she was returning to China for good. Although she had said this before, she sounded more determined this time. She had given notice at work, initiated the purchase of a ticket, and spoke of continuing the divorce procedures she had initiated the previous year. As she explained, she had been in the United States for almost two years. She had given their marriage and life in the U.S. a solid try, but she had decided to go back. She had experienced much bitterness, and would continue to do so if she remained. It was too hard to be married to Elvin, and for someone her age, it was too difficult to do what was necessary to improve their lives. If she had been young enough to return to school or healthy enough to work long hours in a restaurant and not worry about health insurance, it might be different. Compared with China, where she had friends and family, mobility, health care, and a good job, in the U.S. she had very little and was often lonely. With her meager earnings, she paid half the rent for their one-bedroom apartment and paid for her own health insurance. She still had no driver's license, because Elvin would not take her out to practice driving. Without being able to drive, she felt stranded at home and far too dependent on him. She was tired of trying to reason with Elvin, and she could not see any way that life would improve enough. On the weekends and evenings, while Elvin was away at work, she watched the television he had reluctantly agreed to buy, or she sent e-mail messages to friends and family in China.

In anger, Ping once told Elvin that she felt like she was "a wife he had bought" with no freedom to come and go on her own. His response, she said, was that he didn't understand. Western men like Elvin, she said, think Western women are too independent, demanding, and materialistic. They like Chinese women because they expect them to be easily satisfied with very little. But, she explained, these men are wrong: most Chinese women are very independent and strong. Her life was better in Beijing. So she had told him that it was his responsibility to buy her the ticket to go back. A week later, Ping wrote to say that she had not left after all. A friend of hers had spoken to Elvin, and they had agreed to try marriage counseling. By the end of the summer, she was again on the verge of returning to Beijing, but had decided to wait and see how things went, until the two-year mark, when she could file for permanent resident status and possibly a divorce.

Rosie

The historical and political relations that serve as the backdrop to Rosie and Ben's courtship and marriage are different from those in China. Almost everyone I spoke to in the Philippines had friends or relatives living in the United States. Correspondence introductions leading to marriage have been in existence in the Philippines since at least the 1970s, decades longer than in China. From the perspective of family members in the Philippines, as Nobue Suzuki's chapter well illustrates, marriages to men from Japan, Australia, North America, and Western Europe are well known, and generally viewed favorably and as potentially economically beneficial to the woman's family. Instances of trafficking and abuse of women under the guise of marriage are also well known and have circulated via the popular media and the Commission for Filipinos Overseas (CFO). Filipinas were among the first women listed in the printed catalog of U.S.-based introduction agencies in the early and mid-1970s. Such a pattern has continued despite the passage of Republic Act 6955 in the Philippines in 1990, which prohibits recruitment of Filipinas for marriage to foreign nationals.[14] While Chinese women are a growing minority among women listed by introduction agencies, Filipinas (followed by women from Eastern Europe and the former Soviet Union) are the most numerous nationalities listed.

The imagined suitability of Filipinas as prospective spouses is linked to the U.S. colonial and postcolonial military and economic presence in the Philippines. Since before World War II, U.S. servicemen had been becoming involved with Filipinas, and some married and returned to the United States with their wives. Philippine Catholicism, spoken English, and romantic notions about Asian women are among the factors that contribute to the image of Filipinas as suitable wives.

A long-established historical pattern of Filipino emigration to the United States for the "better life" and to help one's family contributes to the popularity of the United States as a desirable destination. Moreover, in China sons have traditionally been considered most responsible for their parents' well-being, and Chinese daughters are expected to marry out to contribute to the well-being of their affines (Watson 1991); in the Philippines, daughters, especially eldest daughters, are expected to contribute to the well-being of their natal families (Tacoli 1996, Suzuki in this volume). This helps explain the prominent role of Filipinas in international labor migration and marriage migration (Constable 1997, Parreñas 2001). Rosie was one of several women I met who was attracted to the idea of meeting and marrying an American. Not only did this fit her romantic personal dreams, but it also provided a means by which to assist her family. Whereas most Filipinas expressed a desire to provide financial assistance to their natal families, most Chinese women said their families did not expect or need such support. Chinese women with a child (none I knew had more than one because of the family-planning regulations) spoke instead of providing a child with the opportunity to emigrate, and those without children spoke of the opportunities for their future children.

By summer 2002, Rosie and Ben had overcome many difficulties and were getting along well. They had met through correspondence several years earlier, much of their early correspondence through postal mail. Ben had been married to an American "career woman" for about a decade. The marriage ended, according to Ben, because he wanted a family, and she did not. This experience made him think about how to meet a woman with whom he could establish a family, so he subscribed to a publication that provided the photographs, names, and addresses of Filipinas. After Ben's first visit to the Philippines, he and Rosie became engaged, and he set up a computer for her and her son to use so that they could correspond with him by e-mail. When they first met, Rosie was in her mid-twenties, Ben was in his early fifties, and Rosie's son, Paul, was under ten.

In her teens Rosie had gone to work as a "helper" (or maid) for a wealthier Filipino family. She became pregnant by her employer's son, and her employer, in the hopes that her son would settle down, required him and Rosie to sign a marriage agreement. The young man showed no signs of settling down, however, and Rosie eventually returned to her *barangay* (village, neighborhood) in Mindanao with her son. She spent the week working in a shop in the small nearby town, depending on her mother for child care. Although she had several romantic prospects, none of them suited her. Meanwhile, one of her friends encouraged her to submit a photograph and brief statement to a pen-pal club. She did so and was surprised at the number of responses she received. When Ben came to visit, he was carefully scrutinized by family members and local elders, who sought assurance of his honorable motives. In the course of his visit, he proposed and she accepted.

When she met Ben, Rosie was unsure of whether she was, in fact, married to Paul's father. She did not consider herself married, especially since they had never lived as "husband and wife," and had not had a church wedding, but she was uncertain whether the paperwork had been filed. When she and Ben discovered that she was indeed legally married, Ben relocated his work to the Philippines and began the long, complicated, and expensive process of having her marriage annulled. Since divorce is illegal in the Philippines, Rosie could not remarry without an official annulment, and would not qualify for immigration to the United States (see Constable 2003b). In any case, Rosie was not particularly keen about going to the United States and would have been very happy to have Ben remain permanently in the Philippines. While they awaited the annulment, Ben worked in Manila and they lived for about a year in an upscale suburb of Manila with household help from some of Rosie's kin.

Eventually the annulment was secured, and despite Rosie's initial reluctance to move, she, Ben, and Paul relocated to the U.S. Midwest in 2000, where Ben had accepted a temporary academic position. I communicated with them several times in 2002, and it was clear that Rosie found the initial adjustment to isolated American middle-class life difficult. She missed her family and Filipino food and disliked the cold midwestern winter. Familiar with the images of racial violence from U.S. television and popular media in the Philippines, she was nervous around her African American neighbors. Like Ping, she felt lonely, but Ben encouraged her to take English-language classes at a nearby community college, and he urged her to get her driver's license. Paul, a friendly and bright child, did well in school and made new friends. When I spoke to Rosie in June 2002, she seemed to be doing well. She sounded relaxed and confident, and her English—which was already good—had noticeably improved. Earlier, Ben had expressed concern about the upheaval of annual relocations in temporary academic jobs, and he had decided to make a permanent job in a region with a significant Filipino population a top priority. Thus they moved to the East Coast, where Ben decided to take a permanent nonacademic job. The move itself was a family adventure. Rosie looked forward to the trip they planned to the Philippines at Christmas. Rosie's mother had built a new house with money they had sent her, and it was large enough for them all to stay in when they visited. Rosie proudly explained that they would have their own bedroom and "powder room" when they visited.

According to Rosie, Ben selected their new neighborhood for several reasons, among them its many Filipino stores and restaurants, so Rosie no longer missed the foods she had craved in the Midwest. In a few short weeks, she had made contact with several Filipinas, and there were Filipino teachers and students at Paul's new private Catholic school. She had been watching television when I phoned, soap operas because she was "bored" since Paul was at school and Ben was at work. Like Ping, she had not anticipated the difficulty of getting around and the ensuing lack of mobility, freedom, and sociality in America. Although she had obtained her driver's license, she was nervous about driving in the more crowded urban setting. We reminisced about my visit to her small *barangay* in the Philippines, where there was no indoor running water and one telephone, and she talked about their plans—plans that Ben had once resisted—to move back to the Philippines in a few years, after Ben had saved enough money and was ready to retire. In contrast to our earlier conversations, she sounded pleased with her adjustments and their future plans and was in very good spirits.

Gendered Mobility and Spatial Hypergamy

Referring to the "power geometry" of migration, Doreen Massey has written that some individuals are more in charge of mobility than others (1994:149). Both Aihwa Ong and Constance Clark suggest, in the case of Chinese women and overseas men, that men are "in charge of mobility" (Ong 1999:153, Clark 2001:105). Yet as the stories of Ping and Rosie illustrate, women who choose to correspond with and marry foreign men are not mobile simply by virtue of men's initiative and power. Women actively seek out such opportunities for mobility and take initiatives to enable themselves to make moves that they view as empowering for themselves and their families. To view women as simply on the "receiving end" of mobility is to downplay their central role in facilitating their own migrations. As Pessar and Mahler write, "people's social locations affect their access to resources and mobility across transnational spaces but also their agency as initiators, refiners and transformers of these conditions" (2001:7–8). To Massey's idea of "power geometry" and their notion of "social location," Pessar and Mahler add the importance of "initiative" and also "imagination and substantive agency" (2001:8), notions that are illustrated by a number of the cross-border marriages described in this volume and by the correspondence marriages of Ping and Rosie.

The majority of correspondence marriages involving U.S. men and foreign women involve a patrilocal postmarital residence pattern. That is, a woman relocates to her husband's homeland. Many older anthropological studies depict such moves as cultural requirements—in which women have little choice—or as indications of male or patrilineal power (Lévi-Strauss 1969, Rubin 1975), but correspondence marriages enable us to see the importance of women's agency and initiative in achieving a patrilocal residence. This move, regardless of the actual living conditions in the United States, is generally considered upward. In cases like Rosie's, where she lived in a small nipa hut without running water in a remote part of the Philippines, her urban apartment in the United States is a step up in terms of living standards, but compared with the spacious modern home she and Ben shared in suburban Manila with household help, her lifestyle in the United States is a step down. Likewise, in Ping's case, her move from her own large two-bedroom flat in Beijing to a one-bedroom small-town flat and from a respected job to a minimum-wage job without benefits should not automatically be considered upward mobility. Yet in the final instance, such mobility is often seen and imagined as upward—at least from the perspective of friends and relatives back home—because of the future opportunities that it potentially offers, regardless of more immediate downward implications (see also Suzuki in this volume).

The marriages described in this chapter thus fit a general pattern of spatial hypergamy, with women's geographic mobility often from a poorer country to a richer one, even though this pattern may, in fact, say little about the particular social or economic mobility of any given individual or of the U.S.-Chinese or U.S.-Filipino couple. As other scholars have noted (Jedlicka 1988, Simons 2001), U.S. men who meet and marry through correspondence do not come from one region, class, educational, occupational, or socioeconomic category in the United States. Many Chinese women and some Filipinas are highly educated and may be white-collar professionals in their countries of origin, but their spouses sometimes have less education and less prestigious occupations. Although most such couples settle in the United States, there are also examples of U.S. men with Asian wives who eventually or temporarily settle in China or the Philippines, where a modest U.S. pension can afford a better standard of living. Chinese or Filipina wives can provide major advantages for men who decide to work and settle abroad. The social locations of such men and women do not simply involve an upward move, but involve complex shifts in the relative importance of— among others—wealth, occupation, education, nationality, race, gender, marital status, and physical appearance in different geographical settings.

The overwhelming majority of international introductions and correspondence, as this volume suggests, involve women who move and men who remain at home. This chapter thus begs the question of why correspondence marriages are so common between U.S. men and foreign women but virtually nonexistent between U.S. women and foreign men. It is not that Western women are unimaginable or unattractive to men in China or the Philippines (Schein 1997, Erwin 1999), or that U.S. women find Asian men in the U.S. unattractive (Pan 2000, Liang and Ito 1999). Marriages do exist between U.S. women and Asian men, but they rarely have the opportunity to meet through correspondence or by way of introduction agencies, and they do not reflect the same popular appeal.

The lack of correspondence opportunities for Chinese or Filipino men and Western women is apparent not only in the relative lack of such listings on introduction-agency Web sites, but is also alluded to by the comments—usually jokes—I heard from Chinese, Filipino, and U.S. men. One Filipino man joked that he wished he could become a mail-order bride, and one Western man who considered relocating to the Philippines, pointing to the reversal of the common logic, joked about becoming a "mail-order husband." The concept of a mail-order spouse was unknown in China, but Chinese men who knew of my research often bemoaned the fact that Chinese women could marry foreigners and that "all of the very best Chinese women, the most beautiful and educated, leave to marry foreign men," whereas the same opportunity was not available for men. One Chinese man, the close friend of the woman manager of an introduction agency in Beijing, complained that even unattractive Chinese women with bad personalities had many foreign suitors, whereas none were available for attractive and financially successful men such as himself (see Constable 2003a).

Relationships between U.S. women and Chinese or Filipino men lack the visibility and the popular appeal of U.S. men-Asian women relationships. One key factor, though one that was not explored in this chapter, lies in the popular and historical U.S. images of Asian women versus Asian men. Whereas Asian women are often depicted in popular media as sexually or romantically appealing and as appropriate partners for Western men, Asian men are commonly depicted as emasculated or violent, and rarely, if ever, as sexually or romantically appealing to Western women (Marchetti 1993, Constable 2003a, Shih 2000).[15] Other cultural beliefs are also relevant. Despite changes and variations in marriage patterns and gender roles in the United States, China, and the Philippines, the beliefs that marriages should ideally be hypergamous (upward for women) or between equals and that men should be the primary breadwinners persist. Such notions, paired with ideas about the relative geographical ranking of the United States in relation to China and the Philippines in terms of wealth and economic development, reinforce the notion that marriages between U.S. men and women from poorer countries are culturally and socially appropriate, whereas those involving U.S. women and foreign men are not.

In sum, this chapter has explored the gendered process of introduction and marriage by correspondence and has pointed to certain social and cultural logics that underlie correspondence marriages of U.S. men with Chinese women and Filipinas. Such marriages, like the others in this volume, reflect a gendered power geometry that allows women like Ping and Rosie (but not their male compatriots) opportunities to achieve mobility through marriage. Such patterns of global hypergamy are commonly considered spatially upward, but often reflect far more contradictory social and individual patterns of mobility. Like the other chapters that describe cross-border marriages in this volume, this chapter raises broader questions about the ways in which marriages are imagined, propelled, and realized across a multitude of borders, and the implications of such marriages for the border-crossing subjects as well as for those who remain at home.

Notes

Chapter 1. Introduction

This project is the outcome of panels I organized for the 2001 American Anthropological Association and Association for Asian Studies meetings; my thanks to the participants. I also wish to thank Nancy Abelmann, Joseph S. Alter, Laurel Kendall, Rubie S. Watson, and an anonymous reader for their comments, suggestions, and insightful critiques; Caren Freeman, Wenfang Tang, Agnes Wen, and Haihui Zhang for help in locating figures and references; and Hung Cam Thai for permission to reprint his previously published chapter. I am grateful to the University Center for International Studies and the Asian Studies Center at the University of Pittsburgh and the Richard D. and Mary Jane Edwards Endowed Publication Fund for providing resources to complete this project. Special thanks to Peter Agree, a most supportive and inspiring editor.

Chapter 2. Cross-Border Hypergamy?

Middlebury College generously supported the Mei Xian research for this chapter during my sabbatical leave in 1995–96. While in China, I benefited immensely from affiliation with the Guangzhou Academy of Social Sciences. Earlier research in India was conducted with a grant from the American Institute of Indian Studies. The Hakka communities of Mei Xian, Calcutta, and Toronto opened their lives to me and helped me in innumerable ways in all dimensions of fieldwork. I am profoundly grateful.

1. The Hakka are a linguistic and cultural group among the Han Chinese, who are found in greatest numbers in southeastern China, especially in Guangdong Province. The term "Hakka" is actually Cantonese for "guest" (*kejia* in Mandarin), and it refers to the notion that the Hakka are thought to have migrated to Guangdong Province and other areas of southeastern China from the north. While the Hakka may have been historically viewed as "guest people" by the predominantly Cantonese population of Guangdong Province, they constitute the vast majority of residents in Mei Xian.

2. During the early decades of the Qing dynasty (1644–1911), the Chinese state banned emigration. Indeed, the Qianlong emperor stated that emigrants had "deserted their ancestors' graves to seek profits abroad" (Duara 1997:43), and emigrants who returned were often executed in order to deter others from leaving (Duara 1997:42). However, in the waning years of the Qing dynasty, the imperial court, much like the reform-minded Communist leaders of the post-

Mao era in China, realized that emigrants might provide an important source of wealth, which could be used profitably to enhance Chinese development. By the 1880s, imperial policy toward emigrants had reversed itself, and by 1902, the Qing government was actually sending envoys to Southeast Asia to encourage the Chinese merchants there to invest in China.

The use of the word *huaqiao,* or "overseas Chinese," also begins in this period. "Hua" simply refers to China or Chinese, and, as Wang Gungwu points out, the word *qiao* is "an ancient word whose main meaning is 'to sojourn, or reside temporarily away from home.' The first clear use of the word . . . occurred in an official document in 1858. . . . Up to this time, a whole range of other terms, some most uncomplimentary, were employed to describe Chinese who resided overseas" (Wang 1985:72).

3. Curiously, while marriage is clearly a form of migration in the Chinese and many other cases, one is at pains to find any mention of this in the traditional migration literatures. A recent summary of work on international migration, for instance, lists a number of migrant categories, including settlers, contract workers, professionals, undocumented workers, refugees, and asylum seekers (Stalker 2001:10–11). Yet in speaking about these categories of migrants and the reasons and ways they move, the author never mentions marriage transactions.

4. The villagers' explanations here are at variance with that of A. Wolf (1968), who sees the issue of family harmony and obtaining a compliant daughter-in-law as more important than poverty in the arrangements behind adopted daughter-in-law marriages.

Chapter 3. Cautionary Tales

Audrey Bilger, Nicole Constable, and Phil Haft read versions of this chapter. I am very grateful for their thoughtful comments and suggestions.

1. *Taohun* is used to describe secretly running off for the purpose of marriage without a specific person in mind. *Paohun* is used to refer to elopement with a particular person.

2. The distinction between *bangjia* and *youguai* (also *guaiyou*) dates back to the nineteenth century and is founded on the assumption that women are neither free agents nor entitled to freedom of movement (Sinn 1994:145–46). According to Sinn (1994), in nineteenth century Hong Kong, where a woman could not be prosecuted for adultery or desertion, deserted husbands sought to punish their wives' lovers by charging the eloping men with kidnapping. Hence, during a period when similar distinctions between abduction and kidnapping existed, kidnapping was also conceptually associated with elopement.

3. The Lijiang case suggests that "hypergamy" in an econometric sense cannot adequately represent what's at stake in new forms of marriage (see Oxfeld and Schein in this volume). Oxfeld questions whether economically advantageous marriages in which husbands migrated abroad, while leaving their brides in China, actually represented mobility for the women involved. Schein questions whether Miao women, for whom migration to Chinese villages in Jiangsu meant being linguistically and culturally isolated, actually improved Miao women's lives. Naxi elopements that are hypogamous (downwardly mobile marriages to men with fewer economic resources) similarly challenge fixed notions of hypergamy (see Lavely 1991). In the Naxi case, parents gauge a daughter's marriage by comparing the economic status of the groom's family with that of the bride's,

but young women conceive of hypergamy in terms of a suitor's potential as well as his family's assets. In Lijiang, the definition of an upwardly mobile or hypergamous marriage is contested and based on generational perspectives corresponding to the different opportunities for mobility during the Maoist and reform eras. As with the Hakka and the Miao, the Naxi case requires a deeper time frame for assessing marriage. In the Naxi case, the examination of hypogamous unions months or years after elopements indicates that such unions (in contrast to hypergamous marriages) enable Naxi women to negotiate the terms of their new lives more effectively.

4. While this description of *paohun* focuses exclusively on female agency, in all but one case I was aware of, the "running" woman was actually being "led by" or accompanied by the young man.

5. In contemporary rural Lijiang, kidnapping and long-distance migration have declined substantially. This may be attributed to the designation of Lijiang town as a UNESCO World Heritage Site and to Lijiang having become a destination for national and international tourism. While kidnapping and long-distance marriage migration occurred primarily in rural Lijiang as opposed to Lijiang town, the economic opportunities generated by tourism in Lijiang town have made long-distance migration and marriage migration less appealing to rural residents (Yang Fuquan, February 17, 2003, personal communication).

Chapter 4. Marrying out of Place

Fieldwork was carried out for short periods in 1999, 2000, 2001, and 2002 against the backdrop of extended research over four stays in the Guizhou Miao community of Xijiang between 1985 and 1993. Research has also been conducted in several American cities of Hmong residence, especially in Fresno, Sacramento, and Minneapolis-Saint Paul. China research sites have included Beijing, Jiangsu, Shenzhen, Guiyang, Kaili, Leishan, Kunming, Wenshan, and other Miao locales. I am extremely grateful to the people of Xijiang and other sites, as well as to Zhang Xiao, Yang Ge, and Gu Wenfeng, for their participation in the project. I thank Rutgers University and the Rutgers Research Council for support of ongoing research. I am also grateful to Nicole Constable and the anonymous reviewers for their critical commentary on earlier drafts of this chapter.

1. Note that *guaimai* is comparable to the term *guaihun* that Chao discusses in this volume, but the former emphasizes the sale (*mai*), while the latter emphasizes the marriage (*hun*).

2. These scenarios take place within the context of the large-scale labor migration, rural to urban as well as interior to coastal, that has been transforming Chinese society in recent years. For more on labor migrants in general see Zhang 2001 and Solinger 1999. On gender and labor migration, see Davin 1999, Fan 2000, X. Huang 1999 and Song 1999. On the desires and experiences of migrant women, see Yan 2003, Ngai 2002, and Schein n.d. For an overview of long-distance marriage migration, see Fan and Huang 1998 and for comparative cases, see Clark 2001 on Shenzhen, Han 2001:159–70 on Anhui, and Bossen 2002:235–40 on Yunnan.

3. I use "patrilocality" here as a shorthand that includes virilocal and neolocal arrangements in which a bride may move to live with a groom in his village,

town, city, neighborhood, etc., but not necessarily take up residence in the same household as the groom's parents.

4. As discussed later in this chapter, in terms of the social, mobility is questionably designated as upward, since the brides often find their new husbands to occupy lower statuses than they did within their own communities.

5. I emphasize, however, that discourses of critique are very much alive among the Hmong in the West as well. Especially vocal in denouncing the transnational quests for women are Hmong feminists—and others interested in women's issues—and Hmong Christians who champion monogamy and morality. A great many Hmong American men speak out as well; indeed, a group of young male filmmaker-activists have produced a courageous documentary, aired on public television, exposing the scandal of a young Hmong woman in Thailand who committed suicide when a Hmong American man failed to follow through on his promised betrothal to her. It opens with the pensive narration: "How many of us have gone back to Thailand? How many of us have asked ourselves why we go? Is it because we miss our homeland? Is it because we miss family and relatives? If we go with honor and honesty, perhaps this young woman would not have died." (see Death in Thailand 2002).

6. See Kelsky 2001 for an in-depth study of Western dreams and cross-border travels on the part of Japanese women over the last century and a half. Kelsky uses the term "internationalism" to describe the subjectivity and practices of women who actually went abroad and of those who participated in the fantasy, which, as she points out, was likewise highly gendered.

7. See, for instance, Shih 1998 on sexual/marital relations between Chinese in mainland, Taiwan, and Hong Kong; Thai (in this volume) for Vietnamese marriages to Vietnamese refugees in the West; and Oxfeld (in this volume) on Hakka in mainland China, India, and Canada.

8. See Schein (n.d.) for a discussion of Neil Smith's and other theories of scale in relation to women's mobility strategies in China.

Chapter 5. Marrying Up and Marrying Down

I wish to thank John R. Shepherd, Susan McKinnon, and Nicole Constable for reading and offering helpful comments on this chapter. I am also grateful to my research assistants, Kim Kyŏngŭn and Kim Jiyŏng and to the many Chosŏnjok women and men who generously invited me into their homes. This chapter is based on my dissertation fieldwork, the various phases of which were funded by USIA Fulbright, Fulbright-Hays, SSRC-IDRF, and the Wenner-Gren Foundation.

1. Both Korean and Chinese terms appear throughout this chapter in accordance with the various geographic locations in which research was conducted as well as the linguistic preferences of my interviewees.

2. The term "Chosŏn" derives from the name of the last dynasty that existed on the Korean peninsula before Japanese colonization. Ethnic Koreans who migrated to northeastern China beginning in the 1860s and throughout the early twentieth century were officially recognized in 1945 as an ethnic minority of the People's Republic of China under the name of Chosŏnjok or the Chosŏn people. North Koreans also use the term "Chosŏn" to refer to their country, while South Koreans use the term "Hanguk."

3. Based on my interviews with ten licensed and unlicensed matchmakers in Seoul, the average cost of a five-day marriage tour was between five and six mil-

lion won or approximately $4,200–5,000, of which half or more was taken home as profit by the matchmaker.

4. At the time of my research, it was a popular saying among middle-aged people in the village that after five years of working what South Koreans commonly call in English a "3D" (dirty, dangerous, and difficult) job in South Korea, one might comfortably retire to the Chinese countryside.

5. Park is referring to the decision made at the Uruguay Round negotiations in 1993, in the face of mounting external pressure, to open South Korean agricultural markets to foreign imports. So emotionally charged were the farmers' protests, which preceded and continued throughout the negotiations, that the minister of agriculture, forests, and fisheries was forced to hand in his resignation (Lee 2000:188).

6. While public opinion in Korea, fueled by the media, tends to focus on the acts of deception committed by Chosŏnjok brides, less publicized accounts depict Korean men as physically abusive of their Chosŏnjok wives or guilty of misrepresenting their socioeconomic situation to their brides-to-be. In these cases, the runaway brides are seen as giving the grooms their just deserts. Matchmakers and ordinary Koreans alike also recognized the existence of "paper marriages," a mutual agreement between brides and grooms to exchange citizenship papers for money. Finally, there is a gray areas of stories in which brides make a sincere effort to adjust to marital life in South Korea, but eventually their disappointed material expectations, feelings of isolation from the larger society, and incompatibilities with their husbands and in-laws push them to leave their marriages.

7. In the most extreme case I encountered, a thirty-seven-year-old Korean man pulled down his collar during an interview to reveal the scars he suffered in an attack on his life. The incident took place in Yanji, China, where the man and his Chosŏnjok wife were peddling merchandise (*pottali changsa*) they had brought over from Korea. Media reports confirm that the wife had conspired with her Chosŏnjok lover to murder her husband and collect the insurance money. An SBS television news broadcast in South Korea ran the story with the headline: "A Human Face with the Heart of an Animal" (*inmyŏn susim pullyun*).

8. It is estimated that one-sixth of the Korean population left the Korean peninsula for Manchuria (now northeastern China) and Japan during the Japanese colonial regime (1910–45). Though a large number returned to mainland Korea between the end of the Second World War and the start of the Korean War, roughly one million Koreans remained in Manchuria (Park 1996:29), where they were physically separated from and entirely barred from communicating with family members living on the southern half of the Korean peninsula for nearly five decades. Grinker notes how the category of "divided families" (*isan kajok*) is symbolically linked to South Korean discourses on national reunification and division (2000:99–126). South Korea's immigration policies with respect to the Chinese Chosŏnjok, which privilege family visitation over other purposes of travel, reflect this symbolic connection between the reunification of divided family members and the reunification of the Korean people.

9. Initially implemented by the Korean government in 1992 to provide skill training for foreign workers already employed by Korean businesses overseas, the industrial-trainee program was broadened in 1994 to recruit overseas workers for small and medium-size businesses in South Korea (Moon 2000:149).

10. Alongside the phenomenon of "paper marriages," a market in "paper mothers and fathers" has emerged, which involves selling the parental rights to visit a married-out daughter on the occasion of major life-cycle events, such as a

wedding ceremony or birth of a child. The forty-five-year-old widow with whom I lived during my fieldwork was offered a chance to travel to Korea as the fictitious mother of a young bride in the village. The bride's parents had already traveled to Korea, so as a charitable gesture, the bride offered to sell her mother's identity and household registration to the widow, who was regarded as one of the most unfortunate in the village community. A male relative would make the journey in the guise of the woman's father. At 60,000 yuan (approximately $7,250), the offer was considered too good to refuse, but in the end, the widow failed to come up with this sum before the proposed date of the (also fictitious) wedding ceremony.

11. At the time of my research, the Korean government set about making the marriage visa application process more costly and complicated to prevent paper marriages. In some cases, couples reported waiting as long as six months to complete the necessary paperwork. In the interval of time between the first meeting in China and arrival of the bride in South Korea, men and women developed their relationship through letters, usually reserving the expensive international telephone calls for practical communication regarding the visa application process.

12. Though large numbers of Chosŏnjok brides hailed from rural parts of China, some were spared having to help their families with the farmwork while pursuing a high school education.

13. Juno wanted me to note that taking in a Chosŏnjok bride was no easy task for the husband, either. He said he had worked hard to help his bride adjust to quotidian novelties of life in a foreign country, from the food and language to how to farm and do the shopping.

14. Repeatedly, Chosŏnjok brides spoke of *inyŏn*, an indefinable force that brings people together in marriage, friendship, and other types of partnerships, and that can be sensed intuitively upon first meeting, as the basis of their decision to marry. While feelings of romantic love might be hoped to be discovered or cultivated later, for the most part they play no role in the initial decision-making process in these cross-border marriages.

15. In June 1998, the Korean government enacted a new naturalization act to help reduce the number of "fraudulent marriages" (*wijang kyŏrhon*). The new law extended the period of time the foreign bride of a Korean national must wait before obtaining Korean citizenship, from ten days to two years.

16. Koreans use the term *chŏng* to refer to the emotional bond between spouses that develops over time as a result of shared life experiences. Unlike the Western notion of romantic love, *chŏng* encapsulates the full spectrum of human emotion and grows more intense with the passage of time.

17. In fact, many South Korean men I interviewed claimed they were initially drawn to China by the expectation that Chosŏnjok women retained so-called traditional Korean virtues of chastity, purity (*sunjinhada*), and obedience (*sunjonghada*) to a greater degree than women living in fast-paced, capitalist South Korean society.

18. This view departs from the findings of Gilmartin and Tan in their demographic study of long-distance marriage migration patterns within the People's Republic of China during the economic reform era. While they consider women's participation in long-distance marriage migrations as "a type of female agency," they postulate that ultimately the resultant marital relationships tend to "reinforce male power" (2002:215).

19. Contrary to the view that marriage migration tends to reinforce male priv-

ilege, the mobility of Chosŏnjok women places Chosŏnjok men in a difficult position in China. (I am grateful to Nicole Constable for pointing out the potentially disempowering effects on men). In northeastern China, the exodus of Chosŏnjok brides has created a marriage squeeze for unmarried Chosŏnjok men. Desperate for a married lifestyle, Chosŏnjok farmers are increasingly opting to set up households with refugee women from North Korea, despite the fact that these "marriages" exist outside the law and North Korean women must live in constant fear of deportation by Chinese authorities.

20. While marriages between South Korean women and Chinese men do exist, they occur in small numbers and are almost exclusively "love marriages" (*yŏnae kyŏrhon*), as opposed to an "arranged marriage" (*chungmae kyŏrhon*) in which the couple meets through the assistance of someone from the senior generation, whether a professional matchmaker, or a relative or friend of the parents (see Lett 1988).

Chapter 6. A Failed Attempt at Transnational Marriage

We are grateful to Sea-ling Cheng for consulting with us on this chapter, and to Nicole Constable, Caren Freeman, Noriko Muraki, and an anonymous reviewer for their extremely helpful comments.

1. A newspaper recently reported on the disabled son of an ophthalmologist who ventured outside of his home for the first time at age twenty-eight (Pak 2003:4, 10, see Sŏ [1963]1990 for a fictional account of disability in South Korea).

2. In the past, non-Korean wives were naturalized upon marriage, but under the new law both non-Korean husbands and wives can be naturalized only after residing in South Korea for two years after marriage (or after having been married for three years and residing in South Korea for one year) and upon completion of a citizenship exam. Thus in redressing gendered inequities in the system of marital citizenship, it has been made decidedly more difficult for non-Korean wives to naturalize; this speaks, we think, to rising concerns over international marriage fraud. Similarly problematic is that because there is no South Korean equivalent of a green card or permanent residency (marriage immigrants are assigned an F1 cohabitation (*tonggŏ*) visa, there are no provisions for non-Korean spouses who do not choose to naturalize to be able to work in South Korea. Furthermore, there are no provisions for dual citizenship. In the aftermath of the IMF crisis, these limitations have become all the more problematic because foreign spouses have been reticent to give up their own national citizenship (the promise of employment at home) in the face of enormous increases in unemployment in South Korea (Rosa-Yoon 1999).

3. In Hyunhee's conversation with Min's Mother in 2002, she spoke about the possibility of finding a poor disabled woman for her son.

Chapter 7. Tripartite Desires

I am grateful to all of my informants and their families in Japan and the Philippines for their patience and understanding of my long-term project. I also thank Nicole Constable, Donald Nonini, and James Roberson for their comments and encouragement, and the Japan Foundation, the Matsushita International Foundation, and the Toyota Foundation for their generous financial support.

1. Marriages between Filipino men and Japanese women constitute 1 percent of all Filipino-Japanese marriages (Ministry of Health, Labour and Welfare 2003). The children constituted on average 10 percent of the category during the 1990s (Ministry of Justice 1999–2000).

2. In Japan, foreign spouses are not automatically granted permanent visas. They must apply for one, usually after five years, but the time period varies depending on the couple's circumstances. Prior to obtaining this visa, as in the case of Reggie, foreigners who lost or are divorced from their Japanese spouses but are the custodians of their Japanese children receive long-term visas. They may eventually apply for a permanent visa as well.

3. Studies of intermarriage have largely dismissed men (Cottrell 1990, Holt 1996) and Japanese men in particular (see Cahill 1990). Even if they are discussed, men's inner feelings tend to be subsumed within national and institutional problems (see Johnson and Warren 1994).

4. Twenty-nine men (67.4 percent) out of forty-three are eldest sons. It is important to keep in mind that the majority of them were born between the 1940s and 1960s, when average birth rates were rapidly decreasing from four to fewer than three, and many men are thus eldest sons if they have only sisters. Therefore, that 67.4 percent of men are eldest is not necessarily peculiar to the husbands of Filipinas.

5. Mitarai married five times—one Japanese, one Korean, three Filipinas, and another Filipina being arranged. Such unusual serial marriages may distance a man's relatives from him.

Chapter 8. Clashing Dreams in the Vietnamese Diaspora

An earlier version of this chapter was published in *Global Woman*, edited by Barbara Ehrenreich and Arlie Russell Hochschild (Metropolitan, 2003). I would like to thank Barrie Thorne, Arlie Hochschild, and Barbara Ehrenreich for comments on drafts of this chapter.

1. All names have been changed to protect the privacy of informants. In most cases, I have also changed the names of peasant villages in Vietnam or small towns in the United States. I have kept the real names of all metropolitan areas.

2. Although Saigon's name changed to Ho Chi Minh City when the South surrendered to North Vietnamese military troops in 1975, most people I met in contemporary Vietnam still refer to the city as "Saigon," or simply "Thanh Pho" (The City). In this chapter, I echo their frames of reference by using the name "Saigon" and "Saigonese" to refer to the locals there.

3. Since April 1975, over two million people emigrated from Vietnam, about 3 percent of the country's current population of eighty million. Approximately 60 percent left as boat refugees; the remaining 40 percent departed from Vietnam and went directly to resettlement countries. Ninety-four percent of those who left Vietnam eventually resettled in western countries. Between 1975 and 1995, the U.S. accepted 64 percent of that group; 12 percent went to Australia and 12 percent to Canada. Among European countries, France received the largest number, although this represents only 3 percent of total resettlements (Merli 1997). As the refugee influx declines, family reunification and family

sponsorship, such as family-forming migration, may dominate Vietnamese out-migration during this century.

4. I would like to thank Pierrette Hondagneu-Sotelo for pointing out the complexity and danger of lumping all migrants—legal and illegal—into one category.

5. Here, "men and women" refer to individuals aged twenty and over since aggregate data from the Immigration and Naturalization Service include the age of eighteen in the bracket of fifteen-nineteen, thus making it impossible to calculate the legal marriage adult age of eighteen into the marriage migration figure. Therefore, we can assume that these percentages are slightly lower than the actual numbers of marriage migrants.

6. In order to understand the types of marriage migrants, I categorize at least three different streams of marriage migration that have earned legitimacy from the state because migrants in all three streams can obtain, with relative ease, the migration paperwork to go abroad. Each stream has its own history, patterns of migration, and cultural images; some women may fall into more than one stream, though it is usually clear in which stream they belong. The first, perhaps most visible and highly represented in the media, is the commercialized mail-order bride stream. From the vantage point of the community of origin in Asia and in Vietnam, and in Eastern European countries where there is a market for mail-order brides, these brides are viewed on a continuum of (mainly) prostitutes to women who search globally through commercialized arrangements for their dream husbands. Men on the receiving end are usually white Caucasians from the U.S., Australia, Canada, and countries in Europe who go to "exotic lands" in search of a submissive wife (Glodava and Onizuka 1994). The second stream of spousal migration is the non-commercialized transracial spousal migrant. Historically, this includes war brides of U.S. servicemen. In contemporary Vietnam and worldwide, where transnational and global workers of large, multinational firms work in corporate branches, men and, to a lesser extent, women, meet their spouses while working there. Another example would be embassy workers or academic researchers in a foreign country who meet and marry locals. The third stream, of which overseas Vietnamese men and women in Vietnam are clearly examples, constitutes the same ethnic individuals who live in different countries and have married each other. This third stream is the topic of my research.

7. Although it is difficult to calculate whether marriage migrants are in transracial relationships, or how many are part of systems of commercialized mail-order brides, the best estimate we have is that about one-third of all marriage migrant couples are transracial and that 2.7 to 4.1 percent are mail-order brides (Thornton 1992, USDOJ-INS 1999a).

8. This study is based on a probability sample of couples in sixty-nine marriages that were registered with the Vietnamese Department of Justice from September to December 1999. Two-thirds of the marriages were from urban Saigon, while the rest were from six villages dotted along a main road in a Mekong Delta province I shall call Se Long. In all, I interviewed ninety-eight individuals in Vietnam and thirty-one in the U.S., including brides, grooms, and family members. The groom phase of the project was based on a non-probability convenience sample of twenty-eight grooms of the brides I met in Vietnam. Although the geography of transpacific grooms included men from eight countries and sixteen U.S. states, the groom phase of my project is predominantly limited to interviewing grooms who live in San Francisco, Los Angeles, Seattle, and Boston,

although I attempt to conceptualize Vietnamese worldwide as a diaspora. Vietnamese emigrants and refugees have settled in over eighty countries worldwide (Tran 1997). I met two of the grooms who come from Australia and France while in Vietnam. The grooms I interviewed in the U.S. accounted for 40 percent of all the grooms in my study and 50 percent of the U.S.-based grooms. I interviewed most of the grooms and some of the brides at least twice, for 181 interviews in all. In addition, eight families in Vietnam allowed me to enter their homes at my leisure and to follow them to various places, such as markets, migration offices, and English classes. This provided me with the opportunity to learn about the effects of marriage to an overseas person on everyday life. Finally, since this was a study about marriage markets, I regularly attended various sites such as dance clubs, bars, and health clubs that catered to overseas Vietnamese men, as well as cooking classes for local women. I found out that people were not meeting each other in public spaces, and why not.

9. In the U.S., from 1960 to 1997, the number of marriage migrants multiplied by approximately three times. In the 1960s, only 9 percent of all immigrants were marriage migrants, while in 1997, an estimated 25 percent of all immigrants were marriage migrants (USDOJ-INS 1999b). In 1997, the latest data we have on marriage migration flows to the United States, for example, there were a total of 201,802 individuals who came to the U.S. through legal marriage migration, of which 84 percent were marriage migrants of U.S. citizens and 16 percent were marriage migrants of permanent residents. Of the marriage migrants of U.S. citizens, 61 percent were women whereas 87 percent of the marriage migrants of permanent residents were women. It is difficult to calculate how many marriage migrants enter through processes of family stage versus family-forming migration (Hondagneu-Sotelo 1994, Hwang and Saenz 1990); these numbers, however, suggest that while women overwhelmingly dominate as marriage migrants, a much larger proportion of women are migrating as spouses of permanent residents than as spouses of U.S. citizens, suggesting that among immigrants, men virtually dominate as the sponsors of marriage migrants.

10. Except in a few cases, the men who do low-wage work are also less educated than their wives; most of these grooms have barely a grade-school education. I do not wish to simply link low-wage work with less or under-education, and vice versa, though education and income are generally linked. I understand, for example, that plumbers may earn more money than teachers. In this chapter, I refer to the men as both "low-wage workers" and "undereducated" men. The brides I describe in this chapter are "highly educated" women compared with most women in Vietnam, meaning that they all have at least a college degree and many have advanced degrees. Most of them, though not all, come from solidly middle-class Vietnamese backgrounds. For this reason, I refer to the women as mostly highly educated, rather than as middle-class women.

11. These calculations are based on Goodkind's (1997) 1990 data. I simply added ten years to each cohort, though I acknowledge that mortality for either sex as a whole may have caused a shift in sex ratio since 1990.

12. When low-wage men travel abroad in search of spouses, many are unlikely to claim they work in low-wage jobs. However, in my study, I believe that most men told their wives, vis-à-vis matchmakers and go-between, that they work in low-wage jobs. Thus, the 55 percent calculation of low-wage men married to highly educated women is based on information provided by the brides and their families and on interviews with some of the grooms of those brides. Of the grooms I interviewed, I did not find any misrepresentations when I compared

their answers with the brides' stories. If anything, grooms are more likely to claim to their future wives that they work in high-wage, rather than low-wage, jobs. Thus, even though I estimate that 80 percent of the grooms in my study are low-wage workers, that number may, in fact, be higher if they told their wives that they work in high-wage rather than low-wage jobs.

Chapter 9. A Tale of Two Marriages

1. For critiques of so-called mail-order marriages, see, for example, Barry 1979 and 1992, Chin 1994, Dateline NBC 2001, Glodava and Onizuka 1994, Maury Povich Show 1998, Meng 1994, Rosca 1995, Villapando 1989. See Simons 2001:chaps. 2 and 3 for an excellent and thorough review and critique of the journalistic, scholarly, and advocacy literature on international matchmaking and so-called mail-order brides.

2. These images also contrast with the images of women in so-called mail-order bride catalogs. On catalogs, see Halualani 1995, Holt 1996, Robinson 1996, Tajima 1989, Tolentino 1996, Tsing 1993, Wilson 1988. For matchmaking between Taiwan and Vietnam, see Wang and Chang 2002. For studies based on interviews and face-to-face interactions, see Julag-Ay 1997, Ordonez 1997, Simons 2001, Constable 2003a and 2003b.

3. Chinese women sometimes had the resources and desire to travel abroad, but U.S. immigration restrictions made it difficult for them to obtain tourist visas. It is generally easier for U.S. men to obtain visas to travel to China or the Philippines than for women to come to the United States.

4. On Japanese marriage tours, see Nakamatsu 2002. The film *Asian Heart* focuses on tours of European men to the Philippines, and Li (2001) describes Hong Kong men's tours in mainland China. See Simons 2001:chap. 4 on U.S. men's tours to Russia and Ukraine. According to Simons, many men use such tours to make initial contacts with women, then continue to correspond after the tour. Others write to women first and arrange to meet during the tour.

5. For an excellent analysis and critique of this report, see Simons 2001:chap. 3.

6. Men I met mostly preferred the "fiancée visa route" because it took less time—usually three to six months—whereas obtaining a spousal visa could take from six months to over a year. Most Filipinas preferred to marry first because it was "more respectable." Some Filipinas had an unofficial ceremony or church blessing in the Philippines, got a fiancée visa, and had an official marriage in the United States as a compromise. Chinese women preferred the fiancée route because—although contrary to the INS intentions—it gave them ninety days to stay in the United States to decide whether to marry or to return home.

7. The Vermont Service Center data from February 1998 classified 5.5 percent of fiancée visa applications as "definitely or probably mail-order introductions" (USDOJ-INS 1999:13). Simons predicts that the number of Russian and Ukrainian women entering with K visas will double over the next decade (2001:313).

8. Another indication of the popularity of international introduction services is that the goodwife.com homepage received over eight million "hits," or visits, in less than six years.

9. A report by Davor Jedlicka based on 260 responses from men who sought brides through correspondence found that 94 percent were white; 50 percent

had two or more years of college; 56 percent identified themselves as politically conservative; 91 percent said sex should be between married or live-in partners. They were generally financially and professionally successful; their median age was thirty-seven; and 84 percent lived in metropolitan areas. Over half had been married at least once, and most had divorced after an average of seven years of marriage; a third had at least one child, and three-quarters hoped to have more children. Roughly half identified themselves as Protestant, about a quarter as Catholic, 15 percent belonged to other religions, and 14 percent had no religious affiliation (Glodava and Onizuka 1994:25–26). I did not conduct a formal survey of the men I encountered, but my impression was that they would fit this general profile. Men who corresponded with Chinese women, however, seemed less religious and of somewhat higher socioeconomic status than men who wrote to Filipinas.

10. For a detailed discussion of Internet and multisited research methodology, see Constable 2003a:chap. 2.

11. These are the same pseudonyms I use in earlier writings to describe the earlier stages of their courtships (Constable 2003a).

12. On marriage advertisements in China as a modern way to meet a partner, see Fan and Huang 1998: 236 and Gilmartin and Tan 2002:210.

13. By 2002, one of Ping's friends had left for the United States on a fiancée visa, and the other had married an Australian and had immigrated to Australia.

14. It is illegal to recruit Filipinas for marriage to foreigners, but introduction agencies get around this law, promoting themselves as "pen pal clubs" geared toward friendship with foreign men.

15. Western women told Lisa Simons that "they would not be interested in a foreign husband because, regardless of how western women complain about men in their own societies being 'not feminist enough' the belief about foreign men is that they were unlikely to view marriage as a partnership of equals" (2001:245 n. 39). Marriages between U.S. women and foreign men are often based on face-to-face meetings and on situations where the social distance and values can be understood on individual rather than broader social and cultural terms.

Works Cited

Abelmann, Nancy. 1996. *Echoes of the Past, Epics of Dissent: A South Korean Social Movement.* Berkeley: University of California Press.

———. 2003. *The Melodrama of Mobility: Women, Talk, and Class in Contemporary South Korea.* Honolulu: University of Hawaii Press.

Abelmann, Nancy, and John Lie. 1995. *Blue Dreams: Korean Americans and the Los Angeles Riots.* Cambridge, Mass.: Harvard University Press.

Aganon, Marie E. 1994. "Migrant Labor and the Filipino Family." In *The Filipino Family: A Spectrum of Views and Issues.* Aurora E. Perez, ed. Pp. 79–96. Quezon City: Office of Research Coordination, University of the Philippines.

Aguilar, Delia M. 1987. "Women in the Political Economy of the Philippines." *Alternatives* 12:511–26.

Aguilar, Filomeno V., Jr. 1996. "The Dialectics of Transnational Shame and National Identity." *Philippine Sociological Review* 44:101–36.

———. 1999. "Ritual Passage and the Reconstruction of Selfhood in International Labor Migration." *Sojourn* 14:98–139.

Ahern, Emily M. 1978. "The Power and Pollution of Chinese Women." In *Studies of Chinese Society.* Arthur Wolf, ed. Pp. 269–90. Stanford, Calif.: Stanford University Press.

Anagnost, Ann. 1997. "Neo-Malthusian Fantasy and National Transcendence." In *National Past-times.* Durham, N.C.: Duke University Press.

———. 2000. "Scenes of Misrecognition: Maternal Citizenship in the Age of Transnational Adoption." *Positions* 8(2):389–421.

Appadurai, Arjun. 1996. *Modernity at Large: Cultural Dimensions of Globalization.* Minneapolis: University of Minnesota Press.

Asis, Maruja M. B. 1994. "Family Ties in a World Without Borders." *Philippine Sociological Review* 42(1–4):16–26.

Baker, Hugh D. R. 1979. *Chinese Family and Kinship.* New York: Columbia University Press.

Barfield, Thomas, ed.. 1997. *The Dictionary of Anthropology.* Oxford: Blackwell.

Barry, Kathleen. 1979. *Female Sexual Slavery.* Englewood Cliffs, N.J.: Prentice-Hall, 1979.

———. 1992. "Sexual Exploitation Violates Human Rights." Coalition Against Trafficking in Women. Fall. Available at http://www.uri.edu/artsci/wms/hughes/catw/barry.htm.

Basch, Linda, Nina Glick Schiller, and Cristina Szanton Blanc. 1994. *Nations Unbound: Transnational Projects, Postcolonial Predicaments and Deterritorialized Nation-States.* Longhorn, Pa: Gordon and Breach Science Publishers.

Batabyal, Amitrajeet A. 2001. "On the Likelihood of Finding the Right Partner in an Arranged Marriage." *Journal of Socio-Economics* 33(3):273–80.

Belanger, Daniele, and Khuat Thu Hong. 1996. "Marriage and the Family in Urban North Vietnam, 1965–1993." *Journal of Population* 2(1):83–112.

Berdahl, Daphne. 1999. "Citizenship and Mass Consumption in Re-Unified Germany." Presented at University of Illinois at Urbana-Champaign Social Cultural Anthropology Workshop. September 10.

Biddulph, Sarah, and Sandy Cook. 1999. "Kidnapping: the Selling of Women and Children." *Violence Against Women* 5(12):1437–68.

Bonacich, Edna. 1973. "A Theory of Middleman Minorities." *American Sociological Review* 38:583–94.

Bossen, Laurel. 2002. *Chinese Women and Rural Development: Sixty Years of Change in Lu Village, Yunnan.* Lanham, Md: Rowman and Littlefield.

Bourdieu, Pierre. 1977. *Outline of a Theory of Practice.* Cambridge: Cambridge University Press.

Brennan, Denise. 2001. "Tourism in Transnational Places: Dominican Sex Workers and German Sex Tourists Imagine One Another." *Identities: Global Studies in Culture and Power* 7(4):621–63.

Cahill, Desmond. 1990. *Intermarriages in International Contexts: A Study of Filipina Women Married to Australian, Japanese and Swiss Men.* Quezon City: Scalabrini Migration Center.

Cannell, Fenella. 1999. *Power and Intimacy in the Christian Philippines.* Cambridge: Cambridge University Press.

Castillo, Gelia T. 1977. *Beyond Manila: Philippine Rural Problems in Perspective.* Los Baños: University of the Philippines.

Chant, Sylvia, and Cathy McIlwaine. 1995. *Women of a Lesser Cost: Female Labour, Foreign Exchange and Philippine Development.* Quezon City: Manila University Press.

Chao, Emily. 1995. "Depictions of Difference." Ph.D. dissertation, University of Michigan.

———. 2002. "Dangerous Work: Women in Traffic." *Modern China* 29(1):71–107.

Cheng, Sea-Ling. 2002. "Transnational Desires: 'Trafficked' Filipinas in US Military Camp Towns in South Korea." DPhil. thesis, Institute of Social and Cultural Anthropology. University of Oxford.

Cherry Blossoms. 2002. Available at http://www.blossoms.com.

Chin, Ko-Lin. 1994. "Out-of-Town Brides: International Marriage and Wife Abuse Among Chinese Immigrants." *Journal of Comparative Family Studies* 25(1):53–71.

China Doll. 2002. Available at http://www.chinese-women.com.

China Statistical Yearbook. 2002. "Number of Marriages and Divorces," Table 22–37. "Number of Marriages and Divorces by Region (2001)," Table 22–38. State Statistical Bureau, Beijing, China: Statistical Publishing House.

Chŏng, Hyŏng-mo. 2003. "Oegugin sinbu tŭl 'paeban ŭi ttang han'guk'" [Foreign brides, "the land of betrayal, Korea"]. *JoongAng Ilbo*, April 14.

Chŏng, Sinch'ŏl. 1995. "Chungguk chosŏnjok in'gu punp'o ŭi pyŏnhwa t'ŭkching e kwanhayŏ" [On the characteristics of the changing population distribution of the Chinese Chosŏnjok]. *Chosŏnhak* [Chosŏn studies]:217–26.

Clark, Constance D. 2001. "Foreign Marriage 'Tradition' and the Politics of Border Crossings." In *China Urban*, Nancy Chen et al., eds. Pp. 104–22. Durham, N.C.: Duke University Press.

Cohen, Myron. 1993. "Cultural and Political Inventions in Modern China: The Case of the Chinese 'Peasant.'" *Deadalus* 122(2):151–70.

Collier, Jane, and Sylvia Junko Yanagisako, eds. 1987. *Gender and Kinship: Essays toward a Unified Analysis*. Stanford, Calif.: Stanford University Press.

Commission on Filipinos Overseas (CFO). 2000. Unpublished tables.

Constable, Nicole. 1997. *Maid to Order in Hong Kong: Stories of Filipina Workers*. Ithaca, N.Y.: Cornell University Press.

———. 2003a. *Romance on a Global Stage: Pen Pals, Virtual Ethnography, and "Mail Order" Marriages*. Berkeley: University of California Press.

———. 2003b. "A Transnational Perspective on Divorce and Marriage: Filipino Wives and Workers." *Identities: Global Studies in Culture and Power* 10(2):163–80.

Constantino, Renato. 1989. *The Second Invasion: Japan in the Philippines*. Quezon City: Karrel.

Cottrell, Ann B. 1990. "Cross-National Marriages: A Review of the Literature." *Journal of Comparative Family Studies* 21(2):151–69.

Creed, Gerald W. 2000. "'Family Values' and Domestic Economies." *Annual Reviews of Anthropology* 29:329–55.

Croll, Elisabeth. 1984. "Marriage Choice and Status Groups in Contemporary China." In *Class and Social Stratification in Post-Revolution China*. James L. Watson, ed. Pp. 175–97. Cambridge: Cambridge University Press.

Cumings, Bruce. 1992. "Silent but Deadly: Sexual Subordination in the U.S.-Korean Relationship." In *Let the Good Times Roll: Prostitution and the U.S. Military in Asia*. Saundra P. Sturdevant and Brenda Stolzfus, eds. Pp. 169–75. New York: The New Press.

Das, Veena. 1995. "National Honor and Practical Kinship: Unwanted Women and Children." In *Conceiving the New World Order*. Faye D. Ginsburg and Rayna Rapp, eds. Pp. 212–33. Berkeley: University of California Press.

Dateline NBC. 2001."Bought and Sold." Geraldo Rivera. March 18.

Davin, Delia. 1999. *Internal Migration in Contemporary China*. London: MacMillan.

Davis, Deborah S., ed. 2000. *The Consumer Revolution in Urban China*. Berkeley: University of California Press.

Death in Thailand. 2002. "Va-Megn Thoj." C.H.A.T. Television Productions, Frogtown Media Productions. VHS.

del Rosario, Virginia O. 1994. "Lifting the Smoke Screen: Dynamics of Mail-Order Bride Migration from the Philippines." Ph.D. dissertation, Institute of Social Studies, the Hague.

Douglas, Mary. 1966. *Purity and Danger: An Analysis of Concepts of Pollution and Taboo*. London: Routledge, Kegan Paul.

Duara, Prasenjit. 1997. "Nationalists Among Transnationals: Overseas Chinese and the Idea of China, 1900–1911." In *Ungrounded Empires: The Cultural Politics of Modern Chinese Nationalism*. Donald Nonini and Aihwa Ong, eds. Pp. 39–60. New York: Routledge.

Dumont, Louis. 1966. *Homo Hierarchicus: The Caste System and Its Implications*. Chicago: University of Chicago Press.

Ehrenreich, Barbara, and Arlie Russell Hochschild. 2003. *Global Woman: Nannies, Maids, and Sex Workers in the New Economy*. New York: Metropolitan Books.

Erwin, Kathleen. 1999. "White Women, Male Desires: A Televisual Fantasy of the Transnational Chinese Family." In *Spaces of Their Own: Women's Public Sphere in Transnational China*. Mayfair Mei-hui Yang, ed. Pp. 232–57. Minneapolis: University of Minnesota Press.

Espiritu, Yen Le. 1999. "Gender and Labor in Asian Immigrant Families." *American Behavioral Scientist* 42(4):628–47.

Everett, Anna. 2002. "The Revolution will be Digitized: Afrocentricity and the Digital Public Sphere." *Social Text* 71, 20(2):125–46.

Fan, C. Cindy. 2000. "Migration and Gender in China." In *China Review 2000*. Chung-ming Lau and Jianfa Shen, eds. Pp. 423–54. Hong Kong: Chinese University Press.

Fan, C. Cindy, and Youqin Huang. 1998. "Waves of Rural Brides: Female Marriage Migration in China." *Annals of the Association of American Geographers* 88(2):227–51.

Farquhar, Judith. 2002. *Appetites: Food and Sex in Post-Socialist China*. Durham, N.C.: Duke University Press.

Farrer, James. 2002. *Opening Up: Youth Sex Culture and Market Reform in Shanghai*. Chicago: University of Chicago Press.

Feng, Yuan. 1990. "Many Abducted Women, Children Rescued." *Renmin Ribao*, p. 3. December 30.

Fitzgerald, Tina Katherine. 1999. "Who Marries Whom? Attitudes in Marital Partner Selection." Ph.D. dissertation, University of Colorado, Boulder.

Foote, Jennifer. 1991. "From Russia—With Love? Mail-Order Brides for Lonely British Bachelors." *Newsweek*, p. 38. May 27.

Fujieda, Eri. 2001. "Filipino Women's Migration to Japan's Sex Industry: A Case of Transnational Gender Subjection." Ph.D. dissertation, University of Illinois at Urbana-Champaign.

Fritzie's Filipina Pen Friends. 2002. Available at http://www.filipinapenfriends.com.

Gates, Hill. 1989. "The Commoditization of Chinese Women." *Signs* 14(4):799–832.

Gilmartin, Christina. 1990. "Violence Against Women in Contemporary China." In *Violence in China: Essays in Culture and Counterculture*. Jonathan N. Lipman and Stevan Harrell, eds. Pp. 203–26. Albany: State University of New York Press.

Gilmartin, Christina, and Lin Tan. 2002. "Fleeing Poverty: Rural Women, Expanding Marriage Markets, and Strategies for Social Mobility in Contemporary China." In *Transforming Gender and Development in East Asia*. Esther Ngan-ling Chow, ed. Pp. 203–16. New York: Routledge.

Glodava, Mila, and Richard Onizuka. 1994. *Mail-Order Brides: Women For Sale*. Fort Collins, Colo.: Alaken.

Godley, Michael. 1989. "The Sojourners Returned: Overseas Chinese in the People's Republic of China." *Pacific Affairs* 62(3):330–52.

Goodkind, Daniel. 1997. "The Vietnamese Double Marriage Squeeze." *International Migration Review* 31(1):108–28.

Goodwife.com. 2000. Available at http://www.goodwife.com.

Grinker, Roy Richard. 2000. *Korea and Its Futures: Unification and the Unfinished War*. London: Macmillan.

Guarnizo, Luis Eduardo, and Michael P. Smith. 1998. "The Locations of Transnationalism." In *Transnationalism from Below*. M. P. Smith and L. E. Guarnizo, eds. Pp. 3–34. New Brunswick: Transaction Publishers.

Guttentag, Marcia, and Paul F. Secord. 1983. *Too Many Women? The Sex Ratio Question*. Beverly Hills: Sage Publications.

Ha, Soekgun. 2002. "Grant Voting Rights to Korean Nationals Abroad." *Korea Focus* 10(4):46–48.

Halualani, Rona Tamiko. 1995. "The Intersecting Hegemonic Discourses of an Asian Mail-Order Bride Catalog: Pilipina 'Oriental Butterfly' Dolls for Sale." *Women's Studies in Communication* 118(1):45–64.

Hama, Natsuko. 1997. *Manira-Iki: Otokotachi no Katamichi Kippu*. Tokyo: Ōta Shuppan.

Han, Min. 2001. *Social Change and Continuity in a Village in Northern Anhui, China: A Response to Revolution and Reform*. Osaka: National Museum of Ethnology.

Hannerz, Ulf. 1996. *Transnational Connections: Culture, People, Places*. London: Routledge.

Hershatter, Gail. 1991. "Prostitution and the Market in Women in Early Twentieth-Century Shanghai." In *Marriage and Gender Inequality in Chinese Society*. Rubie S. Watson and Patricia Buckley Ebrey, eds. Pp. 256–85. Berkeley: University of California Press.

Hirschman, Charles, and Vu Manh Loi. 1996. "Family and Household Structures in Vietnam: Some Glimpses from a Recent Survey." *Pacific Affairs* 69(1):229–49.

Hochschild, Arlie, with Anne Machung. 1989. *The Second Shift: Working Parents and the Revolution at Home*. New York: Viking.

Hollis, Jeffrey Lee. 1998. "Us Versus Maury Povich." Available at http://www.geocities.com/~hollismeister/mauryp.html.

Holt, Elizabeth M. 1996. "Writing Filipina-Australian Bodies: The Discourse on Filipina Brides." *Philippine Sociological Review* 44:58–78.

Hondagneu-Sotelo, Pierrette. 1994. *Gendered Transitions: Mexican Experiences of Immigration*. Berkeley: University of California Press.

Houstoun, Marion F., Roger G. Kramer, and Joan Mackin Barrett. 1984. "Female Predominance in Immigration to the United States since the 1930s: A First Look." *International Migration Review* 18(4):908–63.

Huang, Annie. 1996. "Taiwan Moves to Boost Women's Marriage Prospects." Associated Press. August 30.

Huang, Wei. 1991. "Crackdown on the Abduction of Women and Children." *Beijing Review*, pp. 24–27. July 29.

Huang, Xiyi. 1999. "Divided Gender, Divided Women: State Policy and the Labour Market." In *Women of China: Economic and Social Transformation*. Jackie West et al., eds. Pp. 90–107. New York: St. Martin's Press.

Hwang, Sean-Shong, and Rogelio Saenz. 1990. "The Problems Posed by Immigrants Married Abroad on Intermarriage Research: The Case of Asian Americans." *International Migration Review* 24(3):563–76.

Ishii-Kuntz, Masako. 2003. "Balancing Fatherhood and Work: Emergence of Diverse Masculinities in Contemporary Japan." In *Men and Masculinities in Contemporary Japan: Dislocating the Salaryman Doxa*. James E. Roberson and Nobue Suzuki, eds. Pp. 198–216. London: Routledge Curzon.

Jedlicka, Davor. 1988. "American Men in Search of Oriental Brides: A Preliminary Survey Released as a Courtesy to the Survey Participants." Unpublished report.

JICA (Japan International Cooperation Agency), 2001. "About JICA: Japan's Official Development Assistance." Available at http://www.jica.go.jp/english/about/01.html. November 12.

Johnson, Graham. 1993. "Family Strategies and Economic Transformation in Rural China: Some Evidence from the Pearl River Delta." In *Chinese Families in the Post-Mao Era*. Deborah Davis and Stevan Harrell, eds. Pp. 103–38. Berkeley: University of California Press.

Johnson, Walton R., and D. Michael Warren. 1994. *Inside the Mixed Marriage: Accounts of Changing Attitudes, Patterns and Perceptions of Cross-Cultural and Interracial Marriages*. Lanham, Md.: University Press of America.

Jolly, Margaret, and Lenore Manderson, eds. 1997. *Sites of Desire, Economies of Pleasure: Sexualities in Asia and the Pacific.* Chicago: University of Chicago Press.

JoongAng Ilbo editorial. 2002. "Embracing Ethnic Koreans Worldwide." Reprinted in *Korea Focus* 10(1):53–54 (originally December 1, 2001).

Jowan, Dinah. 1986. "Interview: Watashi no Japayuki Taiken." Interviewed by Hinago Akira. *Bessatsu Takarajima* 54, Japayuki-san Monogatari. Tokyo: JICC.

Julag-Ay, Cecilia. 1997. "Correspondence Marriages Between Filipinas and United States Men." Ph.D. dissertation, University of California, Riverside.

Kang, Hae Sun. 1998. "Chung-han sŏboe hon'in ŭi silt'ae wa chŏnmang" [The current and future outlook for marriages between China and Korea]. 11th seminar of the Korean Family Welfare Institute, "The Current Status of International Marriages between China and Korea and the Welfare of Those Families Involved." Seoul.

Kelsky, Karen. 2001. *Women on the Verge: Japanese Women, Western Dreams.* Durham, N.C.: Duke University Press.

Kendall, Laurel. 1988. *The Life and Hard Times of a Korean Shaman: Of Tales and the Telling of Tales.* Honolulu: University of Hawaii Press.

————. 1996. *Getting Married in Korea: Of Gender, Morality, and Modernity.* Berkeley: University of California Press.

Kibria, Nazli. 1993. *Family Tightrope: The Changing Lives of Vietnamese Americans.* Princeton, N.J.: Princeton University Press.

Kim, Hyun-sook. 1998. "Yanggongju as an Allegory of the Nation: The Representation of Working-Class Women in Popular and Radical Texts." In *Dangerous Women: Gender and Korean Nationalism.* Elaine K. Kim and Chungmoo Choi, eds. Pp. 175–201. New York: Routledge.

Kim, Jinwung. 2001. "From 'American Gentlemen' to 'Americans': Changing Perceptions of the United States in South Korea in Recent Years." *Korea Journal* 41(4):172–98.

Kingston, Maxine Hong. 1975. *The Woman Warrior.* New York: Vintage International.

Koo, Hagen. 2001. *Korean Workers: The Culture and Politics of Class Formation.* Ithaca, N.Y.: Cornell University Press.

Langevin, Louise, and Marie-Josée Belleau. 2001. Trafficking in Women in Canada: A Critical Analysis of the Legal Framework Governing Immigrant Domestic Workers and Mail-Order Brides. Ottawa: Status of Women Canada.

Lavely, William. 1991. "Marriage and Mobility Under Rural Collectivism." In *Marriage and Inequality in Chinese Society.* Rubie S. Watson and Patricia Buckley Ebrey, eds. Pp. 286–312. Berkeley: University of California Press.

Lee, Chae-Jin. 2000. "South Korean Foreign Relations Face the Globalization Challenges." In *Korea's Globalization.* S. Kim, ed. Pp. 170–95. Cambridge: Cambridge University Press.

Lee, So-hee. 2002. "The Concept of Female Sexuality in Korean Popular Culture." In *Under Construction: The Gendering of Modernity, Class, and Consumption in the Republic of Korea.* Laurel Kendall, ed. Pp. 141–64. Honolulu: University of Hawaii Press.

Leonard, Jack, and Mai Tran. 2000a. "Agents Target Little Saigon Crime Groups." *Los Angeles Times,* p. A-1. October 7.

————. 2000b. "Probes Take Aim at Organized Crime in Little Saigon; Crackdown: Numerous Agencies Target Gambling, Drug Sales, Counterfeit Labels and Credit Card Scams." *Los Angeles Times,* p. B-7. October 7.

Lett, Denise Potrzeba. 1998. *In Pursuit of Status: The Making of South Korea's "New" Urban Middle Class.* Cambridge, Mass.: Harvard University Press.

Lévi-Strauss, Claude. 1969. *The Elementary Structures of Kinship.* James H. Bell, John R. von Sturmer, and Rodney Needham, trans. Boston: Beacon.

Li, Wai-ki Viki. 2001. "Seeking the Ideal Wife: Why Hong Kong Men Pursue Mainland Chinese Spouses." M.A. thesis, Chinese University of Hong Kong.

Liang, Zhai, and Naomi Ito. 1999. "Intermarriage of Asian Americans in the New York Region: Contemporary Patterns and Future Prospects." *International Migration Review* 33(4):876–900.

Loewen, James. 1971. *Mississippi Chinese: Between Black and White.* Cambridge, Mass.: Harvard University Press.

Mahler, Sarah J. 2001. "Transnational Relationships: The Struggle to Communicate Across Borders." *Identities: Global Studies in Culture and Power* 7(4):583–619.

Manalansan, Martin IV. 2003. *Global Divas: Filipino Gay Men in the Diaspora.* Durham, N.C.: Duke University Press.

Marchetti, Gina. 1993. *Romance and the "Yellow Peril": Race, Sex, and Discursive Strategies in Hollywood Fiction.* Berkeley: University of California Press.

Margold, Jane A. 1995. "Narratives of Masculinity and Transnational Migration: Filipino Workers in the Middle East." In *Bewitching Women and Pious Men: Gender and Body Politics in Southeast Asia.* Aihwa Ong and Michael G. Peletz, eds. Pp. 274–98. Berkeley: University of California Press.

Marosi, Richard, and Mai Tran. 2000. "Little Saigon Raids Dismantle Crime Ring, Authorities Say; Probe: Asian Syndicate Supplied Most Illegal Gambling machines in Orange County, police say. Fifteen are arrested." *Los Angeles Times*, p. B-3. September 29.

Massey, Doreen. 1994. *Space, Place and Gender.* Minneapolis: University of Minnesota Press.

Maury Povich Show. 1998. February 19.

Medina, Belen T. G. 1991. *The Filipino Family: A Text with Selected Readings.* Quezon City: University of the Philippines Press.

Meng, Eddy. 1994. "Mail-Order Brides: Gilded Prostitution and the Legal Response." *Michigan Journal of Law Reform* 28:197–248.

Merli, Giovanna M. 1997. "Estimation of International Migration for Vietnam 1979–1989." Unpublished manuscript. University of Washington, Seattle.

Migration News. 2002. "Philippines," March, 9(3). Available at http://migration.ucdavis.edu/mn/mar_2002–17.html. March 5.

Minh, Nguyen Huu. 1997. "Age at First Marriage in Vietnam and Its Determinants." *Asia-Pacific Population Journal* 12(2):49–74.

Ministry of Health, Labour and Welfare [Japan]. 2000. *Vital Statistics.* Tokyo: Ōkurashō.

———. 2003. *Vital Statistics.* Tokyo: Ōkurashō.

Ministry of Justice [Japan]. 1999–2000, 2003. *Annual Report of Statistics on Legal Migrants.* Tokyo: Ōkurashō.

Moon, Katharine H. S. 2000. "Strangers in the Midst of Globalization: Migrant Workers and Korean Nationalism." In *Korea's Globalization.* S. Kim, ed. Pp. 147–69. Cambridge: Cambridge University Press.

Na, Chonggŭn. 1997. "Nongch'on ch'onggak kyŏrhon taech'aek sokhi sewŏya" [Measures to help rural bachelors marry must be taken quickly]. *Tong'a Ilbo* [East Asia Daily]. October 13.

Nakamatsu, Tomoko. 2002. *Marriage, Migration and the International Marriage Business in Japan.* Ph.D. dissertation, Murdoch University, Australia.

Nakano, Fe Ceriaquita. 1999. *Nihon ni Totsuide 11-nen.* Tokyo: Bungeisha.

Ngai, Pun. 2002. "Am I the Only Survivor? Global Capital, Local Gaze, and Social Trauma in China." *Public Culture* 14(2):341–47.

Nhat, Hong. 1999. "Hankering for 'Viet Kieu' Money." *Vietnam Economic News* 9:12.

Nonini, Donald M. 1997. "Shifting Identities, Positioned Imaginaries: Transnational Traversals and Reversals by Malaysian Chinese." In *Ungrounded Empires: The Cultural Politics of Modern Chinese Transnationalism.* Donald Nonini and Aihwa Ong, eds. Pp. 203–27. New York: Routledge.

Ong, Aihwa. 1999. *Flexible Citizenship: The Cultural Logics of Transnationality.* Durham, N.C.: Duke University Press.

Ordonez, Raquel Z. 1997. "Mail-Order Brides: An Emerging Community." In *Filipino Americans: Transformation and Identity.* Maria P. Root, ed. Pp. 121–42. Thousand Oaks, Calif.: Sage Publications.

Oxfeld, Ellen. 1993. *Blood, Sweat, and Mahjong: Family and Enterprise in an Overseas Chinese Community.* Ithaca, N.Y.: Cornell University Press.

Pak, Chi-ju. 2003. "Chippak ŭro naogijŏn enŭn tongmul ch'ŏrŏm sarassŏyo" [I lived like an animal before I finally got out of the house]. *Ablenews.* www.able news.co.kr. April 10.

Pan, Esther. 2000. "Why Asian Guys Are on a Roll." *Newsweek,* pp.50–51. February 21.

Parish, William L., and James Farrer. 1993. "Gender and Family." In *Chinese Urban Life Under Reform: The Changing Social Contract,* Wenfang Tang and William L. Parish, eds. Pp. 232–72. New York: Cambridge University Press.

Park, Heh-Rahn. 1996. "Narratives of Migration: From the Formation of Korean Chinese Nationality in the PRC to the Emergence of Korean Chinese Migrants in South Korea." Ph.D. dissertation, University of Washington, Seattle.

Parreñas, Rhacel Salazar. 2001. *Servants of Globalization: Women, Migration, and Domestic Work.* Stanford, Calif.: Stanford University Press.

Patterson, Orlando. 1975. "Context and Choice in Ethnic Allegiance: A Theoretical Framework and Caribbean Case Study." In *Ethnicity: Theory and Experience.* Nathan Glazer and Daniel P. Moynihan, eds. Pp. 305–49. Cambridge, Mass.: Harvard University Press.

Pertierra, Raul, ed. 1992. *Remittances and Returnees: The Cultural Economy of Migration in Ilocos.* Quezon City: New Day.

Pessar, Patricia R., and Sarah J. Mahler. 2001. "Gender and Transnational Migration." Transnational Communities Programme Working Paper Series. WPTC-01–20. Available at http://www.transcomm.ox.ac.uk/working_papers.htm.

Pflugfelder, Gregory M. 1999. *Cartographies of Desire: Male-Male Sexuality in Japanese Discourse, 1600–1950.* Berkeley: University of California Press.

Pierre, Andrew J. 2000. "Vietnam's Contradictions." *Foreign Affairs* 79(6):69–86.

Piper, Nicola. 1997. "International Marriage in Japan: Race and Gender Perspectives." *Gender Place and Culture* 4(3):321–38.

Piper, Nicola, and Mina Roces, eds. 2003. *Wife or Worker? Asian Women and Migration.* New York: Rowman and Littlefield.

Portes, Alejandro, Luis E. Guarnizo, and Patricia Landolt. 1999. "The Study of Transnationalism: Pitfalls and Promise of an Emergent Research Field." *Ethnic and Racial Studies* 22(2):217–37.

Portes, Alejandro, and Ruben G. Rumbault. 1996. *Immigrant America: A Portrait.* Berkeley: University of California Press.

Rebhun, Linda Anne. 1999. "For Love and for Money: Romance in Urbanizing Northeast Brazil." *City and Society* 11(1–2):145–64.

Roberson, James E., and Nobue Suzuki. 2003. "Introduction." In *Men and Masculinities in Contemporary Japan: Dislocating the Salaryman Doxa*. J. E. Roberson and N. Suzuki, eds. Pp. 1–19. London: Routledge Curzon.

Robinson, Kathryn. 1996. "Of Mail-Order Brides and 'Boys' Own' Tales: Representations of Asian-Australian Marriages." *Feminist Review* 52 (spring): 53–68.

———. 2001. "Marriage Migration, Family Values, and the 'Global Ecumene.'" Paper presented at "Conference on Migration and the 'Asian Family' in a Globalizing World." Singapore, April 16–18.

Rosaldo, Renato. 1994. "Cultural Citizenship and Educational Democracy." *Cultural Anthropology* 9(3):402–11.

Rosa-Yoon, Rowena dela. 1999. "Korea: Toward a Multiracial society." *Korea Herald News*. September 1.

Rosca, Ninotchka. 1995. "The Philippines's Shameful Export (Emigrant Women)." *The Nation* 260(15):522.

Rubin, Gayle. 1975. "The Traffic in Women: Notes on the 'Political Economy' of Sex." In *Toward an Anthropology of Women*. Rayna R. Reiter, ed. Pp. 157–210. New York: Monthly Review Press.

Rubin, Lillian B. 1994. *Families on the Fault Line: America's Working Class Speaks About the Family, the Economy, Race, and Ethnicity*. New York: Harper Perennial.

Rumbault, Ruben G. 1997. "Ties That Bind: Immigration and Immigrant Families in the United States." In *Immigration and the Family: Research and Policy on U.S. Immigrants*. A. Booth, A. C. Crouter, and N. Landale, eds. Pp. 3–46. Mahwah, N.J.: Lawrence Erlbaum Associates.

Sadamatsu, Aya. 1996. "Kazoku mondai: Teijugaikokujin no kazoku seikatsu to chiikishakai" [Family problems: The family life of settled foreigners and the regional society]. In *Gaikokujin rodosha kara shimin e* [From foreign workers to citizens]. Takashi Miyajima and Takamichi Kajita, eds. Tokyo: Yuhikaku.

Said, Edward. 1978. *Orientalism*. New York: Vintage.

Schein, Louisa. 1997. "The Consumption of Color and the Politics of White Skin in Post-Mao China." In *The Gender/Sexuality Reader*. Roger N. Lancaster and Michaela Di Leonardo, eds. Pp. 473–86. London: Routledge.

———. 2000. "Forged Transnationality and Oppositional Cosmopolitanism." In *Ethnographic Explorations of Asian America*. Martin F. Manalansan IV, ed. Pp. 199–215. Philadelphia: Temple University Press.

———. 2002. "Mapping Hmong Media in Diasporic Space." In *Media Worlds: Anthropology on New Terrain*. Faye D. Ginsburg, Lila Abu-Lughod, and Brian Larkin, eds. Pp. 229–44. Berkeley: University of California Press.

———. 2004. "Homeland Beauty: Transnational Longing and Hmong American Video." *Journal of Asian Studies* 63(2).

———. N.d. "Negotiating Scale: Miao Women at a Distance." In *Translocal China*. Tim Oakes and Louisa Schein, eds. London: Routledge, forthcoming.

Schiller, Nina Glick, Linda Basch, and Cristina Blanc-Szanton. 1992. *Towards a Transnational Perspective on Migration: Race, Class, Ethnicity, and Nationalism*. New York: Annals of the New York Academy of Sciences.

Scholes, Robert. 1997. "How Many Mail-Order Brides?" *Immigration Review* 28(spring). Available at http://www.cis.org/articles/1997/IR28/mail-order brides.html.

———. 1999. "The Mail-Order Bride Industry and Its Impact on Immigration." In "International Matchmaking Organizations: A Report to Congress" (appendix A). Available at http://uscis.gov/graphics/aboutus/repsstudies .mobappa.htm.

Schwartz, Pepper. 1995. *Love Between Equals: How Peer Marriage Really Works.* New York: Free Press; distributed by Simon & Schuster.

Shih, Shu-mei. 1998. "Gender and a New Geopolitics of Desire: The Seduction of Mainland Women in Taiwan and Hong Kong Media." *Signs* 23(2):287–319.

———. 1999. "Gender and the Geopolitics of Desire: The Seduction of Mainland Women in Taiwan and Hong Kong Media." In *Spaces of Their Own.* Mayfair Mei-hui Yang, ed. Pp. 278–307. Minneapolis: University of Minnesota Press.

———. 2000. "Globalization and Minoritization: Ang Lee and the Politics of Flexibility." *New Formations: A Journal of Culture/Theory/Politics* 40(spring):86–101.

Shim, Young-Hee. 2001. "Feminism and the Discourse of Sexuality in Korea: Continuities and Changes." *Human Studies* 24:133–48.

———. 2002. "Sexuality Policy in Korea in the 1990s: Changes and Factors." *Korea Journal* 42(2):146–51.

Simons, Lisa Anne. 2001. "Marriage, Migration, and Markets: International Matchmaking and International Feminism." Ph.D. dissertation, University of Denver. UMI Microform Number 3020902. Ann Arbor, Michigan.

Sinn, Elizabeth. 1994. "Chinese Patriarchy and the Protection of Women in 19th-Century Hong Kong." In *Women and Chinese Patriarchy: Submission, Servitude, and Escape.* Maria Jaschok and Suzanne Miers, eds. Pp. 141–70. Hong Kong: Hong Kong University Press.

Small, Cathy. 1997. *Voyages: From Tongan Villages to American Suburbs.* Ithaca, N.Y.: Cornell University Press.

Smith, Michael Peter, and Luis E. Guarnizo, eds. 1998. *Transnationalism from Below.* New Brunswick: Transaction Publishers.

Smith, Neil. 1992. "Contours of a Spatialized Politics: Homeless Vehicles and the Production of Geographical Scale." *Social Text* 33:55–81.

Sŏ, Kiwŏn. [1963]1990. "The Heir." In *Modern Korean Literature.* Peter H. Lee, ed. Pp. 169–83. Honolulu: University of Hawaii Press.

Solinger, Dorothy J. 1999. *Contesting Citizenship in Urban China: Peasant Migrants, the State, and the Logic of the Market.* Berkeley: University of California Press.

Song, Lina. 1999. "The Role of Women in Labour Migration: A Case Study in Northern China." In *Women of China: Economic and Social Transformation.* Jackie West, et al., eds. Pp. 69–89. New York: St. Martin's Press.

Stacey, Judith. 1991. *Brave New Families: Stories of Domestic Upheaval in Late Twentieth-Century America.* New York: Basic Books.

Stalker, Peter. 2001. *The No-Nonsense Guide to International Migration.* London: Verso.

Steedman, Carolyn Kay. 1986. *Landscape for a Good Woman: A Story of Two Lives.* New Brunswick, N.J.: Rutgers University Press.

Sunshine International. 2002. Available at http://sunshine-girls.com.

Suzuki, Nobue. 1999. "Women Imagined, Women Imaging: Re/presentations of Filipinas in Japan Since the 1980s." *U.S.-Japan Women's Journal* 19:142–75.

———. 2002. "Gendered Surveillance and Sexual Violence in Filipina Pre-Migration Experiences to Japan." In *Gender Politics in the Asia Pacific Region: Agencies and Activisms.* Brenda S. A. Yeoh, Peggy Teo, and Shirlena Huang, eds. Pp. 99–119. London: Routledge.

———. 2003a. "Battlefields of Affection: Gender, Global Desires and the Politics of Intimacy in Filipina-Japanese Transnational Marriages." Ph.D. dissertation, University of Hawaii at Manoa.

———. 2003b. "Transgressing 'Victims': Reading Narratives of 'Filipina Brides' in Japan." *Critical Asian Studies* 25(3):399–420.

———. 2003c. "Of Love and the Marriage Market: Masculinity Politics and Filipina-Japanese Marriages in Japan." In *Men and Masculinities in Contemporary Japan.* J. E. Roberson and N. Suzuki, eds. Pp. 91–108. London: Routledge Curzon.

Tacoli, Cecilia. 1996. "Migrating 'For the Sake of the Family'?: Gender, Life Course and Intra-Household Relations Among Filipino Migrants in Rome." *Philippine Sociological Review* 44:12–32.

Tahmincioglu, Eve. 2001. "For Richer or Poorer—Mail-Order Brides Make for Big Business Online." *Ziff Davis Smart Business for the New Economy,* p. 40. January 1.

Tajima, Renee E. 1989. "Lotus Blossoms Don't Bleed: Images of Asian Women." In *Making Waves: An Anthology of Writings by and About Asian American Women,* Asian Women United of California, ed. Pp. 308–17. Boston: Beacon.

Tamagaki, Yōichi. 1995. *Firipīna to Kekkon Suru Koto.* Tokyo: Nogizaka Shuppan.

Tawada, Yoko. 1998. "Missing Heels." In *The Bridegroom was a Dog.* Margaret Mitsutani, trans. New York: Kodansha International.

Thai, Hung Cam. 2003. "Marriage Across the Pacific: Family, Gender and Migration in the New Economy." Ph.D. thesis, University of California, Berkeley.

Thiesmeyer, Lynn. 1999. "The West's 'Comfort Women' and the Discourses of Seduction." In *Transnational Asia Pacific: Gender, Culture, and the Public Sphere.* Shirley Geok-Lin Lim, Larry E. Smith, and Wimal Dissanayake, eds. Pp. 69–92. Urbana: University of Illinois Press.

Thornton, Michael C. 1992. "The Quiet Immigration: Foreign Spouses of U.S. Citizens, 1945–1985." In *Racially Mixed People in America.* M. P. Root, ed. Pp. 64–76. Newbury Park, Calif.: Sage Publications.

Tolentino, Roland B. 1996. "Bodies, Letters, Catalogues: Filipinas in Transnational Space." *Social Text* 48, 14(3):49–76.

Tran, Dinh Huou. 1991. "Traditional Families in Vietnam and the Influence of Confucianism." In *Sociological Studies on the Vietnamese Family.* R. Lijestrom and T. Lai, eds. Pp. 27–53. Hanoi, Vietnam: Social Sciences Publishing House.

Tran, Trong Dang Dan. 1997. *Nguoi Vietnam O Nuoc Ngoai* [Vietnamese people overseas]. Hanoi, Vietnam: National Political Press.

Tsing, Anna Lowenhaupt. 1993. *In the Realm of the Diamond Queen: Marginality in an Out-of-the-Way Place.* Princeton, N.J.: Princeton University Press.

Tyner, James A. 1996. "Constructions of Filipina Migrant Entertainers." *Gender, Place and Culture* 4(1):19–35.

———. 2002. "Global Cities and Circuits of Global Labor: The Case of Manila." In *Filipinos in Global Migrations: At Home in the World?* Filomeno V. Aguilar, Jr., ed. Pp. 60–86. Quezon City: Philippine Migration Research Network and Philippine Social Science Council.

United Nations. 2000. *The World's Women, 2000: Trends and Statistics.* New York: United Nations.

USDOJ-INS (United States Department of Justice-Immigration and Naturalization Service). 1999a. "International Matchmaking Organizations: A Report to Congress." Available at http://uscis.gov/graphics/aboutus/repsstudies/Mobrept.htm.

USDOJ-INS (United States Department of Justice-Immigration and Naturalization Service). 1999b. *Statistical Yearbook of the Immigration and Naturalization Service, 1997.* Washington, D.C.: U.S. Government Printing Office.

Vergara, Benito M., Jr. 1996. "Betrayal, Class Fantasies and the Filipino Nation in Daly City." *Philippine Sociological Review* 44:79–100.

Villapando, Venny. 1989. "The Business of Selling Mail-Order Brides." In *Making Waves: An Anthology of Writings by and About Asian American Women.* Asian Women United of California, ed. Pp. 318–27. Boston: Beacon.

Wang, Gungwu. 1985. "South China Perspectives on Overseas Chinese." *Australian Journal of Chinese Affairs* 13:69–84.

Wang, Hong-zen, and Shu-ming Chang. 2002. "The Commodification of International Marriages: Cross Border Marriage Business in Taiwan and Viet Nam." *International Migration* 40(6):93–116.

Watson, Rubie S. 1991. "Afterward: Marriage and Gender Inequality." In *Marriage and Inequality in Chinese Society,* Rubie S. Watson and Patricia Buckley Ebrey, eds. Pp. 347–68. Berkeley: University of California Press.

Weiner, Annette. 1975. *Women of Value, Men of Renown.* Austin: University of Texas Press.

Whyte, Martin King, and William L. Parish. 1984. *Urban Life in Contemporary China.* Chicago: University of Chicago Press.

Wilson, Ara. 1988. "American Catalogues of Asian Brides." In *Anthropology for the Nineties.* Johnetta B. Cole, ed. Pp. 114–25. New York: The Free Press.

Wisensale, Steven K. 1999. "Marriage and Family Law in a Changing Vietnam." *Journal of Family Issues* 20(5):602–16.

Wolf, Arthur. 1968. "Adopt a Daughter-in-Law, Marry a Sister." *American Anthropologist* 70(5):864–74.

Wolf, Margery.1968. *The House of Lim.* New York: Appleton-Century-Crofts.

———. 1972. *Women and the Family in Rural Taiwan.* Stanford, Calif.: Stanford University Press.

Woon, Yuen-Fong. 1989. "Social Change and Continuity in South China: Overseas Chinese and the Guan Lineage of Kaiping County, 1949–87." *The China Quarterly* 118(June):324–44.

Yan, Hairong. 2003. "Spectralization of the Rural: Reinterpreting the Labor Mobility of Rural Young Women in Post-Mao China." *American Ethnologist* 30(4):1–19.

Yi, Tae-ok. 2002. "Yŏngkwangtaek sanŭn iyagi: Nongch'on ŭi chungguktaek, p'illip'intaek tŭl" [Yŏngkwangtaek tells stories: Chinese brides, Philippine brides in farming villages]. *The Hankyoreh 21,* September 11.

Yudice, George. 2001. "Comparative Cultural Studies Traditions: Latin America and the U.S." In *A Companion to Cultural Studies.* Toby Miller, ed. Pp. 217–231. Malden, Mass.: Blackwell.

Yuh, Ji-Yeon. 2002. *Beyond the Shadow of Camptown: Korean Military Brides in America.* New York: New York University Press.

Zhang, Li. 2001. *Strangers in the City: Reconfigurations of Space, Power, and Social Networks within China's Floating Population.* Stanford, Calif.: Stanford University Press.

Zheng, Xinzhe. 1998. "Chaoxianzu renkou liudong jiqi shehui wending wenti yanjiu" [Research on Korean population flow and the problem of social stability]. *Manzu Yanjiu* [Manchu Research] 4(53):74–85.

Zhou, Min, and Carl L. Bankston. 1998. *Growing Up American: How Vietnamese Children Adapt to Life in the United States.* New York: Russell Sage Foundation.

Contributors

NANCY ABELMANN is an associate professor of anthropology, East Asian languages and cultures, and women's studies at the University of Illinois at Urbana-Champaign; she is also a teaching faculty member of Asian American studies. She is the author of *Echoes of the Past, Epics of Dissent: A South Korean Social Movement* (California, 1996); *Blue Dreams: Korean Americans and the Los Angeles Riots* (Harvard, 1996, with John Lie); and *The Melodrama of Mobility: Women, Talk, and Class in Contemporary South Korea* (Hawaii, 2003). She is completing *The Intimate University: College and the Korean American Family,* a transnational ethnography of the educational trajectories of Korean American public college students and the educational histories of their émigré parents.

EMILY CHAO is an associate professor of anthropology at Pitzer College, one of the Claremont Colleges. She has conducted long-term research among the Naxi minority of Southwestern China. Her interests include gender, popular culture, ethnicity, ritual, and globalization.

NICOLE CONSTABLE is a research professor at the University Center for International Studies and a professor of anthropology at the University of Pittsburgh. She is the editor of *Guest People: Hakka Identity in China and Abroad* (Washington, 1996) and the author of *Christian Souls and Chinese Spirits: A Hakka Community in Hong Kong* (California, 1994); *Maid to Order in Hong Kong: Stories of Filipina Workers* (Cornell, 1997); and *Romance on a Global Stage: Pen Pals, Virtual Ethnography, and "Mail Order" Marriages* (California, 2003).

CAREN FREEMAN is a doctoral candidate in anthropology at the University of Virginia, where she is currently completing her Ph.D. dissertation. Her chapter is based on her fieldwork in northeastern China and South Korea on the gendered patterns of marriage and mobility. The working title of her dissertation is "Women on the Move: Gender, Mobility, and Transnational Marriages between China and South Korea."

HYUNHEE KIM is a doctoral candidate at the University of Illinois at Urbana-Champaign. She is currently working on her Ph.D. dissertation entitled "Legal Philanthropy and Ethnic Community: Korean American Lawyers, Korean Immigrants and Citizenship," which explores the changing face of the Korean American community in New York from the legal anthropological perspective.

ELLEN OXFELD, a professor of anthropology at Middlebury College, has conducted fieldwork among Hakka Chinese in Calcutta, India; Mei Xian, China; and Toronto, Canada. She has studied and has published articles about family strategies, ethnic identity, economic culture, and notions of personhood in the Chinese diaspora, as well as ritual, political authority, moral systems, economic culture, and kinship in contemporary rural China. She is the author of *Blood, Sweat, and Mahjong: Family and Enterprise in an Overseas Chinese Community* (Cornell, 1993) and co-editor (with Lynellen Long) of *Coming Home? Immigrants, Refugees, and those who Stayed Behind* (Pennsylvania, 2003). She is presently writing an ethnography of moral and social conflicts in a Chinese village.

LOUISA SCHEIN is an associate professor of anthropology and women's and gender studies at Rutgers University, New Jersey. Her research interests include transnationalism, consumption, media and popular culture, sexuality/gender, ethnic politics, migration, and diaspora. For two decades, she has conducted research among Miao in rural and urban China and among Hmong refugees from Laos in the United States. She is the author of *Minority Rules: The Miao and the Feminine in China's Cultural Politics* (Duke, 2000), and her articles have appeared in such journals as *Social Text, Modern China, Cultural Anthropology, Identities,* and *Postcolonial Studies.*

NOBUE SUZUKI is a research fellow at Oxford Brookes University. Her recent publications include: *Men and Masculinities in Contemporary Japan: Disclocating the Salaryman Doxa* (coedited with J. E. Roberson; Routledge, 2003); "Gendered Surveillance and Sexual Violence in Filipina Pre-migration Experiences to Japan" (in B. Yeoh et al. eds., *Gender Politics in the Asia Pacific Region,* Routledge, 2002); and "Transgressing 'Victims': Reading Narratives of 'Filipina Brides' in Japan" (*Critical Asian Studies,* 2003). She is working on a book on Filipina-Japanese marriages in urban Japan and conducting new research on Filipino entertainment in Japan from the early 1900s to the present.

HUNG CAM THAI is an assistant professor of sociology and Asian American studies at the University of California, Santa Barbara. This chapter is from his forthcoming book, *For Better or for Worse: Marriage and Migration in the New Global Economy* (Rutgers).

Index

China (*continued*)
ping discourse in, 39–42, 59–60; marriage boom in, 88; marriage law in, 29, 34, 38, 51; marriage migration in, 5, 42–43, 56; patrilocality/patrilineality in, 19, 56–58, 78; polygyny outlawed in, 70; residential permits in, 36; revolution of 1949, 25; rural-urban migration in, 5, 20, 36, 51; South Korean diplomatic/trade relations with, 86; spatial hypergamy in Maoist era, 20. *See also* Chinese women
China Doll, 171, 174
Chinese women: Chinese international marriages of, older, 12; independence of, 180; international marriages of, growth of, 5, 15; marriageability of, 12; as mistresses of foreign men, 9, 30, 32–33; modern husbands/marriages sought by, 7, 169; South Korean men married to, 7 (*see also* Chosŏnjok women); Taiwanese men married to, 5; travel to the United States, 197n.3; visas for, 197n.6. *See also* Calcutta Hakka; Miao people; Naxi women
chŏng (emotional bond between spouses), 94, 192n.16
Chosŏn dynasty (Korean peninsula), 190n.2
Chosŏnjok people: ethnic homogeneity of, 95; ethnicity/origins of, 80, 190n.2; Korean bride shortage (*see* Chosŏnjok women); men affected by women's migration, 99, 192–93n.19; "paper marriages"/"paper parents" for, 87, 191–92n.10; reunification with families in South Korea, 86–87, 191n.8
Chosŏnjok women: agency of, 81–82; Chinese consciousness among, 96; ethnicity/nationality paradoxes for, 95–97, 99–100, 192n.17; ethnicity/origins of the Chosŏnjok, 80, 190n.2; gender paradoxes for, 97–98, 99–100, 192–93n.19; geographic-positioning paradoxes for, 98, 100; independence/modern attitudes of, 9, 97–98; on *inyŏn*, 89–90, 192n.14; isolation/disillusionment/hardships of, 89–90, 92–93, 94, 97–98, 109, 192nn.12–13; Juju's marriage, 93–95, 98; marriage migration, ethnographic data on, 82–84; marriage migration of, generally, 6–7, 9, 80–81; opportunism of, 81, 84–85, 87, 91, 99,

109, 191nn.6–7; political/economic reforms and mobility of, 86–87; traditional virtues in, 192n.17; as victims of government-sanctioned trafficking, 81, 84–85, 98–99; Yŏnghwa's marriage, 88–90, 91, 98, 192n.13; Yŏnjae's marriage, 91–93, 96, 97–98; Yunok's marriage, 90–91, 97–98
chu jia (married out), 57
cigarettes, 46
Civil Affairs Department (China), 38
Clark, Constance, 183
class, men's vs. women's status, 57
cohabitation, 38, 48, 51
Commission for Filipinos Overseas (CFO), 180
computers, 12. *See also* Internet
concubines/second wives, 30–31, 32–33, 69
Constable, Nicole, 76, 123. *See also* Filipinas; international matchmaking
consumer culture, 46–47
correspondence marriage, 166–67, 168–75, 184–85, 197n.4
courtship, 44–47, 159. *See also* elopement; marriage
cross-border marriages, generally: distances bridged in, 12–13; frequency/scope of, 3–4; gendered patterns of, 4, 7; meanings of, 31–32; men's motivation in, 8; public concern over growth of, 5–6; women's agency in, 13–14, 15–16, 78–79 (*see also* agency); women's motivation in, 7–8, 15. *See also* marriage migration; *specific peoples and cultural groups*
cultural capital, 46
cultural citizenship, 102
cultural globalization, 128
Cultural Revolution (1966–68), 25

dagong (seek temporary wage labor), 56
Das, Veena, 60
del Rosario, Virginia O., 128
desire, sites of, 7
de-territorialized communities, 32
Dinah, 129
disability, 103, 106, 111, 115–16, 119, 193n.1, 193n.3
divorce, 165, 168, 178, 182
doi moi policy, 149
Douglas, Mary, 19